DRAWING THE FUTURE

DRAWING

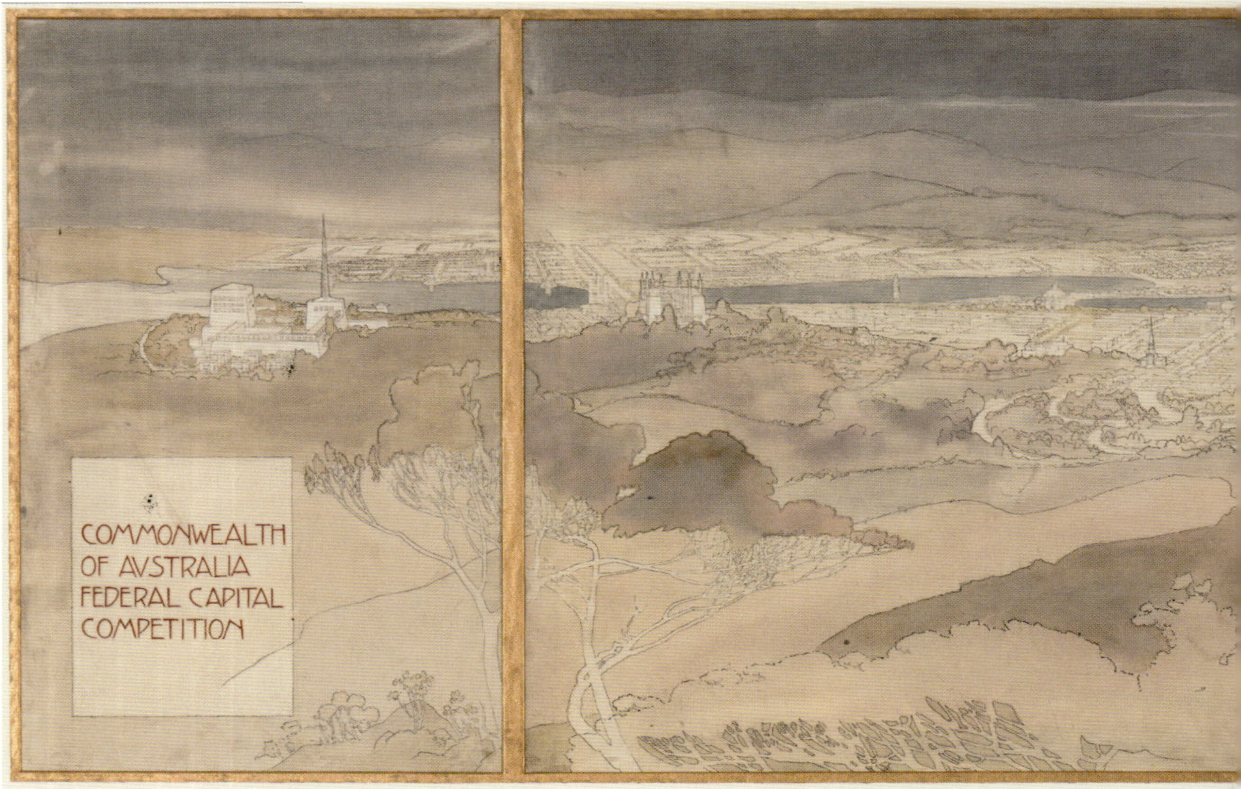

MARY AND LEIGH BLOCK MUSEUM OF ART

THE FUTURE

Chicago Architecture on the International Stage, 1900–1925

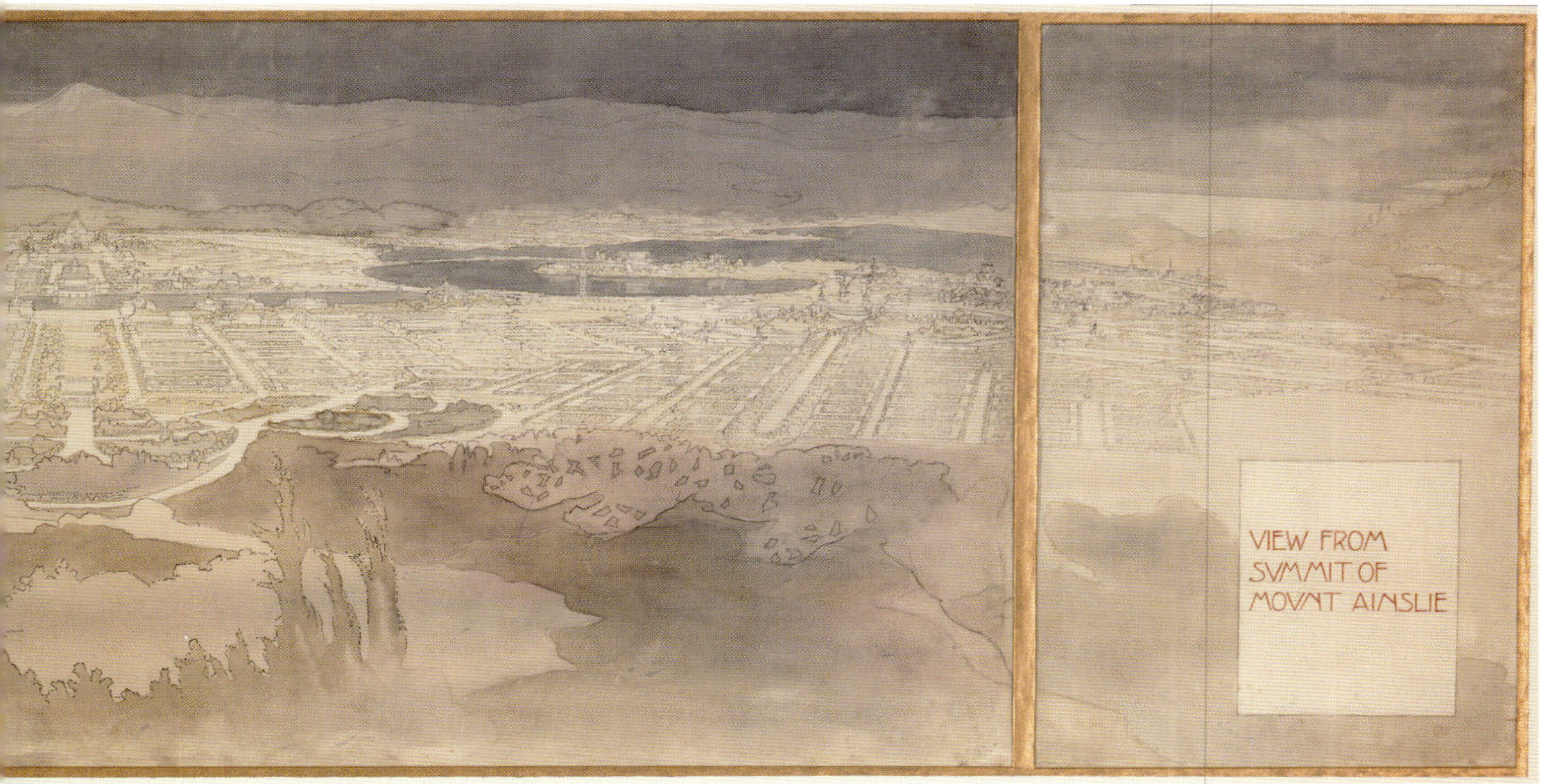

David Van Zanten

Ashley Elizabeth Dunn

Leslie Coburn

NORTHWESTERN UNIVERSITY PRESS / EVANSTON, ILLINOIS

Northwestern University Press
www.nupress.northwestern.edu

Mary and Leigh Block Museum of Art
www.blockmuseum.northwestern.edu

Published in conjunction with the exhibition *Drawing the Future: Chicago Architecture on the International Stage, 1900–1925*, Mary and Leigh Block Museum of Art, Northwestern University, April 19–August 11, 2013.

This publication has been made possible with the generous support of John K. Notz Jr. Further support has been provided by the University Research Grants Committee at Northwestern University, the Myers Foundations, and the Walter Burley Griffin Society of America.

Edited by David Van Zanten
Design and composition by Marianne Jankowski
Printed in China

10 9 8 7 6 5 4 3 2 1

Library of Congress Cataloging-in-Publication Data
Van Zanten, David, 1943–
Drawing the future : Chicago architecture on the international stage, 1900–1925 / David Van Zanten, Ashley Elizabeth Dunn, Leslie Coburn.
p. cm.
"Published in conjunction with the exhibition Drawing the Future: Chicago Architecture on the International Stage, 1900–1925, Mary and Leigh Block Museum of Art, Northwestern University, April 19–August 11, 2013."
ISBN 978-0-8101-2898-9 (pbk. : alk. paper)
1. Architecture—Illinois—Chicago—20th century—Exhibitions. 2. Architecture—Illinois—Chicago—Exhibitions. 3. Chicago (Ill.)—Buildings, structures, etc.—Exhibitions. I. Dunn, Ashley Elizabeth. II. Coburn, Leslie. III. Mary and Leigh Block Museum of Art. IV. Title.
NA735.C4V36 2013
720.977311074—dc23

2012038731

Published 2013 by the Mary and Leigh Block Museum of Art and Northwestern University Press, Evanston, Illinois.

Title page artwork: Marion Mahony Griffin and Walter Burley Griffin; *View from Summit of Mount Ainslie*, 1911–12; National Archive of Austrlia, A710, 48–50

The paper used in this publication meets the minimum requirements of the American National Standard for Information Sciences—Permanence of Paper for Printed Library Materials, ANSI Z39.48-1992.

CONTENTS

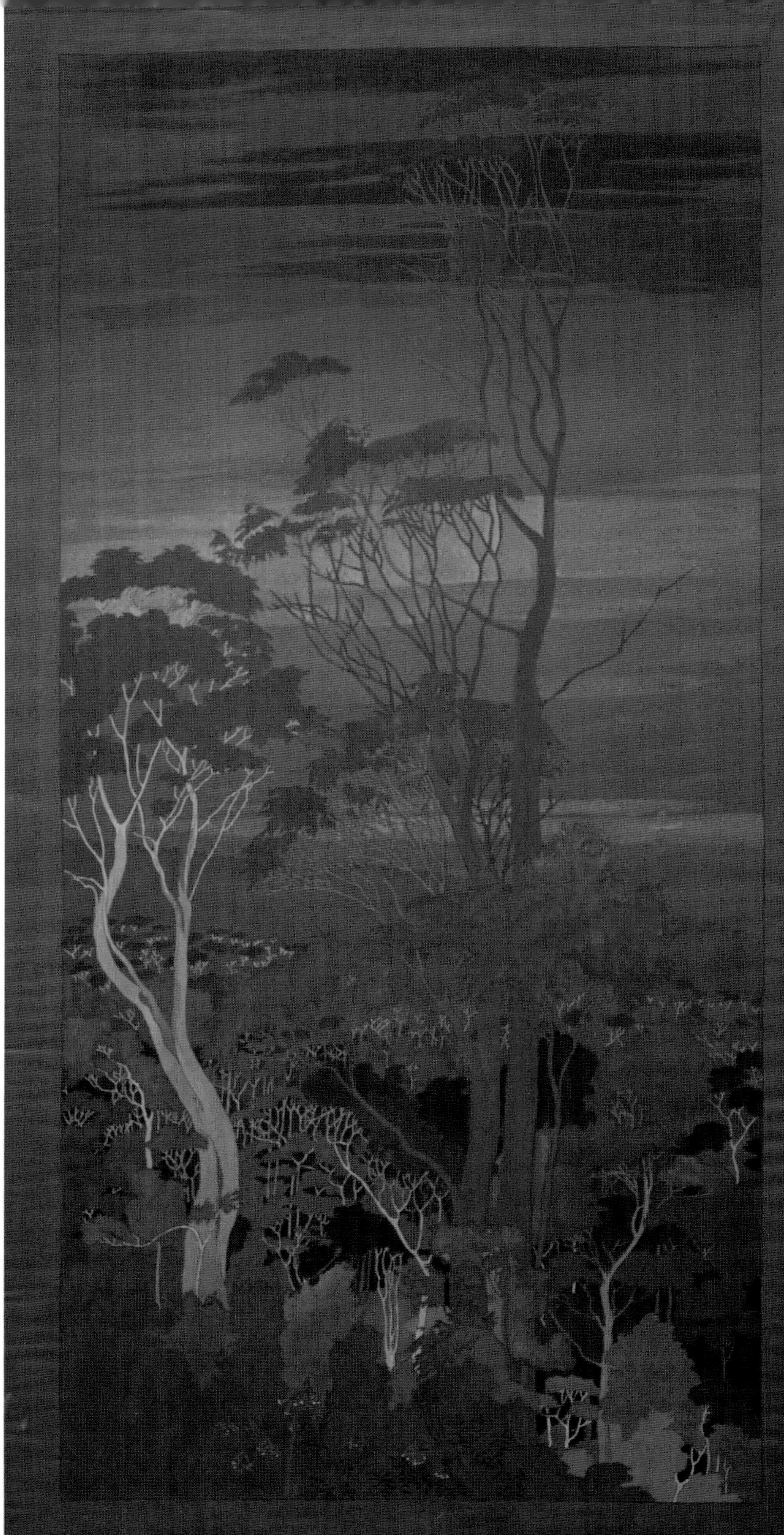

DIRECTOR'S STATEMENT

Lisa Graziose Corrin
Ellen Philips Katz Director,
Mary and Leigh Block Museum of Art
Northwestern University

The Mary and Leigh Block Museum of Art is extremely proud to present *Drawing the Future: Chicago Architecture on the International Stage, 1900–1925,* a collaboration with architectural historian and Northwestern University professor David Van Zanten. On a personal note, this is an especially gratifying start to my career at Northwestern University. I was drawn here by its dynamism, its remarkable faculty, and the legacies of the departments of Art History and Art Theory and Practice, with which the museum has special relationships. I count as friends a number of arts alumni who are outstanding scholars, artists, and professionals. Professor Van Zanten's contribution to this history is considerable. A generous mentor, he is also an indefatigable scholar whose wellspring of knowledge and boundless curiosity have led him to unearth new connections between the practices of Chicago architects and their contemporaries in Europe and in faraway Australia, demonstrating the global impact of our city's early urban planners.

Cornerstones of the Block artistic program are projects in which faculty and students collaborate with the museum staff to develop exhibitions and associated publications. We are committed to providing this critical connection between the museum and the classroom and to the opportunity it affords us to showcase the emerging talent of Northwestern undergraduates and graduate students. Nurturing the next generation is a core value at the Block. Previous faculty-student collaborations include a formidable list of projects that have enhanced teaching and learning and enabled the museum to share new research with a broader public. These include *Caricature in London and Paris, 1800–1900* (2006), *Design in the Age of Darwin: From William Morris to Frank Lloyd Wright* (2008), and *Marion Mahony Griffin: Drawing the Form of Nature* (2005). The latter, also a partnership with Professor Van Zanten, produced a landmark study of a remarkable artist, a large body of whose work lives at the Block in its permanent collection.

Exhibitions such as these are ambitious and could not be achieved without significant partnerships and supportive lenders. We are particularly appreciative of the friendships we have developed over the years with colleagues at Northwestern's extraordinary Charles Deering McCormick Library of Special Collections.

The Block staff has, as always, supported Professor Van Zanten and his students in realizing this project. Special recognition is due Block curator Corinne Granof, who provided invaluable guidance that has shaped the exhibition and this publication, as well as serving as a mentor to Northwestern graduate student Ashley Elizabeth Dunn, a Block fellow. We thank Ashley for her assistance and also for her outstanding essay published here. Thanks also to undergraduate fellow Sophie Jenkins for contributions to exhibition research.

I also join Corinne Granof in thanking the many colleagues, lenders, and funders who have supported this exhibition. We are grateful to them for recognizing the value of this endeavor to our faculty, to our students, to the field, and to the public.

As a graduate student, my admiration for the cultural heritage of the "City of the Big Shoulders" was shaped by Professor Van Zanten's work on the Chicago School. We thank him, and his talented students, for choosing the Block as the platform for this new contribution to the subject.

Marion Mahony Griffin; *Eucalyptus Urnigera, Tasmania/Scarlet Bark, Sunset, Forest Portrait No. 11*, 1918; Mary and Leigh Block Museum of Art, Northwestern University, gift of Marion Mahony Griffin, 1985.1.117. Photograph: James Prinz. See also page 17.

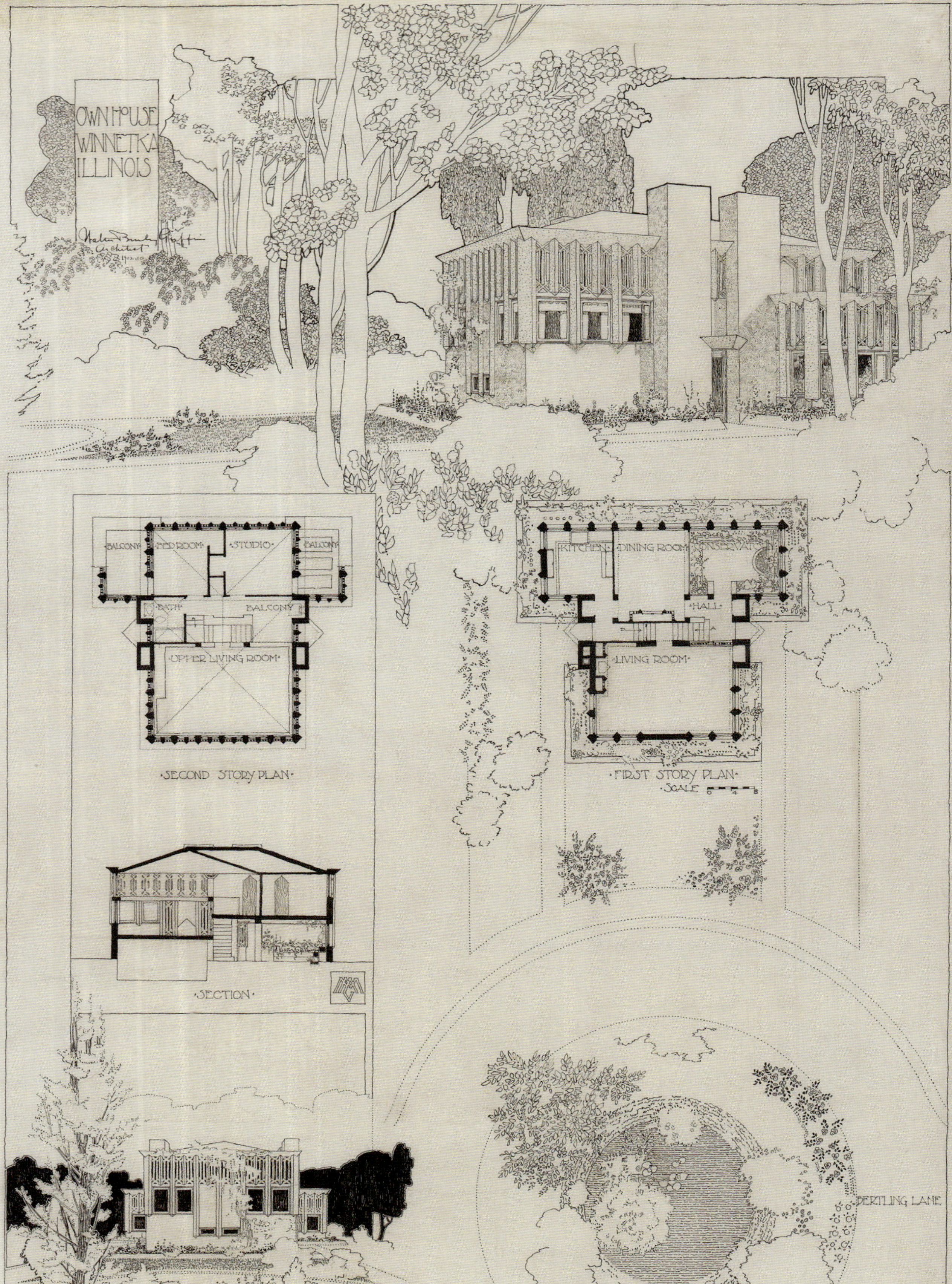

OWN HOUSE
WINNETKA
ILLINOIS
Walter Burley Griffin
Architect
1912.10
BALCONY
BED ROOM
STUDIO
BALCONY
BATH
BALCONY
UPPER LIVING ROOM
SECOND STORY PLAN
KITCHEN
DINING ROOM
HALL
LIVING ROOM
FIRST STORY PLAN
SCALE
SECTION
BERTLING LANE
ALLES ROAD

ACKNOWLEDGMENTS

This project was conceived and shaped working with the staff of the Block Museum of Art at Northwestern University, with Director Emeritus David Robertson and Director Lisa Corrin as well as curators Corinne Granof and Debora Wood with the help of Nicole Druckman. I owe them all the very warmest thanks. In addition I owe a tremendous debt to three scholars with whom I have been discussing this material in detail, first of all Christopher Vernon, but also Neil Levine and Paul Kruty, all working on projects closely parallel. They have been tremendously helpful. Vernon has been especially generous in giving me copies of important documents. No less generous have been James Weirick, David Headon, Ian Batterham, Nicola MacKay-Sim, Anna Rubbo, Donald Leslie Johnson, Alasdair McGregor, Glenda Koporaal, and the late Paul Reid in Australia. I have had enlightening discussions with Otto Antonia Graf, Pierre Vaisse, Wolfgang Sonne, and Iain Boyd Whyte. I am especially indebted to the staff at the Art Institute of Chicago, Lori Boyer, Bart Ryckbosch, Mary Woolever, and Jack Brown, as well as Scott Krafft and Sigrid Perry, Susan Lewis, and Nick Munagian at Northwestern University Library Special Collections, Carl Smith of the Northwestern Department of History, and the graduate students in my seminar winter quarter 2011, including Grace Deveney, Erin Reitz, Leslie Coburn, and Ashley Dunn (these last two contributing essays to this catalog). In addition several scholars have helped with specific matters, for example Gergely Baics finding the Griffins' landing information in New York.

—David Van Zanten

I wish to thank David Van Zanten for his guidance in developing this essay from a seminar paper into the form it takes today and for his generosity in sharing his archival research and the results of his own work as it progressed. I am also indebted to Guillemette Delaporte and the staff at the Bibliothèque des Arts Décoratifs in Paris for aiding in my research there. I am grateful to the Block Museum, especially to curator Corinne Granof, for allowing me the time to work on this paper. Lastly, I wish to thank my fellow graduate students in the art history department at Northwestern University for their feedback at various stages.

—Ashley Elizabeth Dunn

I am indebted to David Van Zanten for his encouragement of this research topic and his many valuable suggestions as this essay has developed. I would also like to thank Corinne Granof, curator of the Block Museum, and Ashley Dunn, Block Museum graduate fellow, for their helpful feedback and assistance as the manuscript was prepared for publication. Thanks are also due to Christopher Vernon, who generously shared his research and knowledge of the Griffins. I am grateful also to the accommodating staff at the Research Center of the Chicago History Museum, especially Lesley Martin, and to Barbara Gilbert and Christine Colburn of the Special Collections Research Center at the University of Chicago Library. Long-distance research was possible thanks to the helpfulness of Inés Zalduendo, archivist at the Frances Loeb Library at Harvard University, and Jean-Robert Durbin of the Rare Books Collection at the Huntington Library, in San Marino, California. Lastly, I would like to acknowledge and thank the Committee on Institutional Cooperation and its Traveling Scholar Program, which made possible my participation in the graduate seminar out of which this essay arose.

—Leslie Coburn

Walter Burley Griffin and Marion Mahony Griffin; *Walter Burley Griffin's Own House, Winnetka, Illinois*, 1912; pen and black ink on drafting linen; Mary and Leigh Block Museum of Art, Northwestern University, gift of Marion Mahony Griffin, 1985.1.108

University museum exhibitions can serve as a vital intersection, bringing ideas explored in classrooms, in seminars, and among academics to a broader public. Such exhibitions can provide access to new currents of thought, new directions in scholarship, and the ideas that shape how we think about the world. A project like *Drawing the Future* is the result of years of research and planning. Throughout the development and preparation, Professor David Van Zanten has been a persistent source of knowledge and energy. This project is his vision and an offshoot of years of researching and teaching architecture. The staff of the Block Museum is grateful that he shared his idea for an exhibition with us, made so many important discoveries, and had the perseverance to see it through in the form of an exhibition that can be shared and enjoyed by visitors to the museum and through this publication.

Many people were involved in realizing this project. John K. Notz Jr. has been a generous supporter of the catalog. His gift is especially meaningful given his depth of knowledge of Chicago architecture and the work of the Griffins. A research grant from the University Research Grants Committee of the Graduate School at Northwestern University provided crucial funds for travel and research. We also thank the Walter Burley Griffin Society of America, whose mission is to preserve the legacy of architects Walter Burley Griffin and Marion Mahony Griffin, for additional funding.

Professor Van Zanten worked with many talented students in the preparation of this project. All the students in his seminar *City Planning Hysteria c. 1905–1914, World War I, "Modern" Town Planning, and What It All Might Have Been About* brought new ideas to the project and participated in discussions that have made an impact on the exhibition and publication. The work of two graduate students, Ashley Dunn and Leslie Coburn, doctoral student at the University of Illinois at Chicago, was selected for expansion and inclusion in the catalog. Ashley Dunn has also taken on the project in her role as the 2011–12 Block Museum graduate fellow. Her intelligence, organization, and commitment have been tremendous assets throughout her year at the museum.

We are fortunate to have many informed scholars, curators, and collectors throughout the city and region who have shared their knowledge and collections. We are indebted to the Art Institute of Chicago and to Douglas Druick, the Eloise Martin Director of the Art Institute; Zoë Ryan, chair of the Department of Architecture and Design and John H. Bryan Curator of Architecture and Design; and Lori Hanna Boyer, exhibitions and collections manager of the department. We have been kindly assisted by Jack Perry Brown, director of the Ryerson and Burnham Libraries at the Art Institute; Christine M. Fabian, library collections conservator; and Mary Woolever, art and architecture archivist at the Ryerson and Burnham Libraries.

The staff at the Chicago History Museum was especially helpful in identifying meaningful loans. We thank Executive Vice President and Chief Historian Russell Lewis; Director of Curatorial Affairs John Russick; Frank DeCurtis, collection manager; Julie Katz, registrar; and Kathy Ludwig, registration technician, for collaborating.

At Northwestern University, we have been fortunate to have worked with and been assisted by Scott Krafft, curator of the Charles Deering McCormick Library of Special Collections. Many of the objects from Special Collections form the core and springboard of our faculty-curated exhibitions, and we are grateful to the people there for sharing their knowledge and assisting us in many ways. In Digital Collections at Northwestern University Library, we are grateful to M. Claire Stewart, department head, and Tom O'Connell, multimedia services assistant. Digital Media Services provided scans and digital imagery of books and plates in the Northwestern University collection. We thank Sarah Pritchard, dean of libraries, and Jeffrey Garrett, associate university librarian, for their support in all our partnerships.

Beyond Chicago, we are indebted to Kris Kiesling, director of archives and special collections, and Barbara Bezat, assistant archivist at the Northwest

Architectural Archives at the University of Minnesota, for their generosity. At the Art, Design and Architecture Museum of the University of California, Santa Barbara, we thank Professor Bruce Robertson, acting director of the museum; Jocelyn Gibbs, curator of the Architecture and Design Collection; and Melinda Gandara, reference archivist, for their assistance.

In Australia, Christopher Vernon, associate professor in the Faculty of Architecture, Landscape and Visual Arts at the University of Western Australia, has been a constant source of information and support. We are also grateful for guidance from Ian Batterham, assistant director, preservation services and projects, at the National Archives of Australia, and David Headon, cultural adviser to the National Capital Authority.

Northwestern University Press has been a key partner on several projects, and we have been fortunate to work with the director, Jane Bunker, and the capable staff there, including Marianne Jankowski, art director; Anne Gendler, managing editor/manager of design and production; Sara Dreyfuss, editor; Ann-Christine Racette, production manager; Mike Levine, acquisitions editor; and Liz Hamilton, administrative assistant.

The staff of the Block Museum has been helpful in so many ways. David Alan Robertson, former director, supported the project from day one. Lisa Graziose Corrin was enthusiastic even before she stepped into her position as the Ellen Philips Katz Director of the Block Museum and has been mindful of the resonance of the project in the Chicago community. Our exhibitions team is dedicated, professional, and thorough. Kristina Bottomley, registrar, ensures the safety of the objects from start to finish, overseeing all details of installation.

Judy Koon, director of education, makes sure the programming is diverse and engaging, and that it speaks to our many audiences. Dan Silverstein, manager of exhibits and facilities, brings vision and life to the exhibitions. Elizabeth Wolf, collections and exhibitions assistant, ensures the safety and care of all the objects on and off the wall. Debora Wood, senior curator, generously shared her knowledge of Marion Mahony Griffin and the works in our collection. Burke Patten, communications manager, is tireless and thoughtful in publicizing all the exhibitions and programs. Nicole Druckman, grants manager, and Helen Hilken, director of development, have worked closely with Professor Van Zanten to match funding donors with the project. All our colleagues at the Block Museum are effective, intelligent, and generous, each contributing to the project in fundamental ways. Particular thanks goes to Pick-Laudati Curator of Film and Director of the Block Cinema Mimi Brody; Aaron Chatman, security assistant; Emily Forsgren, assistant to the director; James Foster, manager of security services; Sophie Jenkins, 2012–13 undergraduate fellow in the Department of Art History, Weinberg College of Arts and Sciences, Northwestern University; her predecessor, Julia Detchon, 2010–11 undergraduate fellow; Kate Wollman, undergraduate in the School of Communication; Sarah Mack, education coordinator; and Rita Shorts, business administrator.

Drawing the Future is the result of participation and assistance by many individuals and institutions, whose contributions have helped bring together many of the rich ideas and discussions that are part of the university culture and teaching. This publication ensures that its ideas will resonate with future students of architecture and the modern city.

—Corinne Granof, *Curator*
Mary and Leigh Block Museum of Art
Northwestern University

DRAWING THE FUTURE

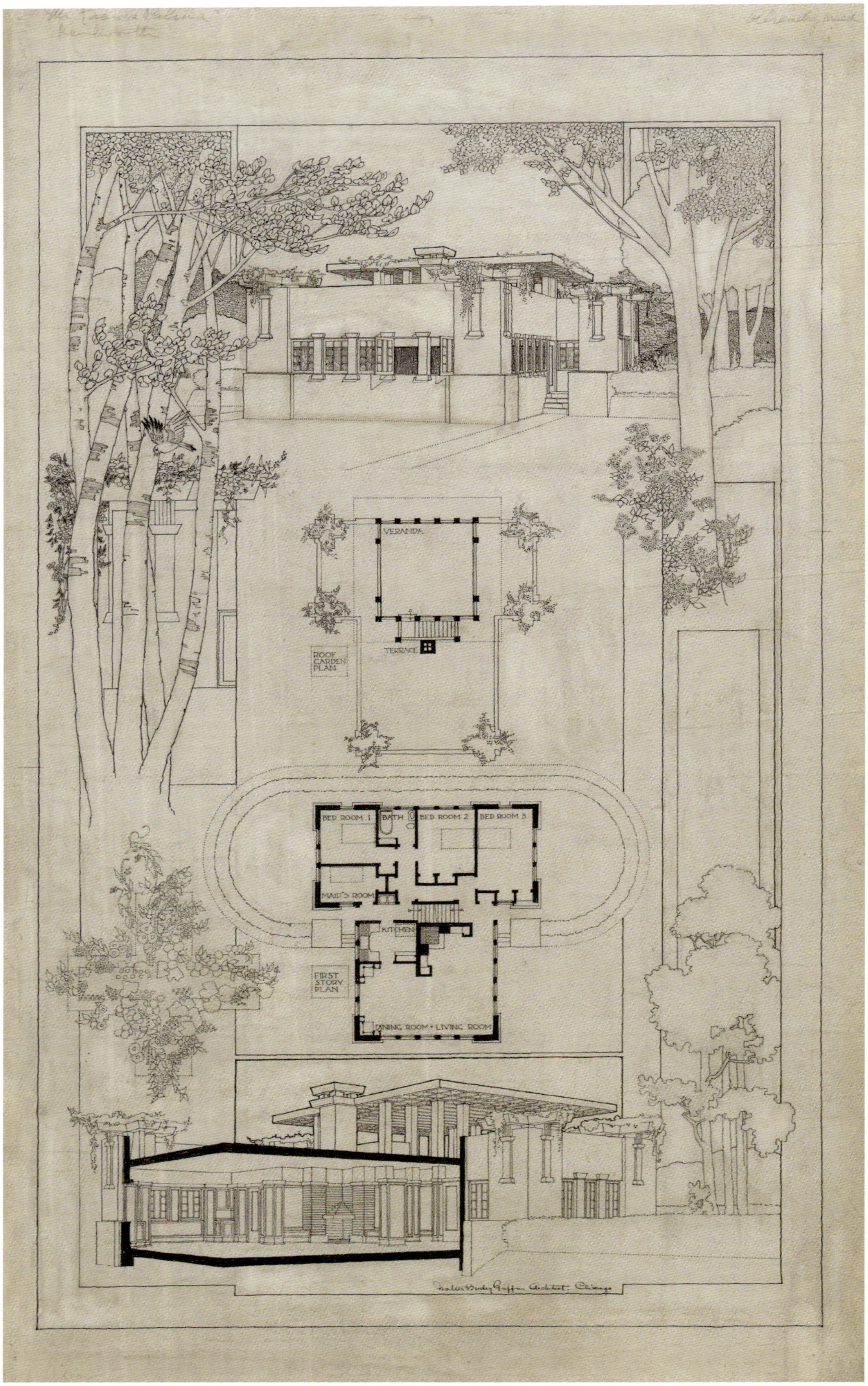
VERANDA
TERRACE
ROOF GARDEN PLAN
BED ROOM 1
BATH
BED ROOM 2
BED ROOM 3
MAID'S ROOM
KITCHEN
FIRST STORY PLAN
DINING ROOM • LIVING ROOM

The Canberra Design Competition

The reach and ambition of Chicago progressive, or "modern," architecture was greater than historians have come to picture. During the decade 1911 to 1921 two of Frank Lloyd Wright's principal assistants, Walter Burley Griffin and his wife, Marion Mahony Griffin, competed for the design of the new Australian capital city, Canberra; won the competition; went there; and as supervising architect, Walter laid out the city. The Griffins also formulated a second competition to design the Parliament building itself, encouraging submissions from progressive architects. The couple toured Europe in March 1914, meeting leading European modernist architects to shape a sympathetic jury, to compose a modernist statement of the requirements for the competition, and to arouse interest in the project. They exhibited Walter's designs in Marion's Japanese-inspired style in Paris and Lyon and would have seen them on to Vienna had World War I not intervened.

This endeavor throws Frank Lloyd Wright's achievement into a broader light. It makes us realize that his "Prairie Style," often considered as chiefly manifest in houses, was only the microcosm of a broader, shared enterprise framing the whole new urban and suburban environment. It makes it clear that Chicago was not isolated from European modernism but a reciprocating part of a broad effort to formulate in space and images the architectural world to come. There were many different names, both narrower and broader, for this modernism—Secession, Prairie Style, Chicago School, Arts and Crafts, even just Progressive—and it was not until 1932 that a consistent definition emerged and was named the "International Style."

Background of the Competition

Before the six colonies that are now part of Australia formed a federation in 1901, they were essentially independent. Each colony issued its own postage stamps, maintained its own defense force, set clocks to its own time, and operated its own railway system, with tracks that differed in width from colony to colony. The colonies even imposed tariffs on goods imported from other colonies.

During the 1800s, communication, trade, and travel among the colonies increased. People throughout Australia developed a growing sense of shared identity as Australians. In 1891, the six colonies met in Sydney to discuss forming a single nation, to be called the Commonwealth of Australia. On January 1, 1901, the new nation came into being.

Australia's two largest cities, Melbourne and Sydney, were fierce rivals to become the capital, and no one could agree which city should get the honor. To settle the dispute, the Australian government decided to build an entirely new capital somewhere in the "bush." The planners eventually decided on a small rural community called Yass-Canberra on the Molonglo River in southern New South Wales. The state of New South Wales ceded some nine hundred square miles of territory surrounding Canberra to form the Australian Capital Territory, a federal zone modeled on the District of Columbia in the United States. Within the territory, private property ownership was forbidden.

In 1911, Australia's minister for home affairs, King O'Malley, launched a competition to plan the new capital city. One hundred thirty-seven architects entered the Commonwealth of Australia Federal Capital Design Competition. The panel of

Walter Burley Griffin and Marion Mahony Griffin; *Frank Pallma Residence ("Solid Rock House")*, Winnetka, Illinois, 1911; pen and black ink on drafting linen; approximately 40 ½ × 23 in.; Mary and Leigh Block Museum of Art, Northwestern University, gift of Marion Mahony Griffin, 1985.1.98

judges consisted of an architect, two engineers, and O'Malley himself, who insisted on making the final decision. He declared that the new city would "rival London in size, Athens in art, and Paris in beauty."

Entrants in the Competition

The third-place project was submitted by the French architect Alfred Agache, founder in 1911 of the Société Française des Architectes Urbanistes. His design was forward-looking in many ways—for example, it was the only one to include an airport. But the judges disapproved of his siting of certain major buildings. Agache later replanned the Brazilian cities of Rio de Janeiro, Recife, and Porto Alegre. Second place in the Canberra competition went to the Finnish architect Eliel Saarinen, author of an influential plan for Helsinki and the father of Eero Saarinen. Saarinen's plan grouped monumental buildings in a stiff arrangement around a series of water basins. George Taylor, the influential editor of *Building* magazine, called it "oppressively formal." The firm of Walter Scott Griffiths, Robert Coulter, and Charles Caswell submitted the only Australian entry, which won fourth place.

The Winning Design

The winners of the Canberra competition were a little-known husband-and-wife team of architects, Walter Burley Griffin and Marion Mahony Griffin of Chicago, Illinois. The Griffins' design envisioned a green, parklike city of about twenty-five thousand to seventy-five thousand people. A chain of ornamental lagoons lay at the heart of the city bordered by parks. The plan featured geometric shapes such as circles, hexagons, and triangles. The city texture centered on two axes aligned with the most important natural features of the valley site. Broad, tree-lined streets ran out from the center like spokes of a wheel, intersected by roads in concentric collars.

Around the Capitol, Walter spread an octagonal matrix of streets, sending two axes across the lagoons to two hexagonal nodes, a commercial and a municipal government center. Additional axes stretched across the plane of the Molonglo River Valley—leaving natural rises free as parkland—to link together a texture of hexagonal neighborhood units meant to grow slowly as the city's population increased. Two hills dominate the valley, Mount Ainslie and Black Mountain, and from their peaks Walter projected two axes to draw this urban matrix together visually. One axis ran north-south linking Mount Ainslie to a low hill that he made the site of the government complex. The other axis intersected it at a right angle down the center of the lagoons and their bordering parks.

The Griffins' design reflected their experience as assistants to Frank Lloyd Wright, their involvement in Chicago urban affairs at the time of the formulation of Daniel Hudson Burnham's monumental Plan of Chicago (1909), and their interest in British socially progressive Garden City planning, which broke cities up into small, dispersed units spread across open farm country.

Marion Mahony (pronounced *MAH hah nee*), who became Marion Mahony Griffin, was the first licensed woman architect in Illinois and also a gifted architectural artist. She had worked in Wright's studio for fourteen years and helped him win fame in Europe with a collection of drawings in 1910, now called the Wasmuth portfolio. The portfolio, *Ausgeführte Bauten und Entwürfe von Frank Lloyd Wright* (Studies and Executed Buildings of Frank Lloyd Wright, 1910), was published by the leading Berlin architectural publisher, Ernst Wasmuth. Marion and Walter married in 1911 and immediately entered the Canberra competition at Marion's instigation.

The Griffins' entry appealed to the judges because of its impressive presentation drawings created by Marion. Instead of modest sketches or plaster models, the Griffins submitted a series of large, sweeping panoramas, exquisitely drawn in complex gouache mixtures on fine stretched linen. Their entry also included a stunning panoramic watercolor titled *View from Summit of Mount Ainslie,* the finished version of which arrived late.

The Griffins, like many of the entrants, had never seen Australia and had to work entirely from contour maps. But their design showed a deep understanding of the Molonglo site, perhaps because of the presence in Chicago of the Australian writer Stella Miles Franklin, who had grown up nearby. They regarded hills, for example, not "as obstacles to be wiped out of existence, but as opportunities to be made the most of," dividing the town into neighborhoods spread across low areas, kept separate by unbuilt-on higher ground. Their plans fit Canberra's setting of vast open spaces, wide skies, and unobstructed views. Their buildings seemed to sprout naturally from the earth; Marion's renderings even captured the rich gold, ocher, russet, and sepia coloring of the Australian landscape.

The Griffins in Australia and India

In October 1913, the Australian government appointed Walter Burley Griffin as director of design and construction for the federal capital. When the Griffins arrived in Australia six months later, they found scanty funds for building the new city and little political support for the project. The outbreak of World War I a few months later only made the situation worse. Walter also lacked experience at managing a large construction project. By the time he resigned in 1921, almost no work had been done except to stake out the main roads. At the start of the year, Walter left the project. It was finally brought to completion, in a modified form, in the 1960s.

The Griffins stayed in Australia for another twenty-one years and became one of the country's most distinguished architectural partnerships. They designed and developed the suburb of Castlecrag in Sydney, the towns of Griffith and Leeton in New South Wales, and Newman College at the University of Melbourne.

In 1935, the Griffins went to India and set up an architectural practice. Walter died there a year and a half later after falling from a scaffold. Marion returned to the United States, where she lived into her nineties.

Collections of the Griffins' Work

The National Archives of Australia in Canberra has the original copies of Marion's magnificent competition renderings. Her twenty colored silk *japoniste* (Japenese-style) house renderings shown in Paris in 1914 are now in the Avery Architectural and Fine Arts Library at Columbia University. The drawings arrived there in the original tin box the Griffins used to store them during their European trip. Many of Marion's renderings for the couple's Indian projects are there as well. The ink layout drawings for the Canberra competition are in the collection of the Art Institute of Chicago, and similar outline drawings for the house silks are in the Mary and Leigh Block Museum of Art at Northwestern University, together with a body of working drawings divided between those two institutions. A rich collection of drawings and office papers from Griffin's Australian partner, Eric Nicholls, is now at the National Library of Australia. Two copies of Marion's unpublished manuscript biography of Walter, "The Magic of America," survive—one at the New-York Historical Society and one at the Art Institute. The latter is available online at www.artic.edu/magicofamerica/.

THE AMBITION AND REACH OF

This essay documents an event and an idea. The event was a trip by the Chicago architects Walter Burley Griffin and his wife, Marion Mahony Griffin, to Paris, Vienna, and London in early 1914 to arrange a competition for the design of the new Australian Parliament building in Canberra. The idea was the social and aesthetic "program" (to use their own word) which was behind their plan for the capital and which they used the trip to further.

The Griffins' journey was not a leisurely European tour but the coordination of an international impetus centering on the Parliament House design competition. The essay examines just which interlocutors the Griffins chose to promote their cause, what they hoped of their advocates, what they learned on their tour, and what they themselves left behind. The principal item that remained after their trip was a long, narrow tin box containing a set of renderings of their work. The renderings were displayed in Paris in June and July 1914, and were scheduled to be displayed afterward in Vienna. The Griffins also sent subsequently a set of their Canberra plans that were displayed in Lyon in May of that year. But defining just what they left behind is difficult because of the European appearance of the Wasmuth portfolio, *Ausgeführte Bauten und Ent-*

Figure 1
Marion Mahony Griffin and Walter Burley Griffin; *Section A–B Northerly Side of Water Axis: Black Mountain to Lake Park*, 1911; ink, watercolor, gouache, and metallic paint on linen 30 × 240 in.; National Archives of Australia, A710, 39–42

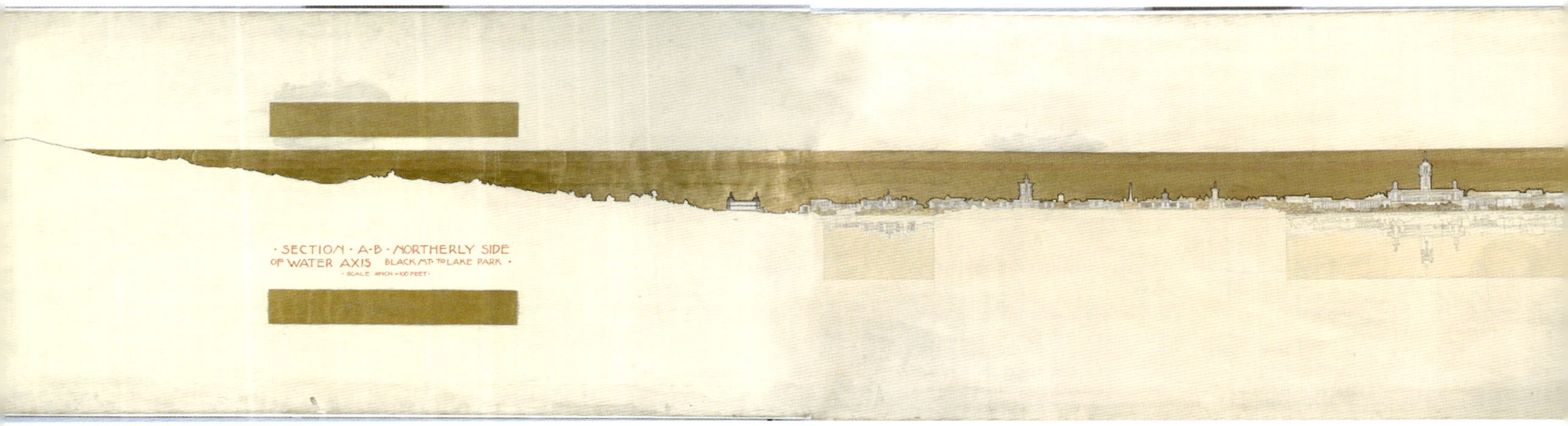

Chicago Progressive Architecture

würfe von Frank Lloyd Wright (Studies and Executed Buildings of Frank Lloyd Wright, figure 12), published in 1910 and distributed in 1911 (presented in Marion's rendering style), and the Griffins' arrival in Europe on the eve of World War I. Two male architects presented their work through the graphic vocabulary of the same draftswoman, Marion.

Furthermore, there is a thick lens through which all this is necessarily seen, induced by the emergence of a new universal architectural technology in concrete, the possibility and definition of a consistent new architectural style, and a new professional ethos holding the architect to be all-knowing, good, and rightly all-powerful.

The Canberra Competition Project

Walter Burley Griffin, after graduating in architecture from the University of Illinois in 1899, worked in Frank Lloyd Wright's Oak Park studio from 1901 to 1906. There he met Marion Mahony, who had graduated in architecture from the Massachusetts Institute of Technology in 1894 and served as Wright's draftswoman and renderer beginning in 1895. In 1909, Wright left his wife and six children and departed to Europe with his neighbor's wife, Mamah Cheney. During his absence, Marion ran the practice for Wright's successor Herman von Holst in Steinway Hall in Chicago. Walter and Marion renewed their acquaintance there in 1909, when both worked in a drafting studio in the attic of Steinway Hall. The couple married in June 1911.[1] Several weeks earlier, the Australian government had announced an international competition for architects and urban planners for the design of Canberra, a new capital for the unified country. Marion persuaded Walter to prepare an entry and coordinated the rendering of it. In May 1912, the Griffins received a telegram informing them that their design had won. There followed some months of confusion about whether Walter would actually be named to execute the design, culminating in a trip to Australia in August 1913. Australia appointed him as director of design and construction for the national capital on October 18 of that year, with six months' leave to wind up his practice in Chicago and to visit Europe to organize a second competition for the design of the Parliament building that stood at the center of his design.[2]

Marion's Canberra competition drawings as a set are extraordinary to examine, even on tightly packed sliding screens in the National Archives of Australia

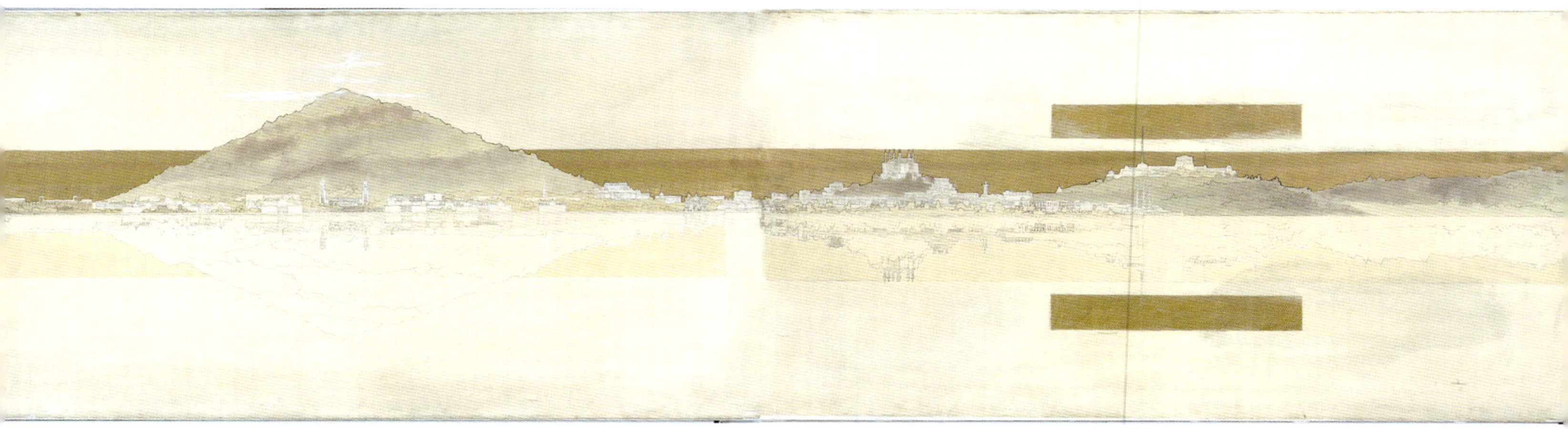

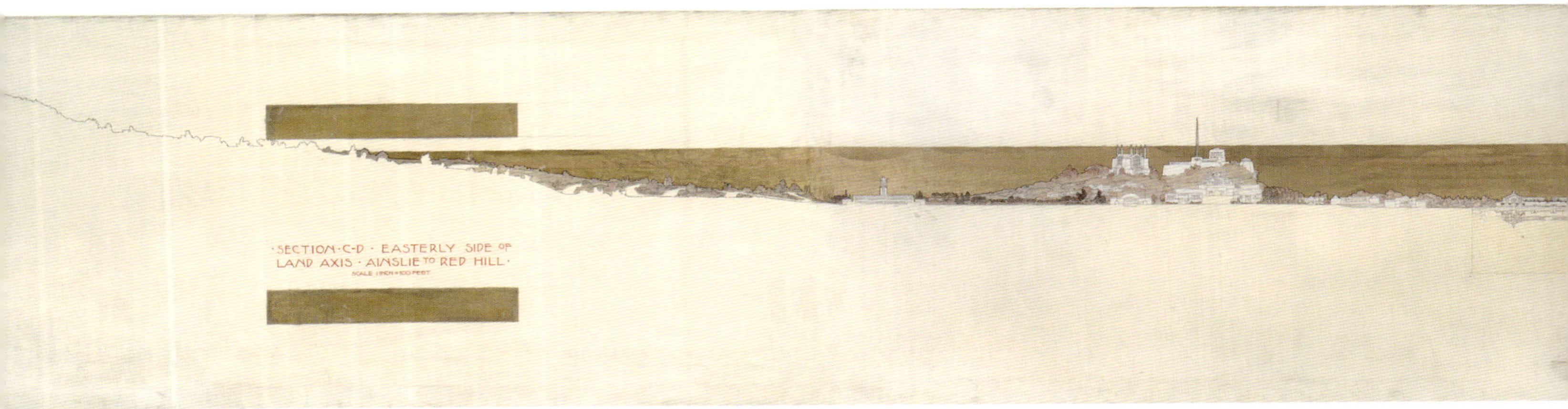

Figure 2
Marion Mahony Griffin and Walter Burley Griffin; *Section C–D Easterly Side of Land Axis: Ainslie to Red Hill,* 1911; ink, watercolor, gouache, and metallic paint on linen; 30 × 240 in.; National Archives of Australia, A710, 44–47

Figure 3
Marion Mahony Griffin and Walter Burley Griffin; *Section B–A Southerly Side of Water Axis: Government Group*, 1911; ink, watercolor, gouache, and metallic paint on linen; 30 × 60 in.; National Archives of Australia, A710, 43

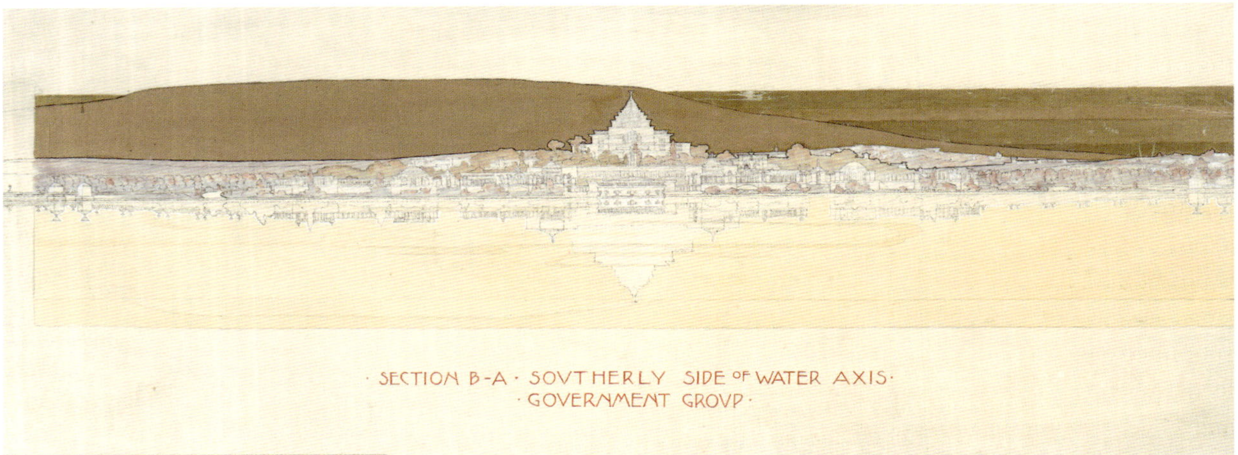

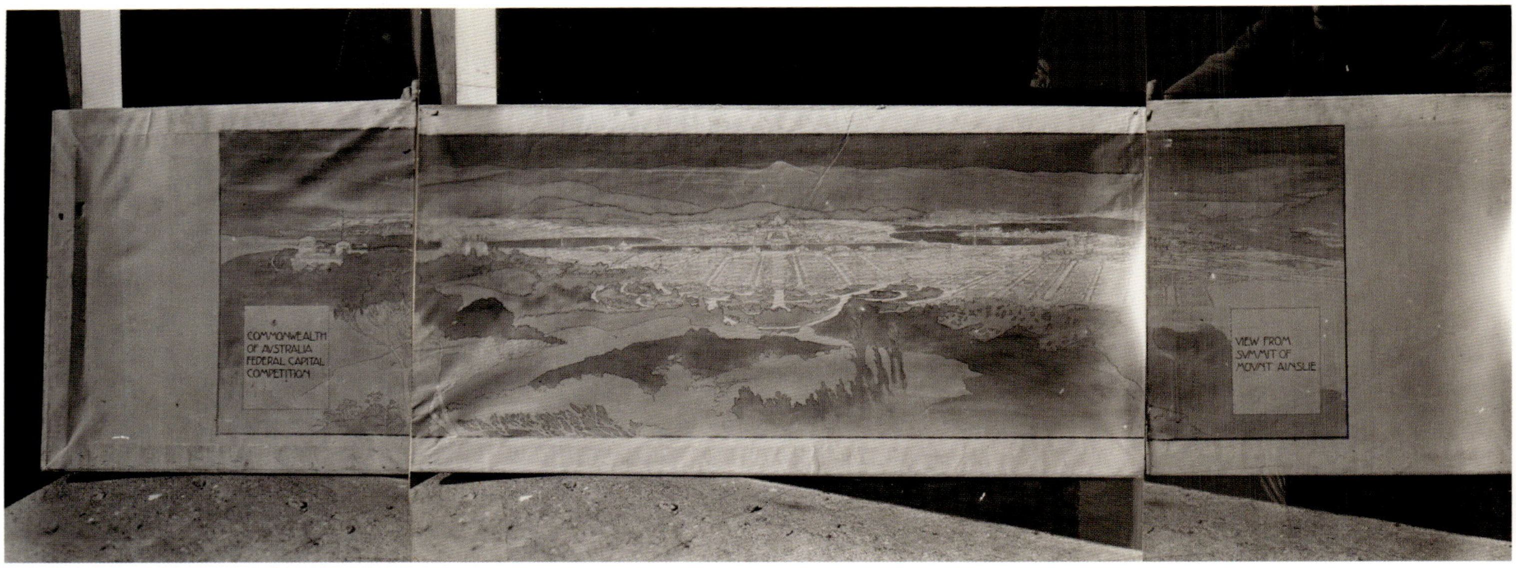

Figure 4
Marion Mahony Griffin and Walter Burley Griffin; *View from Summit of Mount Ainslie*, undated photograph, gift to the author from Peter Harrison.

annex outside the capital. They include fifteen large panels meant to be assembled into two four-part cross sections—one labeled "Section C–D" looking east and one labeled "Section A–B" looking north through the lagoons, both some three-by-twenty feet (figures 1 and 2). Other drawings in the Griffins' entry include a three-by-five foot elevation—a drawing of the exteriors—of the Government Group, the buildings that would house the nation's political institutions (figure 3). Still other drawings include a four-by-ten foot three-panel perspective looking south from Mount Ainslie in one large and two small sections together (figure 4). The Griffins also submitted a relatively small plan sheet (two by five feet) providing a detailed layout of the city (figure 5) and a two-sheet inscription of the plan over the topographical map of the site.[3] (David Headon explains that the perspective was not ready on time and a line drawing for it was sent ahead, the functions of the buildings in the plan being marked on it.)

Marion did not render these drawings on paper, but on fine window-shade linen, with outlines printed in black from layout drawings now in the Art Institute of Chicago (figures 6 and 7). The final drawings were colored in a complex mix of media, ranging from watercolor to gouache, a paint in which a gum additive is mixed with watercolors to produce an opaque appearance. Marion mixed metallic powders into the gouache in silver, gold, and copper, applying the metallic paint in stripes across the lower areas of the sky (something which does not come through in photographs).[4] She also employed this metallic gouache in the lagoon area of the plan and in the Government Group elevation, greatly thinned.

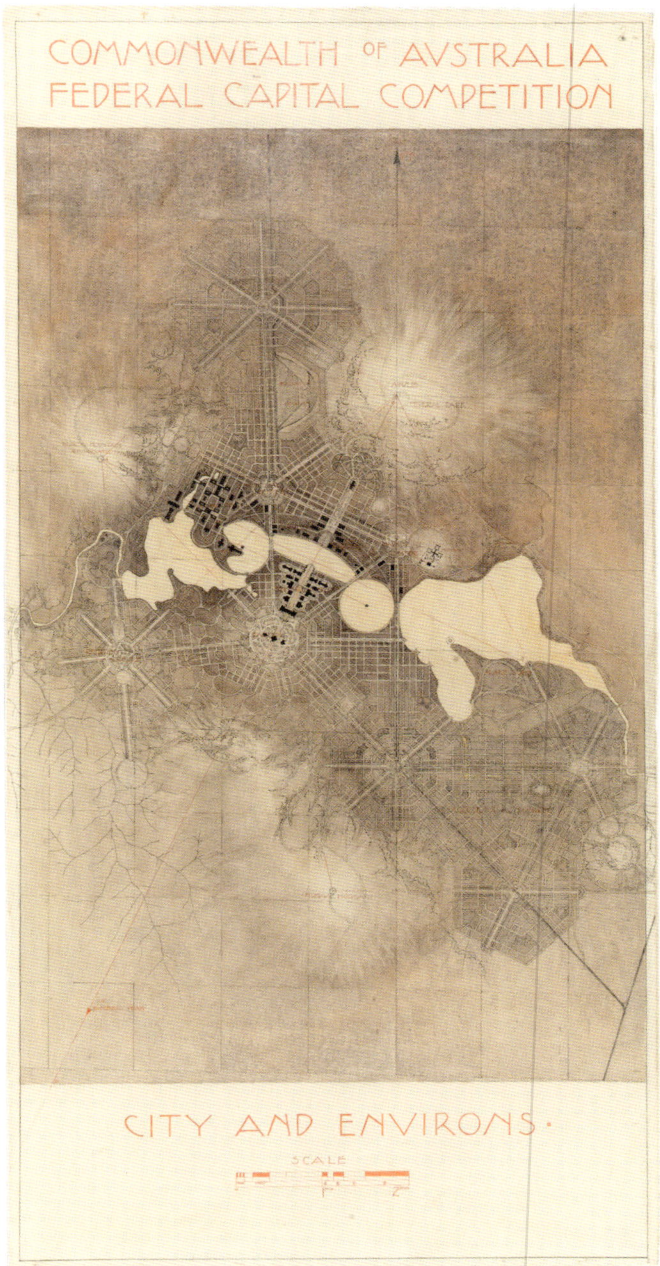

Figure 5
Marion Mahony Griffin and Walter Burley Griffin; *Commonwealth of Australia Federal Capital Competition: City and Environs*, 1911; ink, watercolor, gouache, and metallic paint on linen; 60 × 30 in.; National Archives of Australia, A710, 38

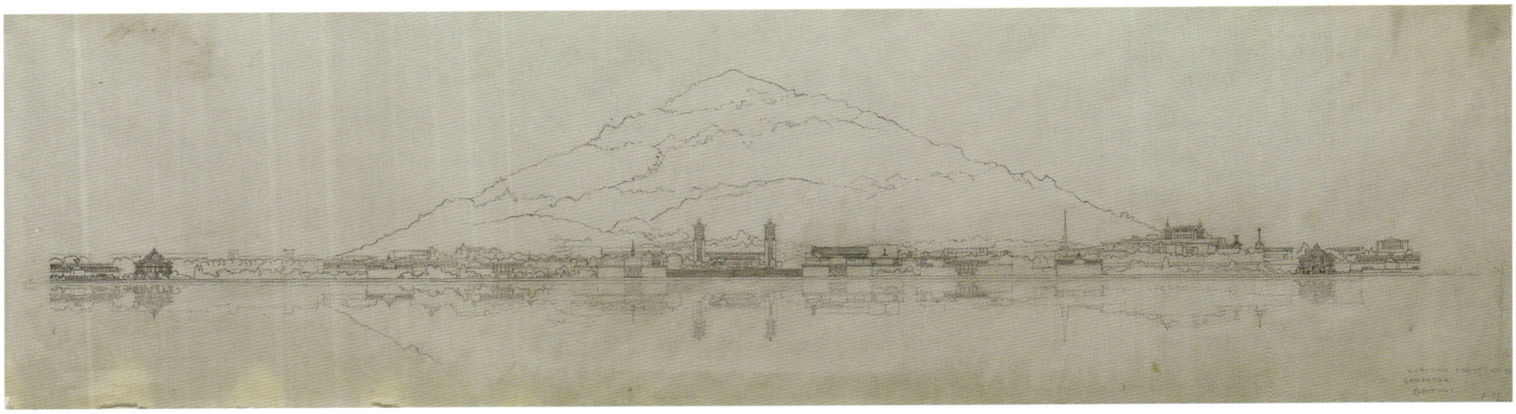

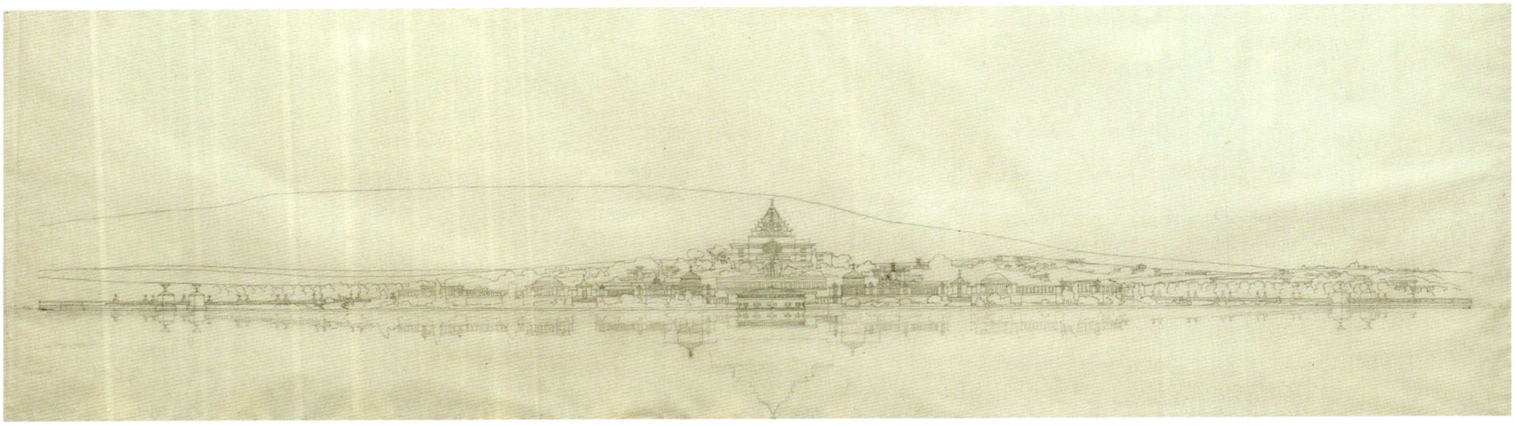

Figure 6 *(top)*
Marion Mahony Griffin and Walter Burley Griffin; *Canberra City Plan: Sectional View Through Lake Showing Mount Ainslie in Background*, circa 1912; ink on linen; 18 ¼ × 67 in. Gift of Marion Mahony Griffin through Eric Nicholls, 1988.418.2, The Art Institute of Chicago. Photograph copyright © The Art Institute of Chicago.

The technique varied from panel to panel as Marion and her assistants, among them Emily Hofman and her sister-in-law Genevieve Griffin, experimented and hurried to finish. Entries were due at the end of January 1912, giving the Griffins only about nine weeks to complete their work and send it by ship to Australia.

There are extraordinary explorations and subtleties in the execution of the images—the elegant Japanese-style whiplash clouds, forming long, sweeping curves over Mount Ainslie and the Government Group elevation, the echoing whiplash reflections in the Government Group water rendering, and the watercolor representation of the "autumn" foliage between Marion's sketches of colonnaded buildings, what might be called a kind of architectural *staffage*. The trees would not have been autumnal in fact; Australian flora is strongly multicolored all year round.

Marion's most important stylistic technique is almost invisible: the minute impasto crescents, thick applications of white paint spread across her architectural surfaces. She adopted that trick from the publication of the Austrian architect Josef Olbrich's work by the German publisher Ernst Wasmuth, and she used it in her renderings.[5] The result is a subtle flicker.

James Weirick feels that these huge drawings are not based on Japanese prints (as is usually assumed of Marion's work) but on painted and gilded Asian screens. Marion's images are much bigger (the scale in the cross sections is 1 = 100 feet) than Eliel Saarinen's and Alfred Agache's second- and third-prize drawings on conventional paper, rendered in pen, ink wash, and watercolor (figures 8 and 9).[6] Indeed, Marion's three-part perspective from Mount Ainslie may have been hinged, like a screen.

Others surmise that Marion's drawings are intended more as murals than as screens, taking off from the watercolor panorama of the Molonglo site provided in the competition materials, but also like a mural of fairies and herons painted by Marion more than twenty years later at the George B. Armstrong International Studies Elementary

Figure 7 *(facing page)*
Marion Mahony Griffin and Walter Burley Griffin; *Canberra City Plan: Sectional View Showing Elevation of City from Waterfront,* circa 1912; ink on linen; approximately 19 × 63 ¾ in. Gift of Marion Mahony Griffin through Eric Nicholls, 1988.418.7, The Art Institute of Chicago. Photograph copyright © The Art Institute of Chicago.

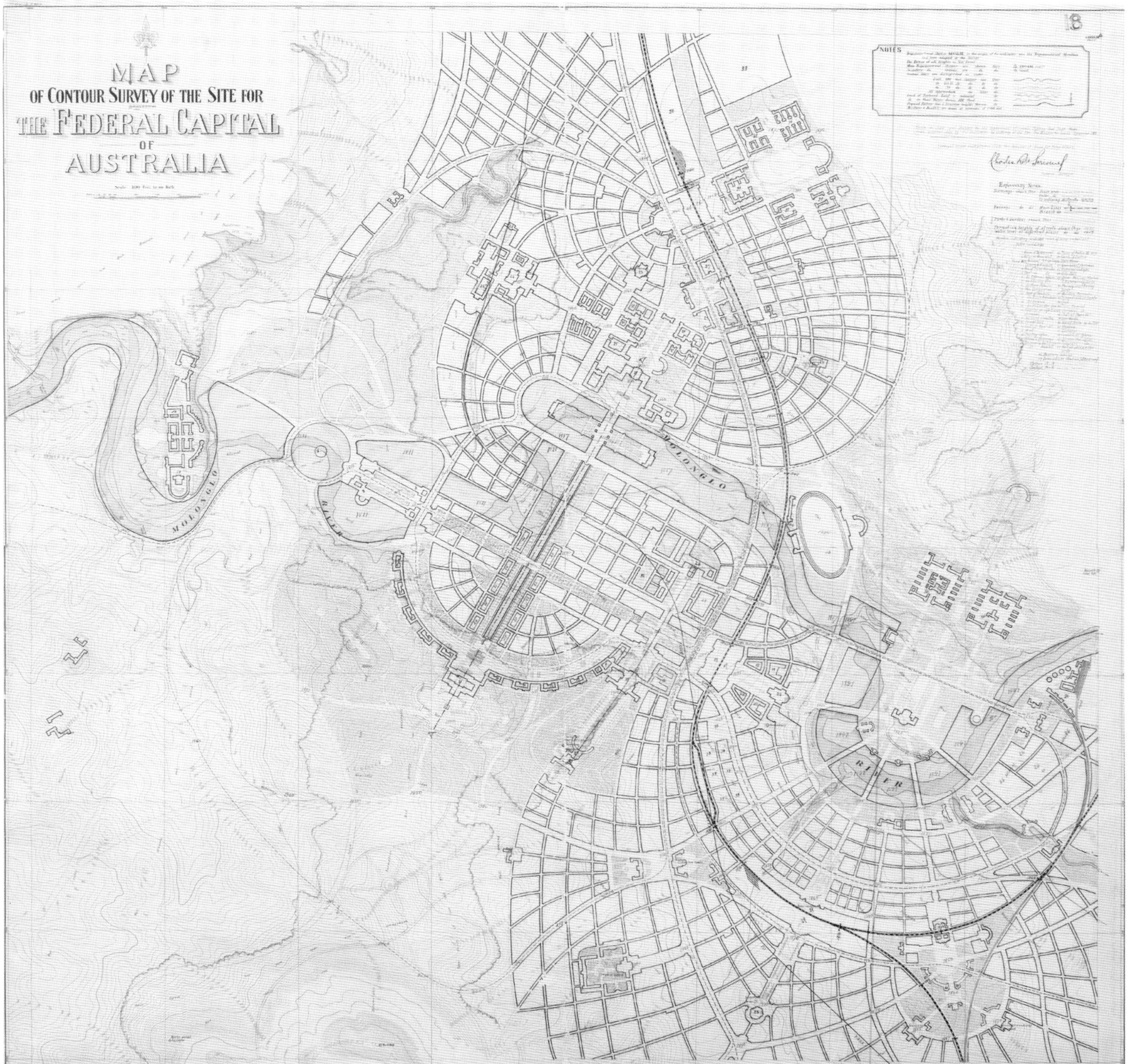

Figure 8
Eliel Saarinen; *Map of Contour Survey of the Site for the Federal Capital of Australia,* 1911; drawing on existing contour map; 55 × 55 in.; National Archives of Australia, A710, 30

Figure 9
Alfred Agache; *Enumeration of Public Buildings for the Federal Capital of Australia,* 1911; drawing on existing contour map; 55 × 52 ¾ in.; National Archives of Australia, A710, 1

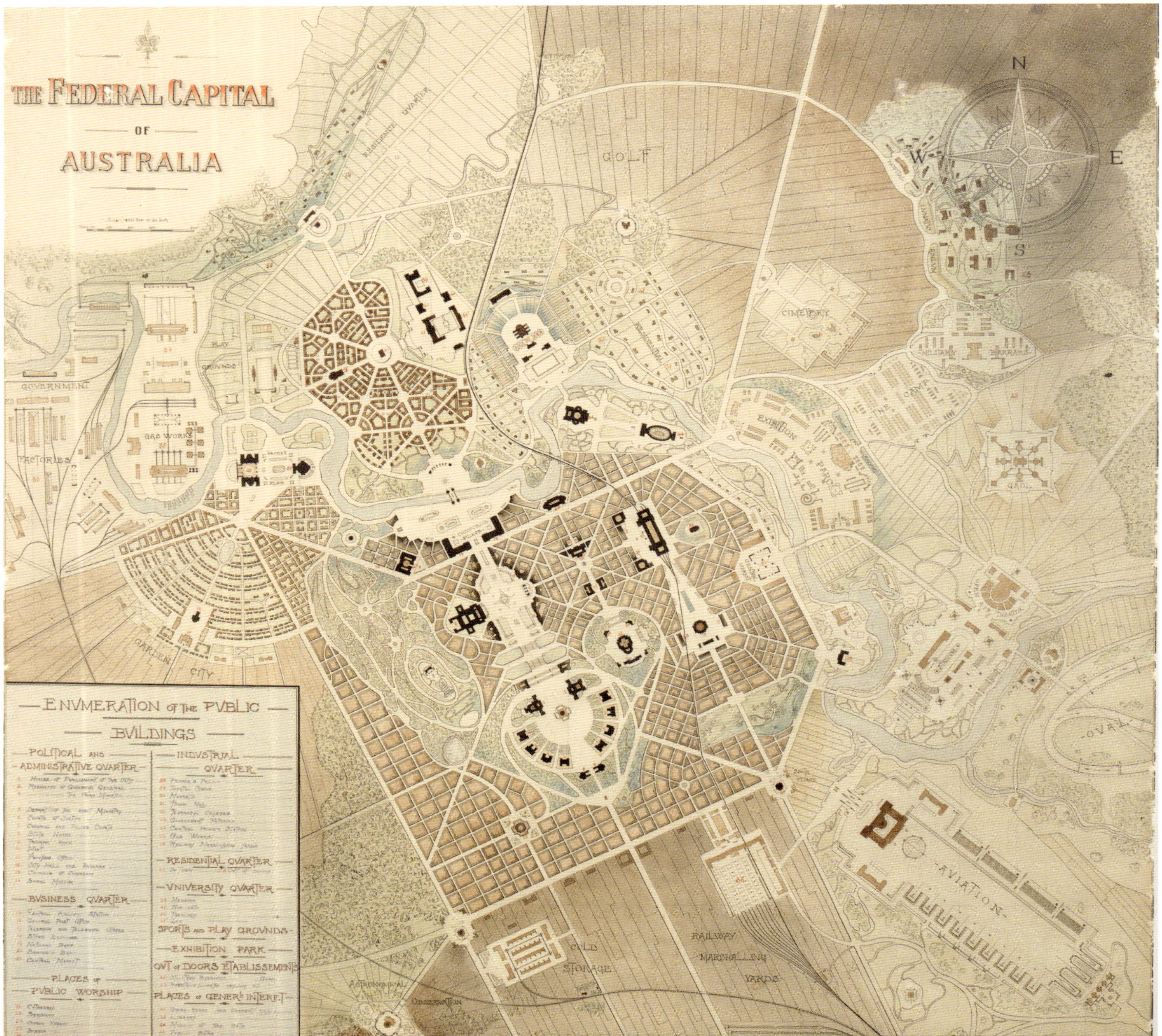

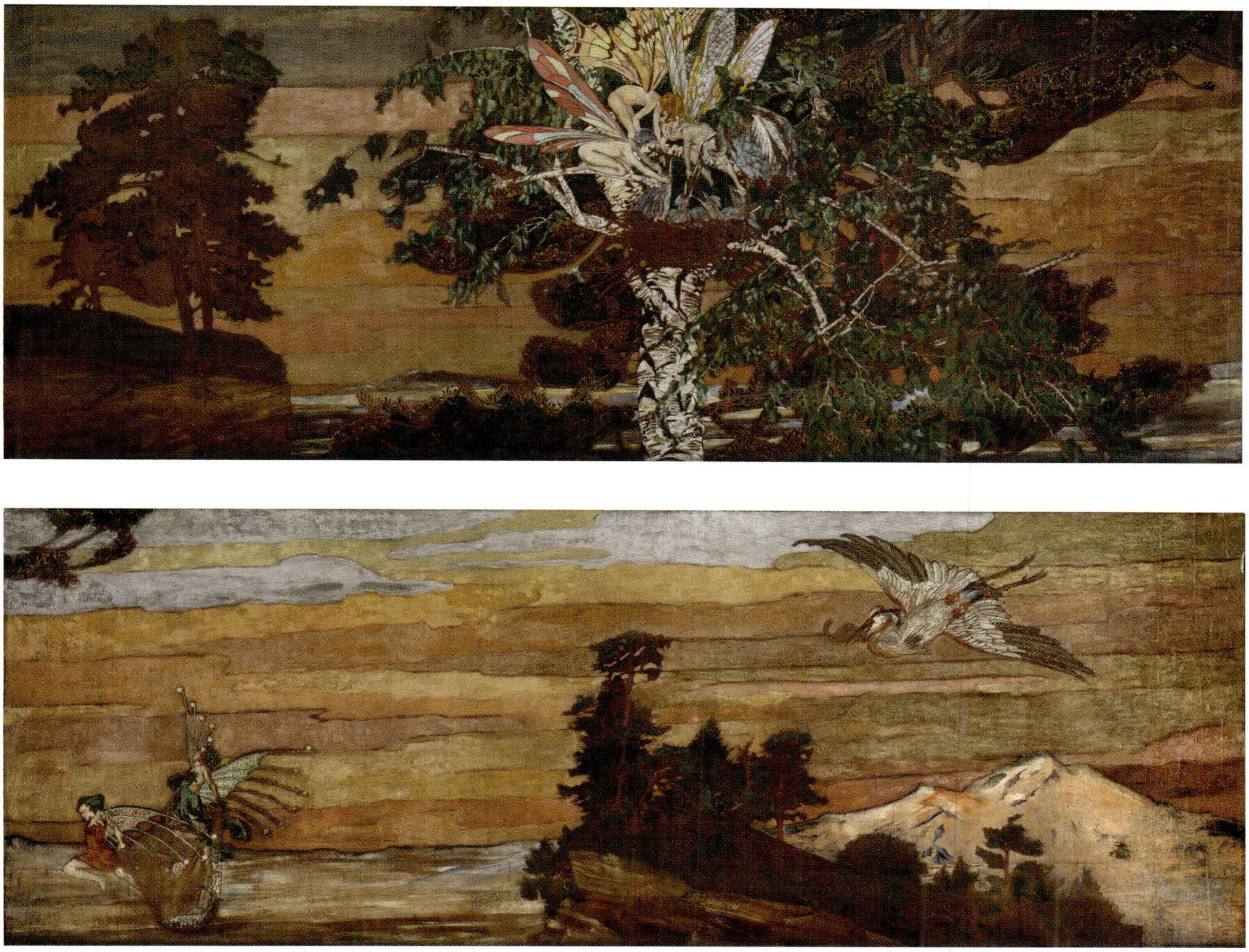

Figure 10
Marion Mahony Griffin; *Fairies Feeding the Herons,* 1931; oil with metallic paints on canvas, two panels, approximately 4 x 12 ft. each; courtesy George B. Armstrong International Studies Elementary School, Chicago. Photograph: James Prinz.

School in Rogers Park, Chicago (figure 10).[7] In type one might compare them to Jules Guerin's architectural murals depicting international trade in Daniel Burnham's Continental Bank Hall, or to Guerin's historical scenes flanking Daniel Chester French's statue of Abraham Lincoln at his memorial in Washington. But Marion's colors are much more intense, and her surfaces are more heavily worked.[8] Those rugged surfaces suggest that the viewer stand back to embrace them, but the extreme fineness of their detail lures the viewer slowly forward to examine them closely, first their startling architectural *staffage,* then the luminous building surfaces achieved by her stippling, and finally the silhouettes, reflections, and halos she evokes. This *staffage* of buildings—which are identified in the preliminary perspective—seems purposefully varied, from the formal classical vocabulary of the Government Group to the fantasy forms of the lagoon-front recreational structures. Walter urges in his competition text that the buildings be executed in reinforced concrete, a new and popular architectural material in the early twentieth century.[9]

How the Griffins' Plan Worked

The overall plan was a different problem than the sections or the perspective. Walter's idea was to interweave built-up areas and parklands, spaced by the lagoons and by hilltops (meant not to be built on), from which an organizing network of axes spreads across the site. The principal axis extends

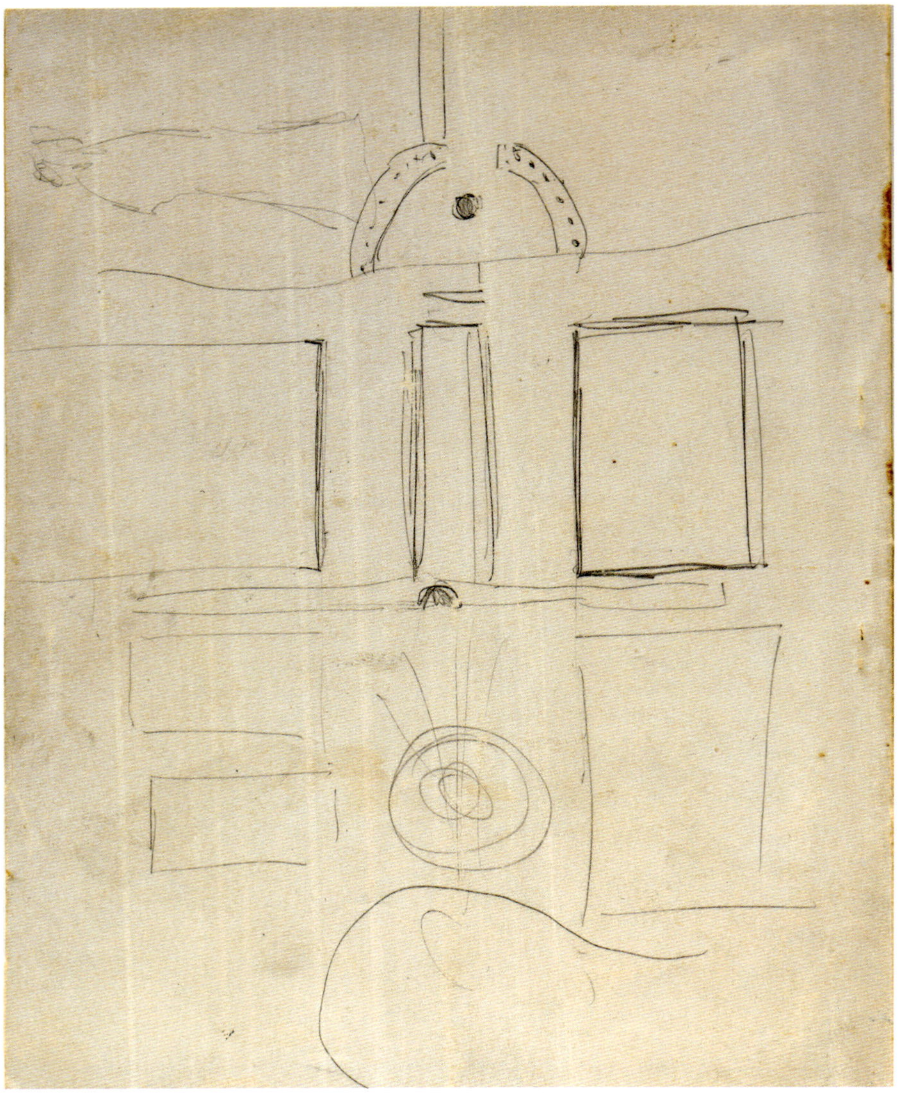

Figure 11
Attributed to Daniel Hudson Burnham; Sketch for Court of Honor at World's Columbian Exposition, 1891; graphite on paper; approximately 9 x 7 in.; private collection; photograph by Tom Van Eynde

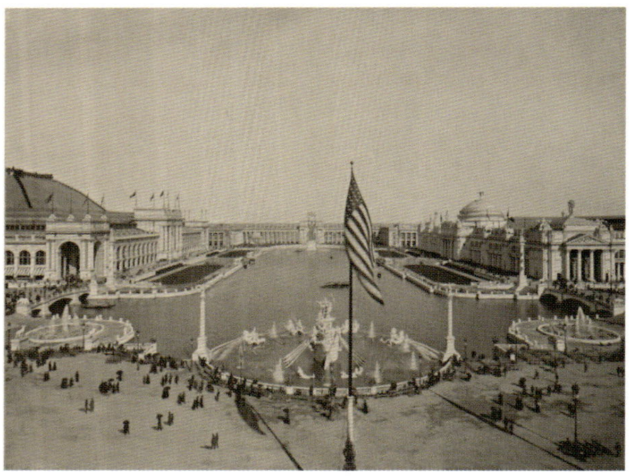

(right) Court of Honor, Looking East, 1894; architecture by Daniel Hudson Burnham, photograph by William Henry Jackson; Charles Deering McCormick Library of Special Collections, Northwestern University Library.

from the abrupt conical Mount Ainslie to distant Mugga Mugga across the low Capital Hill. The secondary axis runs at right angles from Black Mountain on the city's western edge eastward down the Molonglo Valley. The Griffins' knowledge of the site is as amazing as their success in building within it—so dramatically proved when it was actually executed in the Molonglo Valley. One is curious to know whether they had talked with the writer Miles Franklin, then living in Chicago, who knew the site well as a child.[10] In October 1913, after his first actual visit to the Canberra site, Walter explained:

> Taken altogether, the site may be considered as an irregular amphitheatre—with Ainslie at the north-east in the rear, flanked on either side by Black Mountain and Pleasant Hill, all forming the top galleries; with the slopes to the water, the auditorium; with the waterway and flood basin, the arena; with the southern slopes reflected in the basin, the terraced stage and setting of monumental Government structures sharply defined rising tier on tier to the culminating highest internal forested hill of the Capitol, and with Mugga Mugga, Red Hill and the blue distant mountain ranges, sun reflecting, forming the back scene of the theatrical whole.[11]

This, of course, is the tableau represented in Marion's three-part perspective. An important document of the conception of Daniel Hudson Burnham's Court of Honor for the World's Columbian Exposition of 1893 is the architect's pencil sketch on the back of a copy of John Wellborn Root's funeral service of January 18, 1891 (figure 11). In the sketch, what became the domed Administration Building appears as a lookout indicated by a series of concentric circles emitting a spray of sight lines down the lagoon and out into Lake Michigan past what, in the 1891 plan, was a single semicircular file of columns. Marion's use of Mount Ainslie to elevate her view, furthermore, repeats Guerin's remarkable 1907 aerial view of Chicago from over Lake Michigan created for Burnham's project to improve the city, the Plan of Chicago (figure 15).[12]

The drawings that the Griffins executed in Chicago, however, have a more immediate context than rendering techniques used in city planning, first of

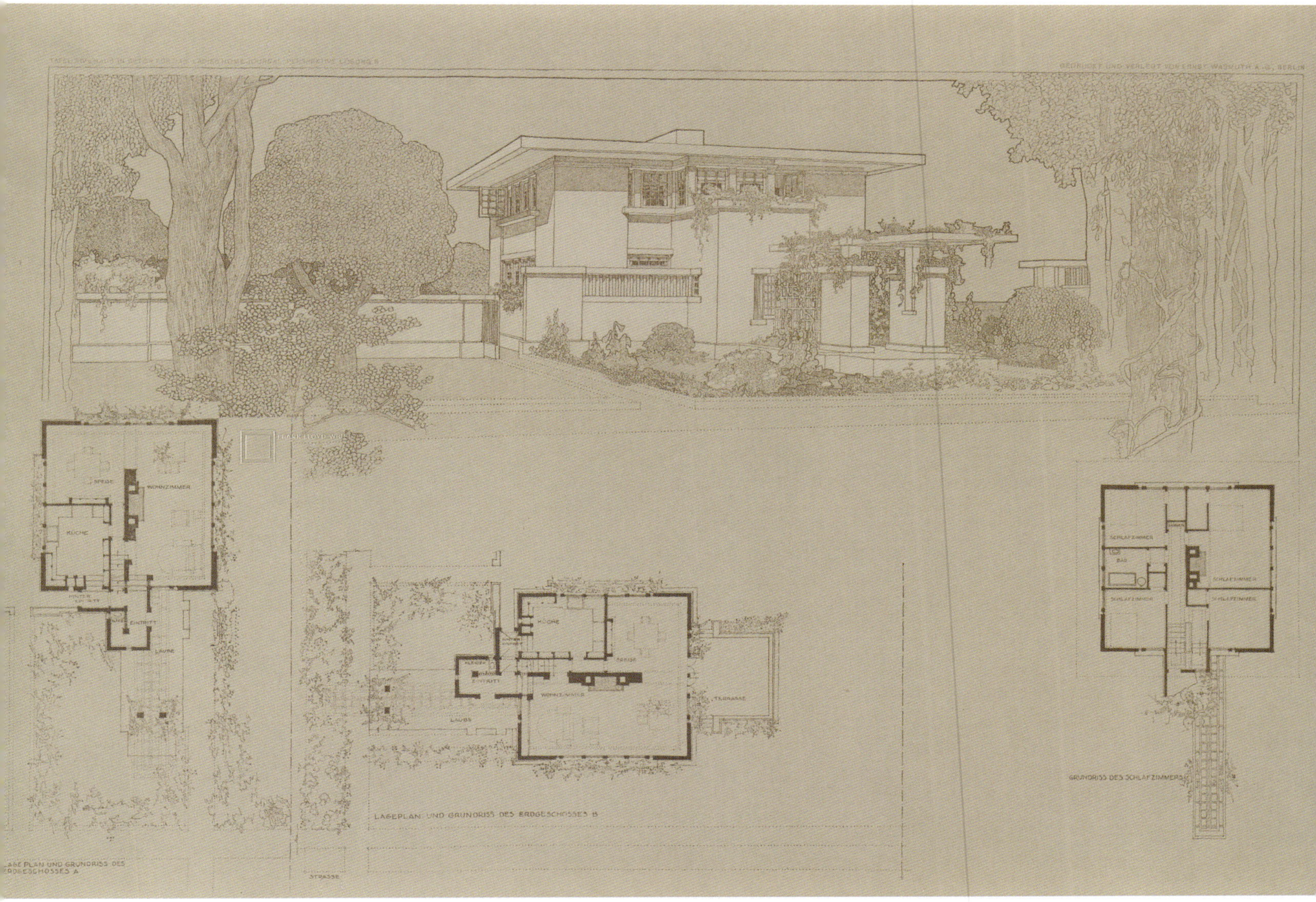

Figure 12
Frank Lloyd Wright; *Concrete House for Ladies' Home Journal*; from *Ausgeführte Bauten und Entwürfe* (Studies and Executed Buildings) *von Frank Lloyd Wright* (Berlin: Wasmuth, 1911); 16 × 26 in.; Charles Deering McCormick Library of Special Collections, Northwestern University Library. Copyright © 2012 Frank Lloyd Wright Foundation / Artists Rights Society (ARS), New York.

all in the exploration Marion herself carried out for Frank Lloyd Wright in her 1905–6 Unity Temple representations (as Paul Kruty has documented).[13] This technique became the signature vocabulary of the portfolio of one hundred lithographs of Wright's drawings, *Ausgeführte Bauten und Entwürfe von Frank Lloyd Wright,* assembled in 1910 for Wasmuth, a Berlin publisher of art books (figure 12). Marion was simultaneously pushing her technique much further in her presentation work for Walter around the time of their marriage in June 1911, building off his scroll format that he originated in 1906 for Chicago Architectural Club exhibitions.[14] And there is Marion's largely lost work as an artist and muralist—barely discernible in frustratingly vague photographs of her altar wall for the destroyed All Souls Unitarian Church in Evanston, Illinois (1904), visible in her 1916 "forest portraits" of Tasmanian landscape (figures 13 and 14), and most elaborately executed in her 1932 mural at the Armstrong School in Chicago, "Fairies Feeding the Herons" (figure 10). But for her using color was a broad enterprise—given the opportunity at the Sydney suburb of Castlecrag, she painted and stippled interior surfaces, as in the Fishwick House. Louise Lightfoot, who lived with the Griffins, reminisces that Marion flecked the interior where they lived in yellow splashes, "to bring the sunshine into the house."[15]

The ultimate precedent for the Canberra set was not Marion's at all, however, but Daniel Burnham's Plan of Chicago drawings by Jules Guerin (figures

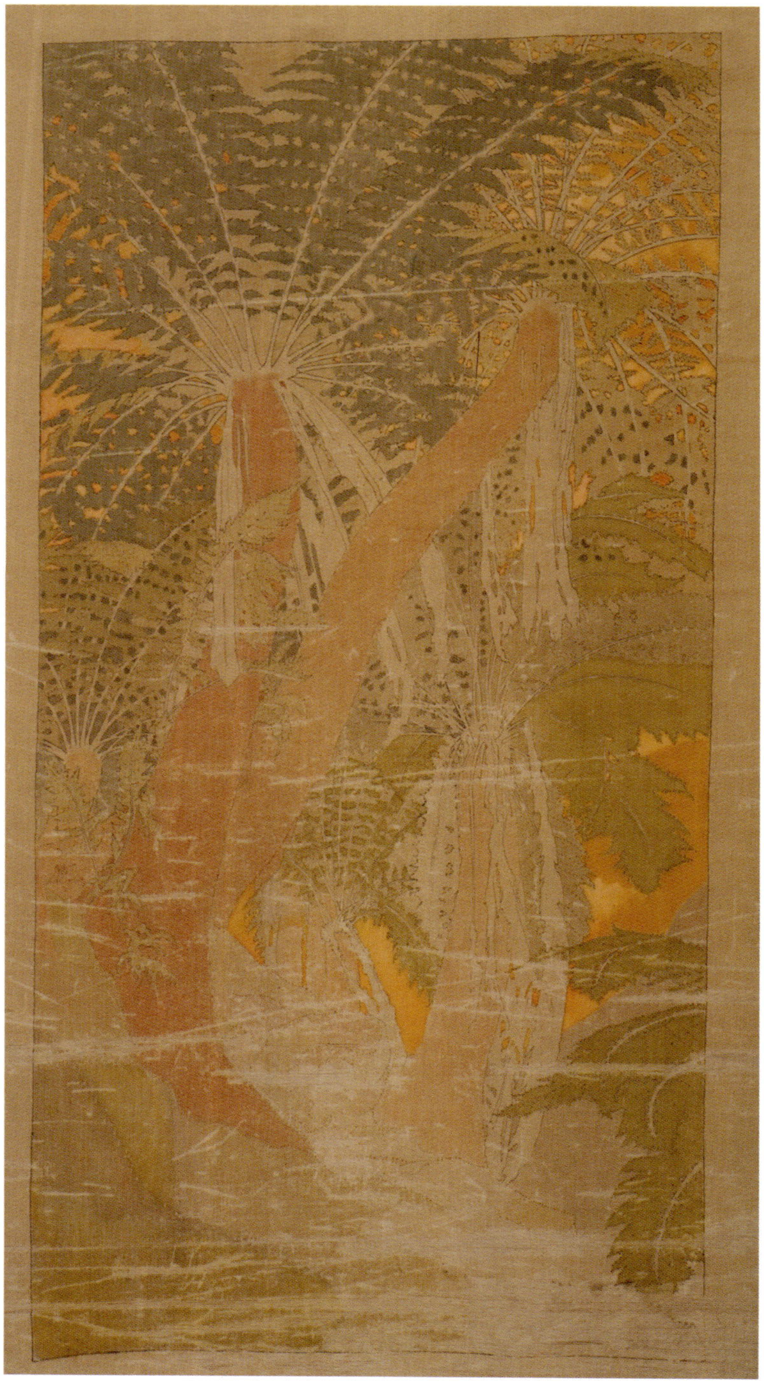

Figure 13
Marion Mahony Griffin; *Tree Fern Gully, Forest Portrait No. 9*, 1919; pen and black ink with brush and colored inks and dyes on gold silk; 43 ½ × 25 ¾ in.; Mary and Leigh Block Museum of Art, Northwestern University, gift of Marion Mahony Griffin, 1985.1.88. Photograph: Tom Van Eynde.

15 and 16). Like Marion Griffin's, Guerin's drawings are huge in format and brilliant in color (although clearly influenced by the paintings of Édouard Vuillard and Ker-Xavier Roussel). These drawings were not to be mailed off in a competition. Instead, they became the elements of an amazing public unveiling of the project on July 5, 1909, in the northeast first floor gallery of the Art Institute on Michigan Avenue, before publication in Burnham's gorgeous book *Plan of Chicago* (1909) (figures 17, 18, and 19).[16] It was Burnham who took two steps which were to be fundamental for Marion's breakthrough: first, the adoption of great size to lift the plan from document to proclamation; second, the use of novelty in rendering style (rather than architectural vocabulary) to achieve an atmosphere of futurity.[17] The architectural historian Christopher Vernon would add a third gift of Burnham to the Griffins: the concept of organizing a city around axes fixed by existing features, demonstrated subtly in Burnham's 1902 McMillan Commission Plan for the development of Washington, D.C., oriented on Capitol Hill and the White House, and shown much more systematically in his 1905 plan for the Philippine summer capital, Baguio.

How did the three Australian judges—only one an architect and he of little experience—manage to award first prize to the Griffins' project (even if in a two-to-one decision)? How did Minister for Home Affairs King O'Malley—though bold, socialist, and (unadmittedly) American-born—manage to accept their decision? The project was described in Walter's accompanying text as harnessing Australia's natural state and potential resources for a luminous future, and that may have been the very point. And visually the plan was tremendously lucid—you could read it at a glance and see what it was about. Conceptually, the plan was divided into its functional elements—which Walter later neatly diagrammed in his explanatory text—and arranged in the symmetrical, hierarchical pattern admired in "Beaux-Arts" planning and also evident in Chicago progressive functionalism. At the center, the capital complex and the civic and market nodes were linked by boulevards into an equilateral triangle across

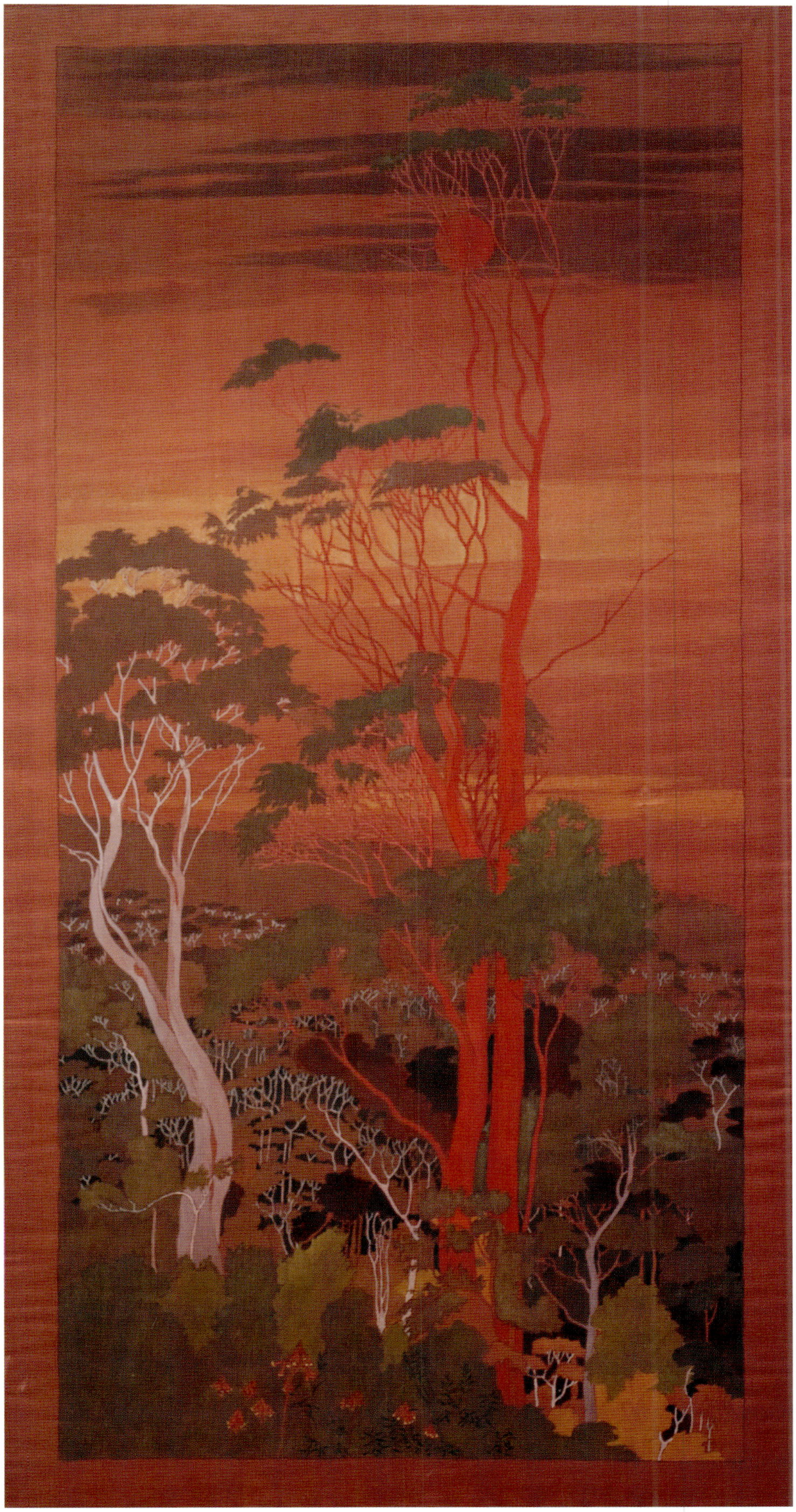

Figure 14
Marion Mahony Griffin; *Eucalyptus Urnigera, Tasmania/Scarlet Bark, Sunset, Forest Portrait No. 11*, 1918; pen and black ink with brush and colored inks and dyes on red silk; 45 × 22 ¾ in.; Mary and Leigh Block Museum of Art, Northwestern University, gift of Marion Mahony Griffin, 1985.1.117. Photograph: James Prinz.

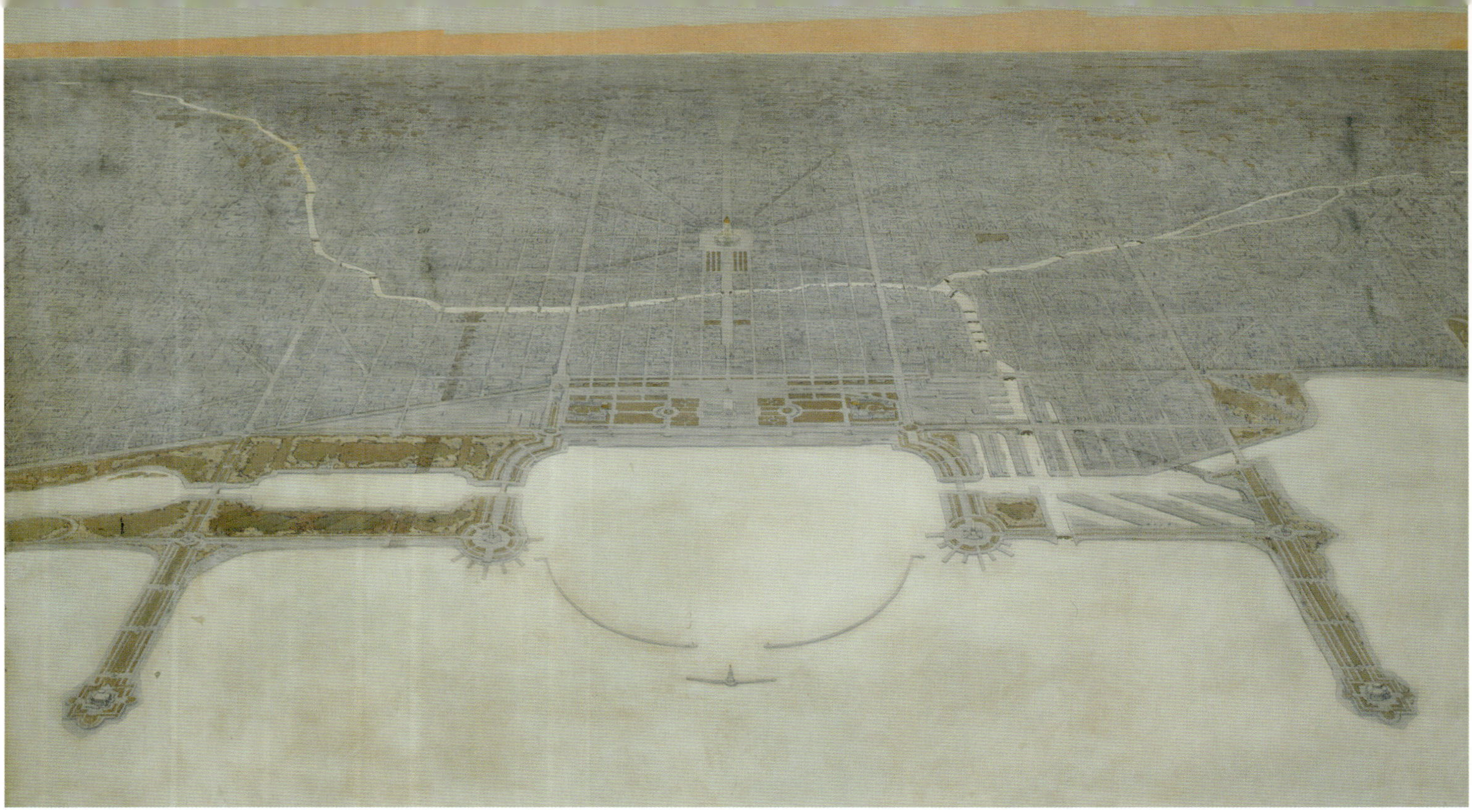

Figure 15
Jules Guerin, Edward Herbert Bennett, and Daniel Hudson Burnham; *Plan of Chicago, Plate 87: View Looking West over the City, Showing the Proposed Civic Center, the Grand Axis, Grant Park, and the Harbor,* 1907; watercolor and graphite on paper; approximately 55 × 90 ½ in.; gift of Patrick Shaw, 1991.1381, The Art Institute of Chicago. Photograph copyright © The Art Institute of Chicago.

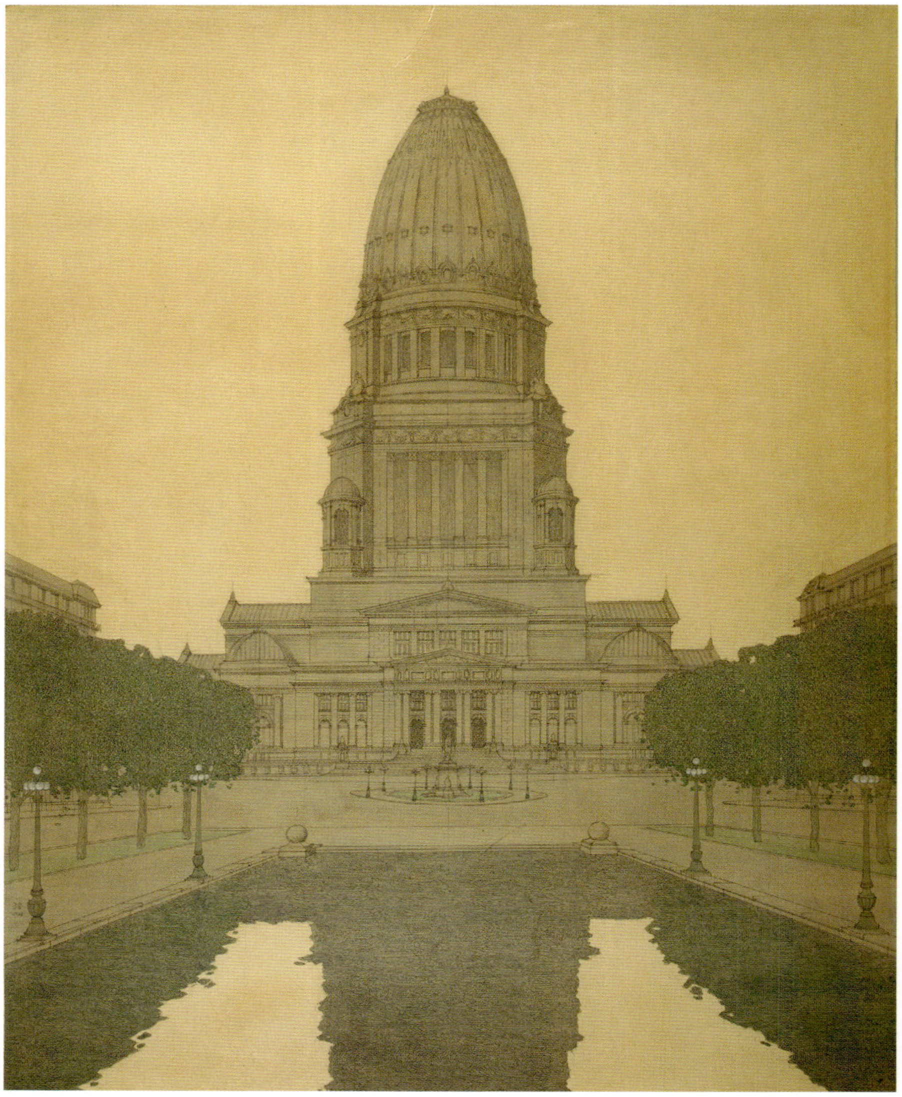

Figure 16
Jules Guerin, Edward Herbert Bennett, and Daniel Hudson Burnham; *Plan of Chicago: Civic Center,* 1908; ink, colored inks, graphite, and watercolor on toned paper; approximately 30 × 23 in.; gift of Edward H. Bennett, Jr., 1989.457, The Art Institute of Chicago. Photograph copyright © The Art Institute of Chicago.

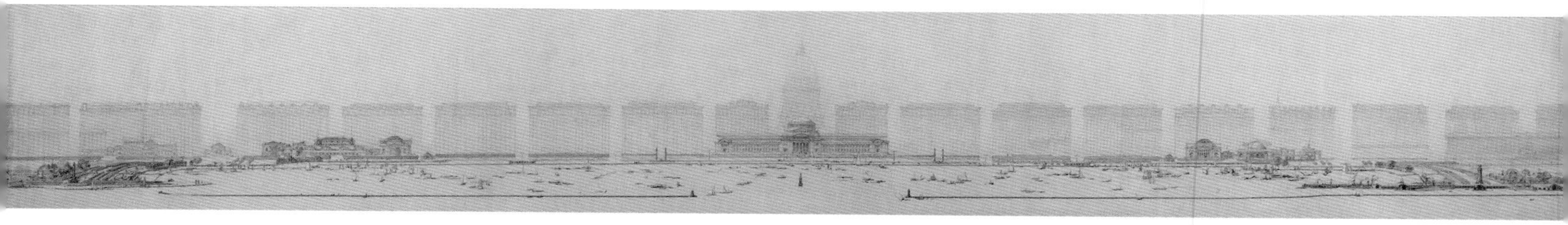

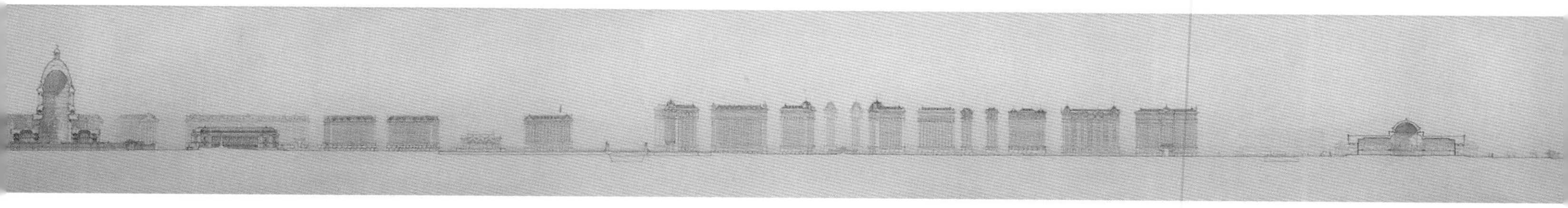

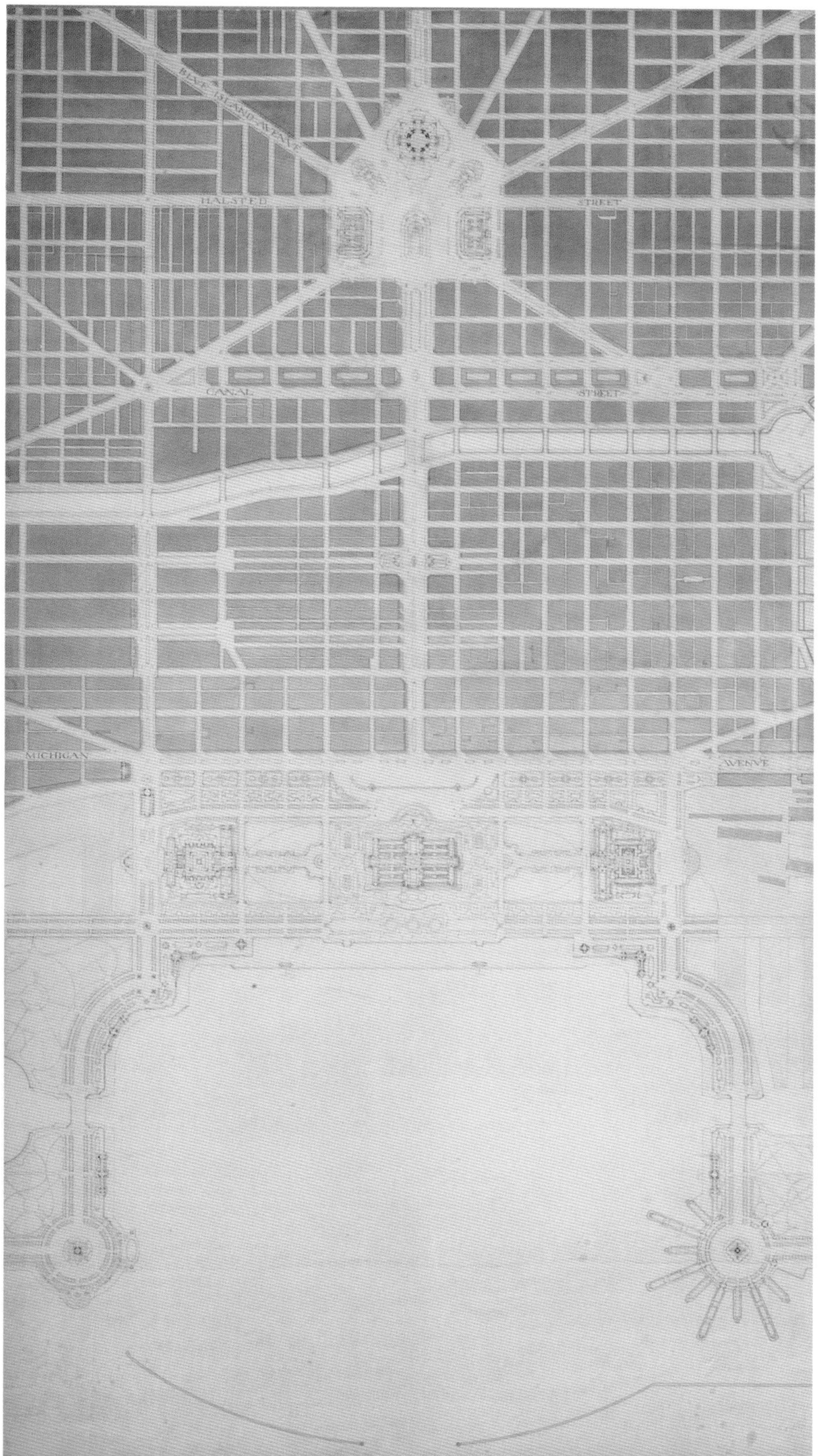

Figure 17 *(top)*
Daniel Hudson Burnham and Edward Herbert Bennett; *Plan of Chicago, Plate 125: Elevation of Grant Park and Harbor; the Eastern Facade of the City on Michigan Avenue, and the Dome of the Administration Building of the Civic Center, Looking from Lake Michigan*, 1909; ink, graphite, and watercolor on paper; 16 × 126 ½ in.; on permanent loan from the City of Chicago to the Art Institute of Chicago, 23.148.1966. Photograph copyright © The Art Institute of Chicago.

Figure 18 *(above)*
Daniel Hudson Burnham and Edward Herbert Bennett; *Plan of Chicago, Plate 126: Section Looking North, Taken Through Proposed Grand Axis of the City, Showing the Civic Center and Grant Park*, 1909; ink and graphite on paper; 11 ¾ × 109 in.; on permanent loan from the City of Chicago to the Art Institute of Chicago, 24.148.1966. Photograph copyright © The Art Institute of Chicago.

Figure 19 *(left)*
Daniel Hudson Burnham and Edward Herbert Bennett; *Plan of Chicago, Plate 129: The Business Center of the City, Within the First Circuit Boulevard, Showing the Proposed Grand East-and-West Axis and Its Relation to Grant Park and the Yacht Harbor, the Railway Terminals Schemes on the South and West Sides, and the Civic Center*, 1909; graphite, ink, and wash on paper; approximately 67 × 35 ½ in.; on permanent loan from the City of Chicago to the Art Institute of Chicago, 25.148.1966. Photograph copyright © The Art Institute of Chicago.

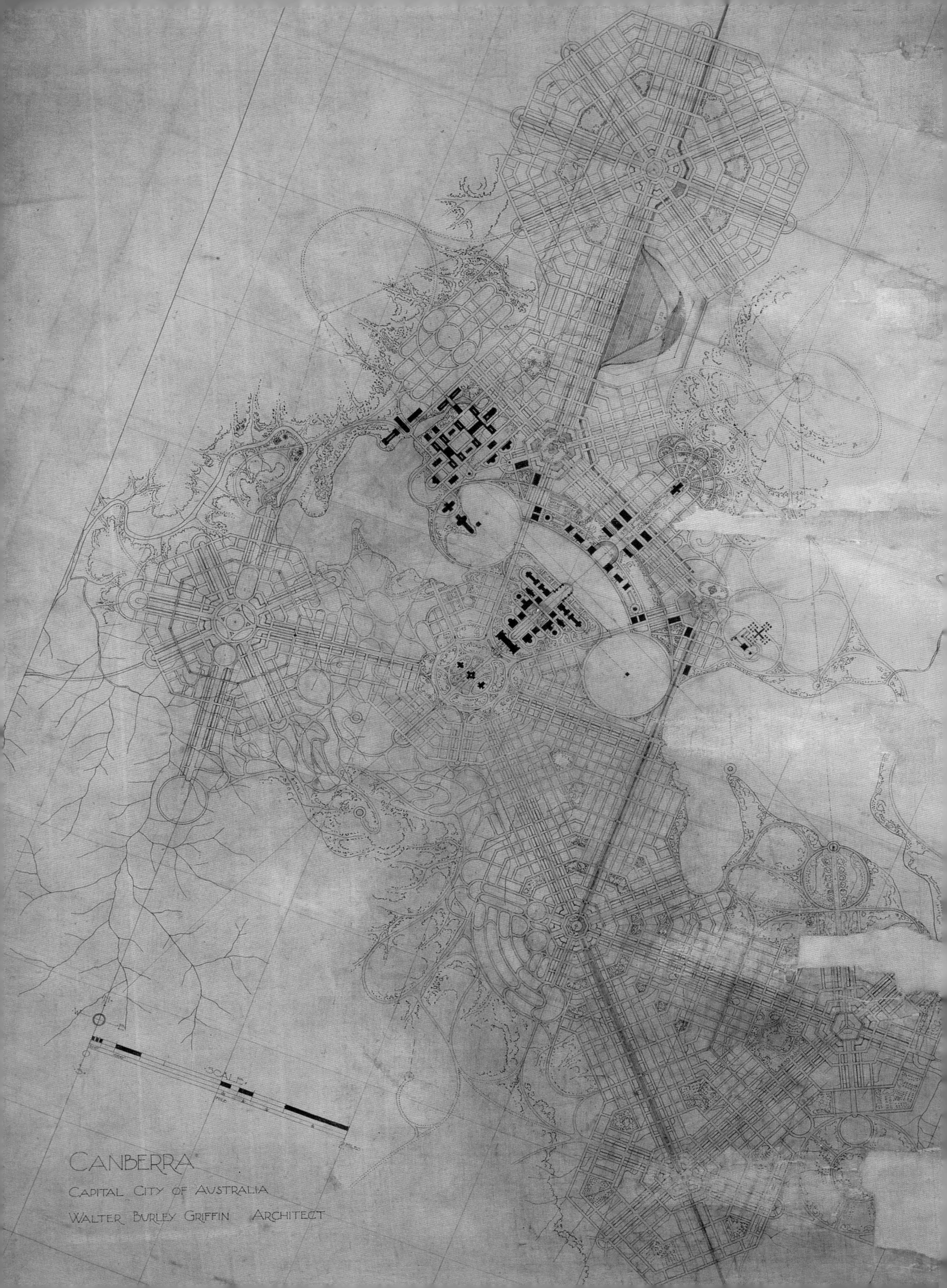
SCALE
CANBERRA
CAPITAL CITY OF AUSTRALIA
WALTER BURLEY GRIFFIN ARCHITECT

a trilobed lagoon (figure 20). From this matrix, further axes radiated out to a series of neighborhoods expanding outward in counterplay with the topography: an industrial suburb to the north, an elite suburb to the west, and three middle-class "garden suburbs" down the Molonglo Valley to the east. Once Walter was named director of design and construction, this lucidity of scattered units disappeared as Walter compressed the plan and bound it together with two broad, curving boulevards for practical execution.

The respected Dutch architect Hendrik Petrus Berlage visited Chicago in 1911 on a lecture tour of the United States. He presented at the Art Institute, met Griffin, and examined the Canberra plan in process.[18] Berlage remarked of Wright's work in Zurich in 1912 that he must have been a student at the École des Beaux-Arts. The young Swiss architect Charles-Édouard Jeanneret (Le Corbusier) later elaborated this idea: "On sentait dans les plans de Wright la *bonne école* de l'Ecole des Beaux-Arts d'ici, c'est à dire, une inclination vers l'ordre, vers l'organisation, vers une création de pure architecture." (One sensed the good tradition of the École des Beaux-Arts in Wright's plans, that is to say, an inclination toward order, toward organization, toward a creation of pure architecture.)[19] In 1912, Berlage illustrated an article on new American architecture in *Schweizerische Bauzeitung* (Swiss Building Journal) with the plan of Wright's Darwin Martin House. This quality of Beaux-Arts organization is even more evident in the Canberra plan in its clear separation of parts and axial interrelation.

The immediate lucidity of the Griffins' plan is all the more striking in contrast to the convolutions of Eliel Saarinen's second-place project—both magisterial and labyrinthine, fascinating and confusing—and the fragmentation of Alfred Agache's third-place design (figures 8 and 9). Interestingly, Griffin's 1918 revision of the plan moves closer to Saarinen's conception in its even pattern of continuous curving streets and boulevards across the Molonglo Valley.

Figure 21
Ebenezer Howard; *Group of Slumless Smokeless Cities*; from *To-Morrow: A Peaceful Path to Real Reform* (London: S. Sonnenschein, 1898)

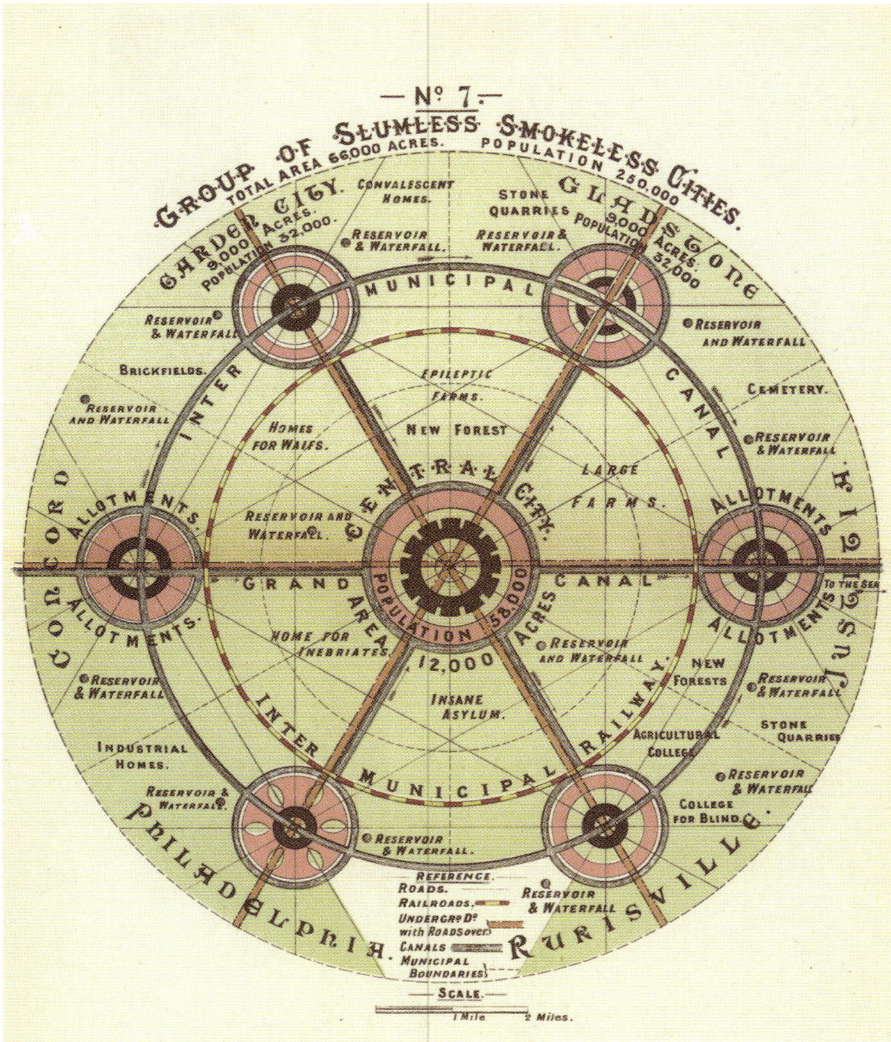

Figure 20 *(facing page)*
Marion Mahony Griffin and Walter Burley Griffin; *Canberra City Plan: Plan of Canberra City, and Environs*, circa 1912; ink on linen; 41 × 30 in.; gift of Marion Mahony Griffin through Eric Nicholls, 1988.418.8, The Art Institute of Chicago. Photograph copyright © The Art Institute of Chicago.

What the École des Beaux-Arts taught, at this high point in its reputation and influence, was the division of an architectural problem into constituent units, then their arrangement in an order simultaneously functional and symbolic—what was called a *parti,* a word Walter himself (trained in this ethos at the University of Illinois) used in the first paragraph of his explanation of his Canberra competition plan.[20] The *parti* was the functional arrangement and underlying organizational geometry of an architectural plan, sympathetic to both the Beaux-Arts and the progressive practices. But Griffin clearly was also looking to a parallel authority in his broad scattering of parts across the Molonglo basin, namely Ebenezer Howard's Garden City model of 1898, a utopian disaggregation of the city into a texture of small circular town nodes spread across open agricultural land linked together by a network of railroads (figure 21). This model Griffin pushed together and linked with streetcars to achieve an anti-urban city, like what Howard's followers Raymond Unwin and Alfred Mottram were imagining in 1911 when Unwin visited Chicago to lecture about the Garden City movement (figure 22).[21]

Concrete as a New Building Material

Marion, furthermore, drawing the panoramic cross sections of the Canberra competition set, filled this landscape with a surprising new cast-concrete architecture. Concrete as a building material was an issue of great import in the first decade of the twentieth century, partly for the unexpected forms it made possible, partly for its wonderful economy.[22] Every Midwestern suburb has its concrete house (or houses), in blocks or cast whole. Thomas Alva Edison led the way with his experiments from 1901 to 1909, culminating in eleven cast "cement" (actually concrete) houses for his employees in Union, New Jersey.

There were exhibitions of cement products and competitions to design concrete houses, the two often linked as in Chicago in June 1911, when Walter served on the jury for such a competition

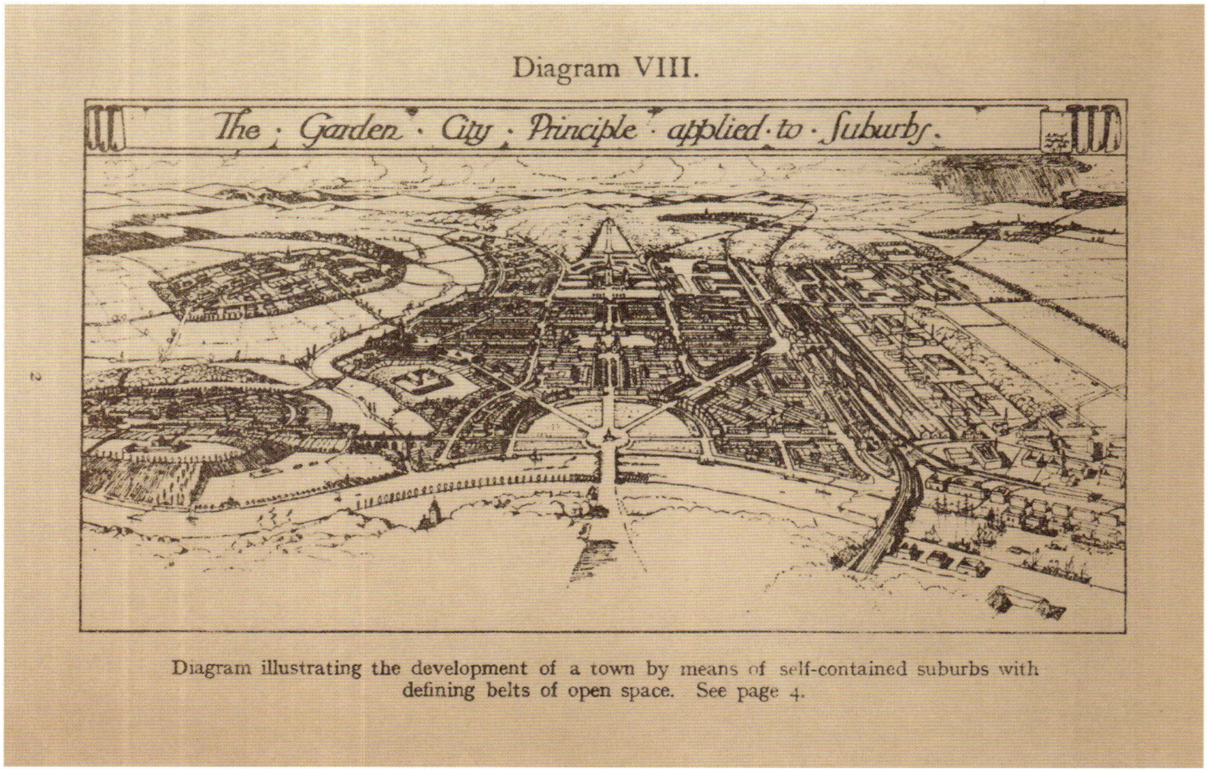

Figure 22
Alfred Mottram, *The Garden City Principle Applied to Suburbs;* from *Nothing Gained by Overcrowding!* by Raymond Unwin (London: P. S. King and Son, 1912)

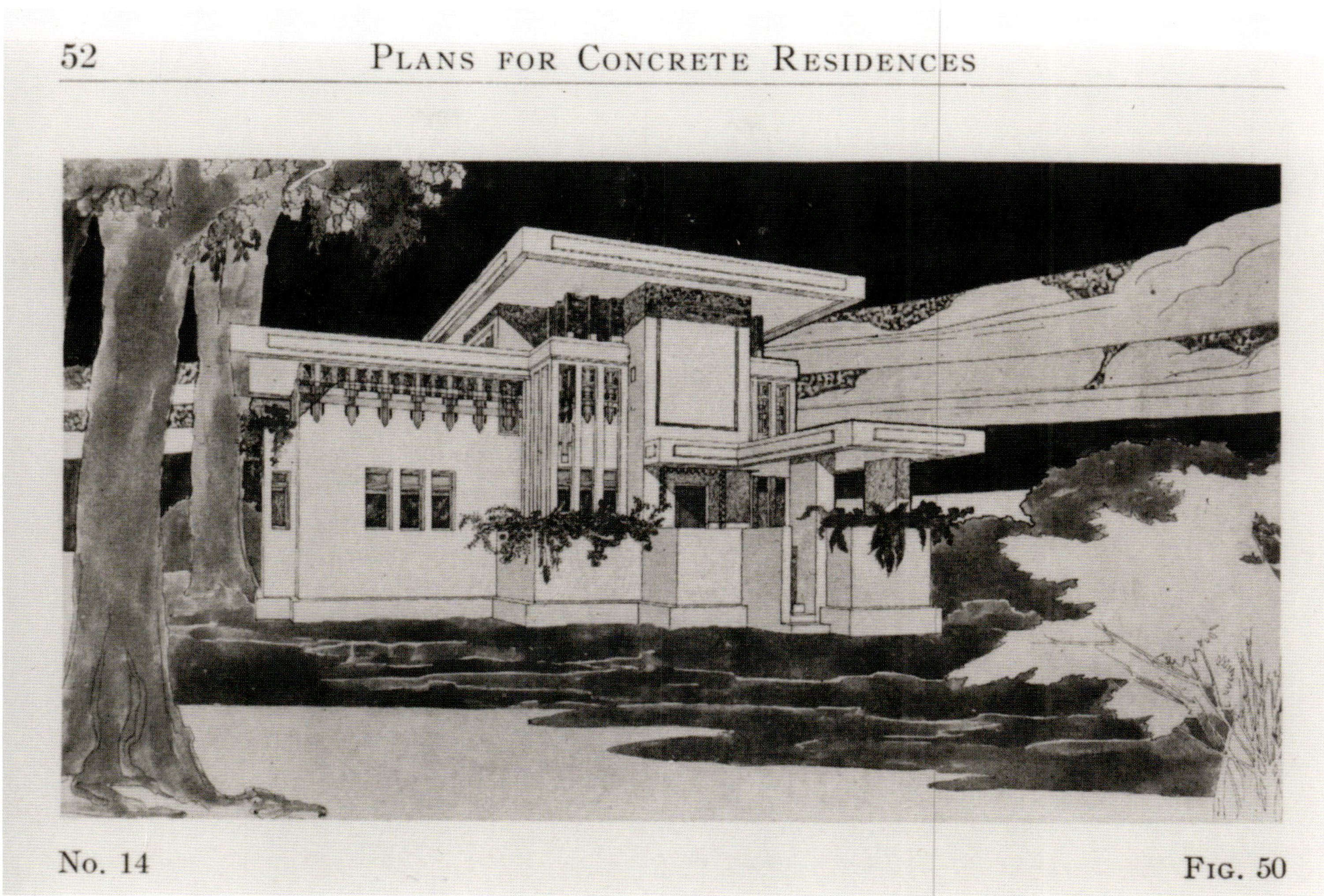

Figure 23
Marion Mahony Griffin; from *Plans for Concrete Residences: Being a Selected Number of Designs with Descriptions and Estimates of Cost, Submitted in a Competition of the Chicago Architectural Club for Prizes Offered by the Universal Portland Cement Co.* (Chicago: Universal Portland Cement Company, 1909); Avery Architectural and Fine Arts Library, Columbia University

and awarded a prize to his former employee Harry Robinson.[23] Later both Walter Burley Griffin and Frank Lloyd Wright were commissioned to design pavilions for the Universal Portland Cement Company.[24] Earlier, in 1909, Marion had submitted a project in her own right to the company's concrete house competition (figure 23).[25] *The Ladies' Home Journal* published a model concrete house in 1906 (figure 12, designed by Frank Lloyd Wright, aided by Walter and rendered by Marion).

The *American Architect* mounted a discussion of the possibilities of concrete construction, soliciting comment from architects all over the country, including Louis Sullivan and Dwight Heald Perkins.[26] Wright had used the material to great effect, first in the Larkin Building (1902–6) and Unity Temple (1905–6), then—after Marion's 1911 Canberra drawings—in his Midway Gardens (1913–14) and Tokyo Imperial Hotel (1913–23).[27] Walter founded his Solid Rock Construction Company in 1911, the "Solid Rock House" in Kenilworth, Illinois, being his flagship building.

In 1916, a French observer cited the Griffins' work as a model for cheap concrete reconstruction after the world war.[28] This reflected a general misapprehension of Prairie work that the Griffins' experiments resolved. In 1910, a German survey of American architecture, Rudolf Vogel's *Das amerikanische Haus*, mistook Wright's Heller and Willits houses for concrete construction, and in 1912 the *Schweizerische Bauzeitung* published the Griffins' Bovee Houses (correctly labeled "Eisen- und Eisenbeton" [iron and ferroconcrete]) in the context of a portfolio of Wright's work[29]—leading Le Corbusier to assume Wright was providing a model for concrete construction, as the architectural historian Paul Turner has documented. The French architect Tony Garnier, whom Le Corbusier knew and admired, just then accepted concrete as the tool to realize the idea of a utopian new industrial city.[30]

The Griffins in Europe

Er ist im Einklang mit unserem Programm . . .
(He is in agreement with our program)
—WALTER BURLEY GRIFFIN (1914)

The design competition the Griffins had won in 1912 was, theoretically, only for the plan of the new Australian capital city, in spite of the extraordinary architectural *staffage* in Marion's drawings. A second competition was specified to choose a design and designer for the Parliament House building itself. Walter was put in charge of organizing the project, writing a competition brief with an important statement of "Design Principles" and setting off on an extended tour to publicize the event and to recruit a jury. He returned through San Francisco at the time of the planning of the Panama-Pacific International Exposition, and the director of the exposition requested that a model of the Canberra project be made for display. Then the Griffins journeyed on together to France, Germany, Austria, and Great Britain.[31]

By the time the trip was over, Walter had the enthusiastic confirmation of the architects Otto Wagner of Austria, Victor Laloux of France, and John James Burnet of Britain to serve as jurors (joining Louis Sullivan and the Australian John Sulman, later replaced by George T. Poole). Walter also collected invitations to display the set of drawings for the Canberra competition at the Exposition Internationale Urbaine (International Urban Exhibition) at Lyon as well as Marion's house renderings at the Musée des Arts Décoratifs (Museum of Decorative Arts) in Paris, which later were to go on to Vienna for display under Otto Wagner's aegis.

Walter Burley Griffin's intentions for the competition are handwritten on several sheets of paper in the National Archives of Australia. He inscribed, "The importance of this event cannot be considered limited to that of the foremost building of the Commonwealth, but as establishing an architectural standard not only for the future seat of government in Australia but for a great democracy of such scope, climatic advantages and other modern conditions differing radically from any prototype in Europe or elsewhere."[32] In the printed text, this goal expanded to:

> The Australian Commonwealth, with no historically evolved suitable architectural style, but with unique scope in its unlimited open continent for national growth, with this virgin city site under unified control, and possessed of modern building science, appliances and materials, is in a position to exact unity in plan and homogeneity in expression and harmony with the whole natural environment beyond any ordinary opportunity. Since the city is to evolve gradually, the desired unity cannot be assured by personality, nor can it under popular government be established by authoritative decree of any arbitrary type. Hence it is desired that the standard of design be the expression of actual functions through practical organic planning; through the direct adaption of the inherent characteristics of the materials used, avoiding the intrusion of irrelevant features, however time-honoured, on the one hand, or individual, on the other; and through recognition of the peculiar site conditions. Parliament House, with the whole Government Group, is but an element in a larger system of parallel-set public buildings, all regulated by the same standard, which is intended to extend through the entire city and to characterize it.[33]

This statement is precisely what Griffin's opponents in the government bureaucracy would eliminate when the competition was revived in 1916, restricted to citizens of the British Empire.[34]

Paris

The Griffins' six-month leave can be sketched as follows (I am greatly indebted to Christopher Vernon here): departure from Sydney on November 15, 1913; departure for Europe (from Chicago?) on February 15, 1914; departure from Paris on March 7; in Vienna March 9 (visiting Otto Wagner that day); in London March 23 (attending a Royal Institute of British Architects dinner); departure from Southampton on the ship *St. Louis,* March 25; arrival in New York, April 5; arrival in Sydney via Chicago, May 12.[35] Swift as it was, Griffin planned his trip with care. He speaks of obtaining letters of introduction to "leading architects and prominent men in England, France, Germany and Austria."[36] The American architect Andrew Rebori provided suggestions. Griffin cites a letter requested of the architect Irving K. Pond, and he clearly had spoken with Louis Sullivan.[37] In addition, Griffin had already been contacted by William Morton Fullerton, an American journalist representing the London *Times* in Paris, a friend of Henry James's, a lover of Edith Wharton's, and some sort of agent of the mayor of Lyon, Édouard Hériot.[38] Hériot was arranging a town planning exhibition for the summer of 1914, the Exposition Internationale Urbaine. He wanted to include the Canberra plan (as well as the Burnham Plan of Chicago) and tried unsuccessfully to meet the Griffins in Paris. Fullerton had been in Chicago in October 1913 to publicize this coming exhibition and attended a board meeting of the City Club of Chicago, of which Walter Griffin was a member.[39] Passing through San Francisco on his way back from Australia, Griffin made the acquaintance of the French delegate to the Panama-Pacific International Exhibition, Joseph de Montarnal.

The Rebori letter in the Eric Milton Nicholls Collection in the National Library of Australia indicates Griffin's attitude in meeting progressive architects:

> Patrons of ateliers at the "Beaux-Arts," Paris, whose students are doing work in a modern spirit, giving expression to the problem at hand according to the requirements and conditions involved,
>
> M. Pascal
>
> M. Redon
>
> L'Ecole Spéciale d'Architecture, boulevard du [*sic*] Montparnasse, Paris.

Jean-Louis Pascal, a French teacher of architecture, had traveled around the United States in 1899 when he had served on the jury of the University of California campus plan competition. He was a patron of the brilliant Paul Philippe Cret, since 1903 professor of architecture at the University of Pennsylvania and winner in 1907 (with Albert Kelsey) of the competition to design the headquarters of the Organization of American States in Washington, D.C.[40] Gaston Redon was the brother of the symbolist artist Odilon Redon. The École Spéciale d'Architecture had been founded in the 1860s by the engineer Émile Trélat as a radical rationalist alternative to the École des Beaux-Arts, with the support of the architect Eugène Viollet-le-Duc. In 1913, the school was managed by Trélat's son Gaston, producing such designers as Robert Mallet-Stevens, imitating Viennese Secession design as an alternative to the conservatism of the art establishment of the time.[41] In 1910, Trélat had organized a competition to design an ideal Olympic city.[42]

There also survives in the National Library of Australia an envelope of calling cards left for the Griffins at their Paris hotel, the Normandie on the Rue de l'Echelle near the Avenue de l'Opéra. The cards read:

> Morton Fullerton
>
> 8, Rue du Mont Thabor 3:30–5:00; after 5:00 33 boulevard des Batignoles
>
> Louis Bonnier Directeur des Services d'Architecture of Paris [Director of Architectural Services of Paris][43]
>
> Carroll Greenough [two cards, inviting the Griffins to visit him in Neuilly near the Porte Maillot]

Christopher Vernon has found that the *New York Times* (April 10, 1915) noted Greenough's marriage, mentioning that he worked with a French architect and lived at 21 Rue Bonaparte—the address of the teacher and architectural experimenter Gustave Umbdenstock. After the war, Greenough collaborated with the American architect Ralph Adams Cram in building the Gothic-style American Church in Paris. Fullerton and Bonnier were to be very important in a second step in the Griffins' project—the display of the couple's work in Paris and Lyon in the summer of 1914.

There are two small pages of pencil notes from a loose-leaf pocket notebook surviving among the Nicholls papers that start with an interesting list of names and addresses:

> France
>
> Emile Vaudremer, quai de Conti, 23, 85 years old, L. H. Sullivan patron, Saint Pierre de Montrouge

[a Paris church that was Vaudremer's first and best-known work.]

Cordonnier, Palais de la Paix [Louis-Marie Cordonnier had won the 1906–7 international competition to design the Palais de la Paix (Palace of Peace), which now houses the World Court, in The Hague, Netherlands.]

Deglanne, av. D'Antin, porte C, atelier deGlane, grand prix man [Henri Deglane was the *maître d'atelier* (studio teacher) of Burnham's two sons at the École des Beaux-Arts.]

DeMontarnal, 213—7e—rue de l'Université, San Francisco Fair [There were two architect brothers at this address, E. Joseph and Jean de Montarnal. Joseph de Montarnal had designed the iron-and-glass art nouveau office building at 118, Rue de Réaumur.]

Toni [*sic*] Garnier, Lyons, Grand Prix [circled by Griffin]

On the back of this sheet a number of further names appear, as if Griffin were adding to his initial list:

Jacques Hermant, av MacMahon 19, classmate of L. H. S. [Louis Henry Sullivan] in atelier Vaudremer, important work

Also work of Vaudremer Prison Mazas [Vaudremer's second-best-known work].

Jacques Hermant had visited Chicago in 1893 and had reviewed the city's architecture, making particular mention of Sullivan's recently finished Schiller Building, stating that they had shared an *atelier* in Paris, and proceeding to critique it as their teacher Émile Vaudremer might have done.[44] Hermant was one of the most successful and visible of Vaudremer's students, executing the large Caserne des Célestins on the Boulevard Henri IV, the iron-and-glass interior of the Société Générale on the Boulevard Haussmann behind the Opéra, and a number of admired *maisons de rapport* (apartment houses). Hermant was a leading advocate of reinforced concrete construction.

The second page of Griffin's loose-leaf extends this, on one side showing him following Rebori's advice:

Atelier Pascal (Louis) Boulevard St Denis 8

Gaston Redon Boulevard Raspail 131 [his home address]

Atelier Redon Louis Blanc 61

The other side shows—in addition to practical matters such as addresses of the American Express Company and the Hotel Regina—the names and addresses of three further architects important for planning and progressive design:

Alphonse Rey

Um[b]denstock, rue Bonaparte 21, 8 rue de la Beaulieu

Agache 11 Eugène Flachat[45]

Rey was a leading designer of public housing in concrete, having won the famous 1905 Rothschild competition for which Tony Garnier submitted an unsuccessful but now celebrated project. Gustave Umbdenstock was the author of a general design book, *Recueil de compositions architecturales* (Collection of Architectural Compositions, 1922). Agache was a participant in the Canberra competition and the prime mover of the newly created Société Française des Architectes Urbanistes, founded in 1911.[46]

Interestingly, there is also the note "J. G. Melson, Hotel Normandie" indicating that Joshua Melson—the Griffins' important Mason City, Iowa, patron—was in Paris at the same time they were.

Finally, there is a very small sheet by itself with five names written on it in a column:

Bonnier

Girault

Laloux

Pontrimoli [*sic*]

Toni Garnier [again underlined by Griffin]

Was this the list of the jurors Griffin was considering? Louis Bonnier was the city architect of Paris. Charles Girault was architect of the huge arch and museum complex in the Parc du Cinquantenaire (Park of the Fiftieth Anniversary) in Brussels. Emmanuel Pontremoli designed the exquisite Villa Reinach, Kerylos, on the Côte d'Azur—one of the most famous buildings of the moment. No one

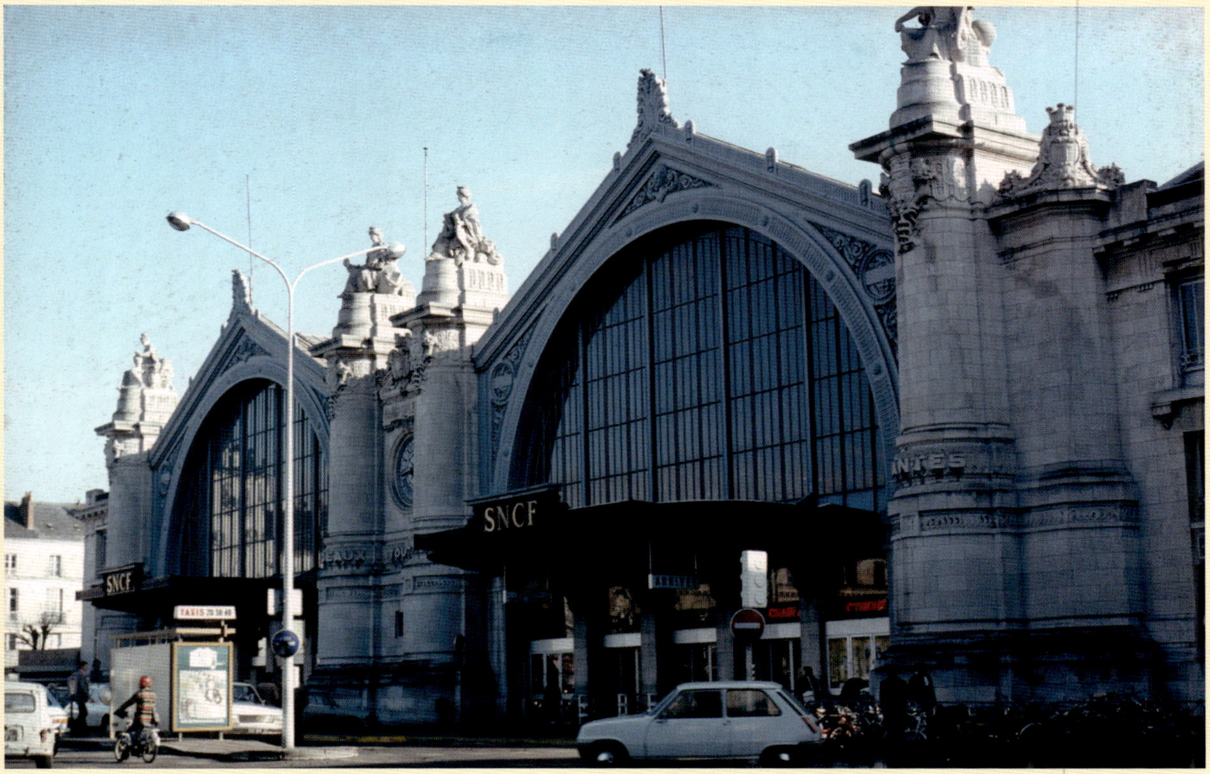

Figure 24
Victor Laloux; Tours Railway Station, façade, 1896–98. Photograph: David Van Zanten.

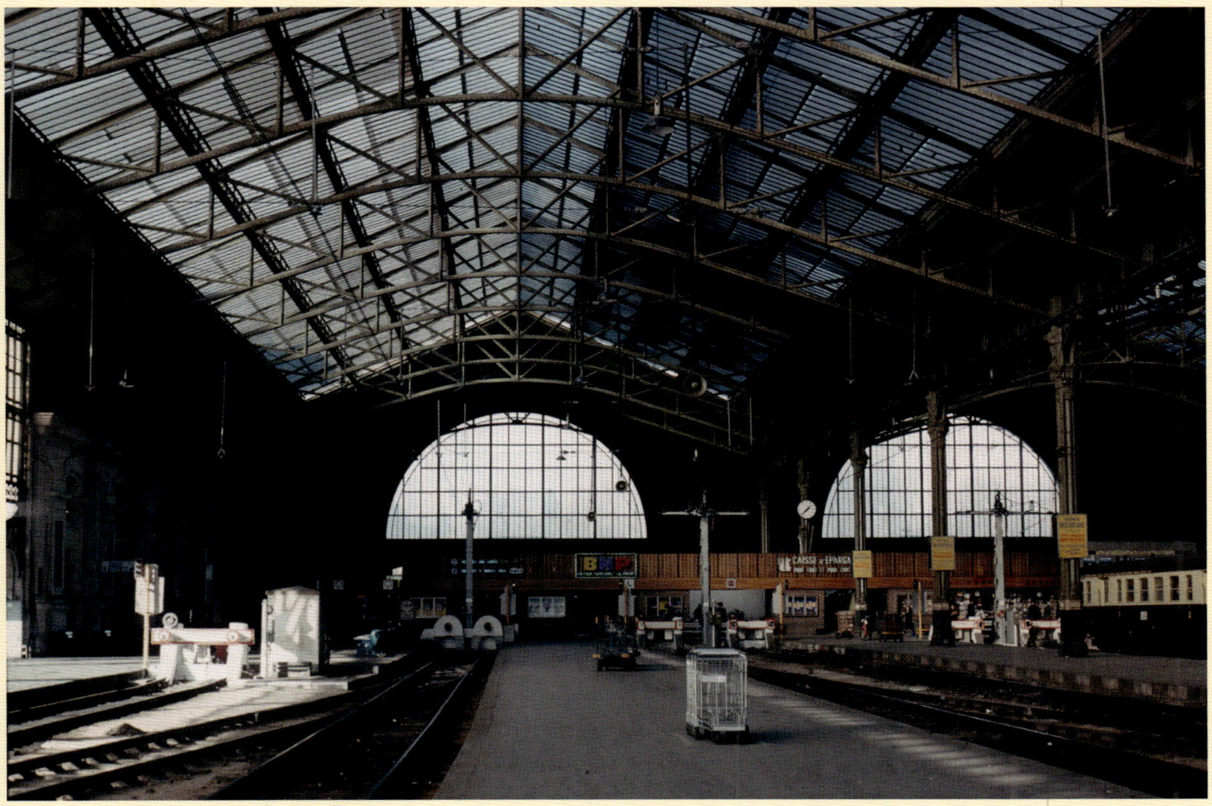

Figure 25
Victor Laloux; Tours Railway Station, interior, 1896–98. Photograph: David Van Zanten.

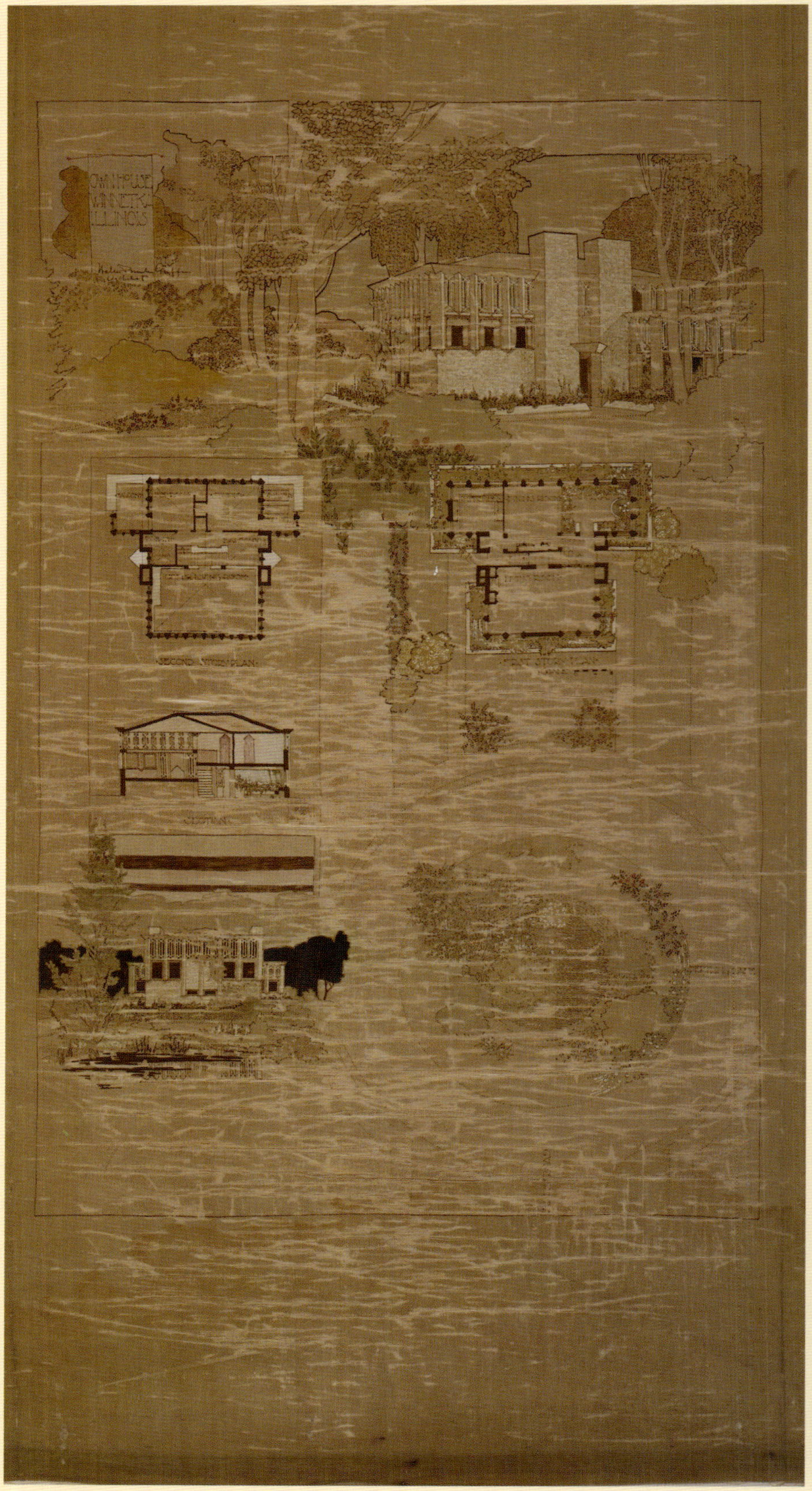

Figure 26
Walter Burley Griffin and Marion Mahony Griffin; *Griffin House, Winnetka, Illinois,* 1912; various coloring agents on silk; approximately 46 x 25 in.; Avery Architectural and Fine Arts Library, Columbia University

knows how Griffin arrived at approaching Victor Laloux—who, like Pascal and Redon, managed a progressive atelier (significantly, with a large number of Americans studying there). Laloux had been the architect of two major railway stations, the Gare d'Orsay in the center of Paris, now the Musée d'Orsay, and the main railway station in Tours (figures 24 and 25).[47] It was Laloux who recommended that Griffin ask John James Burnet in London to join the jury—perhaps after William Lethaby declined.

Louis Bonnier arranged the exhibition Esquisses d'architecture de l'architecte américain Walter-Burley Griffin (Architectural Sketches of the American Architect Walter Burley Griffin) at the Musée des Arts Décoratifs in Paris from June 20 to July 13, 1914. It consisted of twenty silk renderings of Walter's work by Marion—including the Griffins' own house in Winnetka, Illinois (figure 26)—plus five line drawings on linen. (The exhibition is the subject of Ashley Dunn's essay in this catalog.) The Nicholls Collection letters give us some idea of the exhibition's inception. It starts with a telegram to Walter Griffin in London, at the Hotel Surrey, "Remerciements reçevrons dessins avec plaisir pour exposition, Bonnier" (Thank you we would receive with pleasure drawings for exhibition, Bonnier). The message indicates that the two men had met in Paris and discussed an exhibition of the Griffins' work, evidently at Bonnier's initiative, although no one knows what inspired his interest. Bonnier had just been named to the board of the Union Centrale des Arts Décoratifs (Central Union of Decorative Arts or UCAD), the body in charge of the museum, and—one presumes—had consulted with the board and gotten their permission for the exhibition. That telegram is answered by Griffin forwarding to Bonnier the renderings he had brought with him before sailing from the United Kingdom, explaining, "I greatly appreciate your interest and courtesy [regarding] the exhibition which I feel will be of great benefit to our Australian project if it interests the young men to enter into the spirit of our competition." He thus indicates what, officially, was his purpose in visiting Europe—to advance progressive design. He mentions that the renderings should be sent on to Otto Wagner in Vienna and that the publisher Albert Lévy would like to photograph "two or three" of them for publication.[48] Because architectural journals suspended publication at the outbreak of the war in 1914, those images never appeared.

Lyon

The Fullerton-Lyon connection is more complex and involved the hurried completion of a second set of Canberra renderings during the short time the Griffins were in Chicago on their way from Europe to Australia. ("It is going to punish Mrs. Griffin to get them ready in the few days we have but they have precedence over all else," Walter Griffin wrote Fullerton on July 23, 1914.) Fragmentary correspondence starts with Fullerton, dated February 4, 1914 (likely dated in error and actually written in March),[49] expressing distress that he didn't connect with Griffin at his hotel. The correspondence continues with a detailed letter from Griffin of March 28, 1914, thus written on shipboard, preserved in the Lyon Archives Municipales—explaining the sizes and shapes of the drawings about to be sent. A letter of April 24 from the Griffins' associate Barry Byrne (left in charge of the Chicago office after the couple's second departure for Australia) informs the Lyon authorities of the drawings' dispatch. In fact, what was sent may have been reproductions.

The correspondence ends with a letter dated July 23, 1914, from Fullerton to Griffin in Australia, quoting Édouard Hérriot, "Les très interessantes réproductions qu'a bien voulu nous addresser M. Walter Griffin sont exposer [*sic*] en bonne place dans le Pavillon reservé aux 'Places des Villes.'" (The very interesting reproductions that Mr. Walter Griffin has kindly sent us are displayed in the city spaces pavilion.) On June 22 to 27, 1914, the Société Française des Architectes held its annual convention, starting in Lyon (with a tour of the exposition led by Tony Garnier) and ending in Paris: the Griffins' two displays could not have had a larger professional audience.

Vienna

The evidence of the Griffins' Vienna visit is very different from that for their Paris stay, but complementary because it permits a glimpse of their immediate relationship with the most important progressive architect of the period, Otto Wagner (figure 27). Wagner's text *Moderne Architektur* of 1895 had been available to Walter Burley Griffin as a student at the University of Illinois through a translation by the dean, Nathan Ricker.[50] Wagner's correspondence with Griffin, comprising fifteen letters and a number of manuscripts, survives both in his original office folder (now in private hands in Chicago) and in the National Archives of Australia, as well as the Akademie der Bildenden Künste (Academy of Fine Arts) in Vienna. The manuscripts include an announcement to the architects of Austria-Hungary and Germany of the Parliament House competition, in handwritten draft (dated July 22, 1914) and typed versions; the Parliament House competition program in Fullerton's French translation, plus both a handwritten draft in German and a typed final version; and the program for a Neighborhood Center Competition framed by the City Club of Chicago and dated June 20, 1914—both the original printed pamphlet and its translation into German in two typed copies. The brief competition announcement ends, "Ein Umstand, der den Wettbewerb besonders interessant macht, ist die Wettbewerbs-

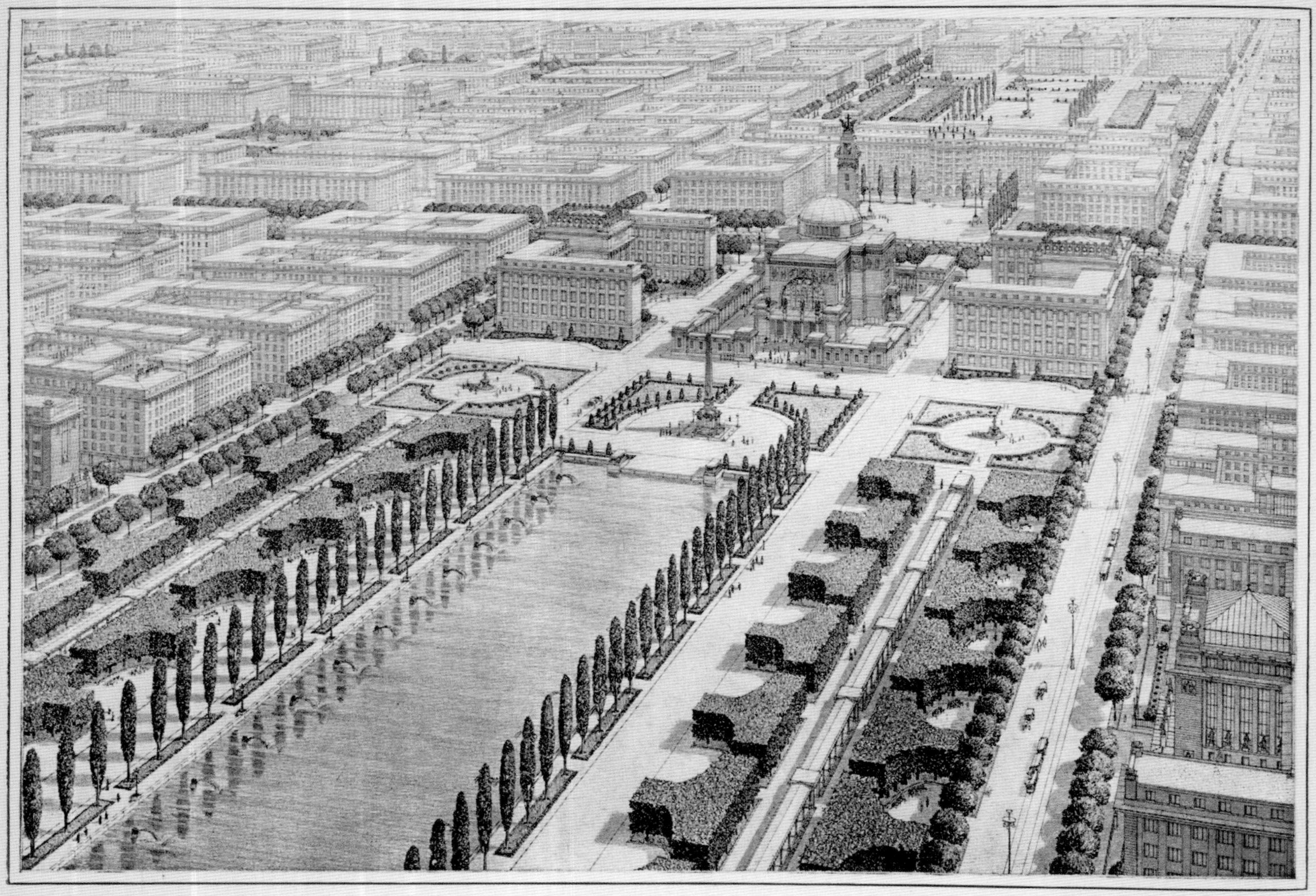

Figure 27
Otto Wagner; *View of the Future Twenty-Second District of Vienna;* from *Die Groszstadt* (Vienna: A. Schroll, 1910); Joseph Regenstein Library, University of Chicago

Bedingung, dass in der künstlerischen Durchführung des Bauwerkes jede Stilarchitektur une jeder Hinweis auf Tradition ausgeschlossen sein soll, also zum ersten Male offiziell die Bauerscheinung im 'Stil der kunst unserer Zeit' verlangt wird." (A detail that makes this competition especially interesting is the requirement that in the aesthetic elaboration of the building every architectural style or traditional detail is forbidden so that, for the first time, an architectural conception "in the style of our time" is officially demanded.)

The personal material starts with two sheets of notes dated March 9, 1914, clearly recording a visit to Wagner by Griffin. These notes record dates and addresses and include the cards of Griffin in Chicago and in Australia (that address written over a second copy of his card), and the card of L. H. Eisenmann, "Correspondent of the Daily News and Leader," evidently functioning as a go-between as Morton Fullerton did in Paris. Wagner lists the jurors: Sullivan, Laloux, and Wagner, and he notes W. R. Lethaby.[51] ("W. R. Lethaby" is, likewise, written on Eisenmann's card.) Next comes a letter from Wagner to Griffin (March 11, surviving in drafts in German and French plus the typed original), saying that Wagner has searched in the Akademie library but has found nothing about Lethaby. Then comes a letter from Griffin in Chicago (in German)[52] of April 10 listing the names of the jury—Sulman, Burnet, Laloux, Wagner, and Sullivan—and instructing Wagner to contact Louis Bonnier in Paris about the exhibition of Griffin's "Skizzen" (renderings) in Vienna. Burnet, Griffin explains, was suggested by Laloux, and "Er [Burnet] ist im Einklang mit unserem Programm, obwohl er in seinen Bauten nicht viel davon zeigt, mit Ausnahme vielleicht in dem Gebäude der 'Kodac [*sic*] Limited' in London" (He is in agreement with our program even if he does not show it except in his Kodak Limited building in London).

On April 23, Wagner sends letters to Bonnier and Burnet, introducing himself, plus a letter to Griffin saying that he is translating the Parliament House competition program (complaining about the bad French, surmising that an English speaker—known to have been Fullerton—produced it) and hoping that the most capable architects of Austria and

Figure 28
John James Burnet; Kodak Building, Kingsway, London, 1911.
Copyright © Courtauld Institute of Art.

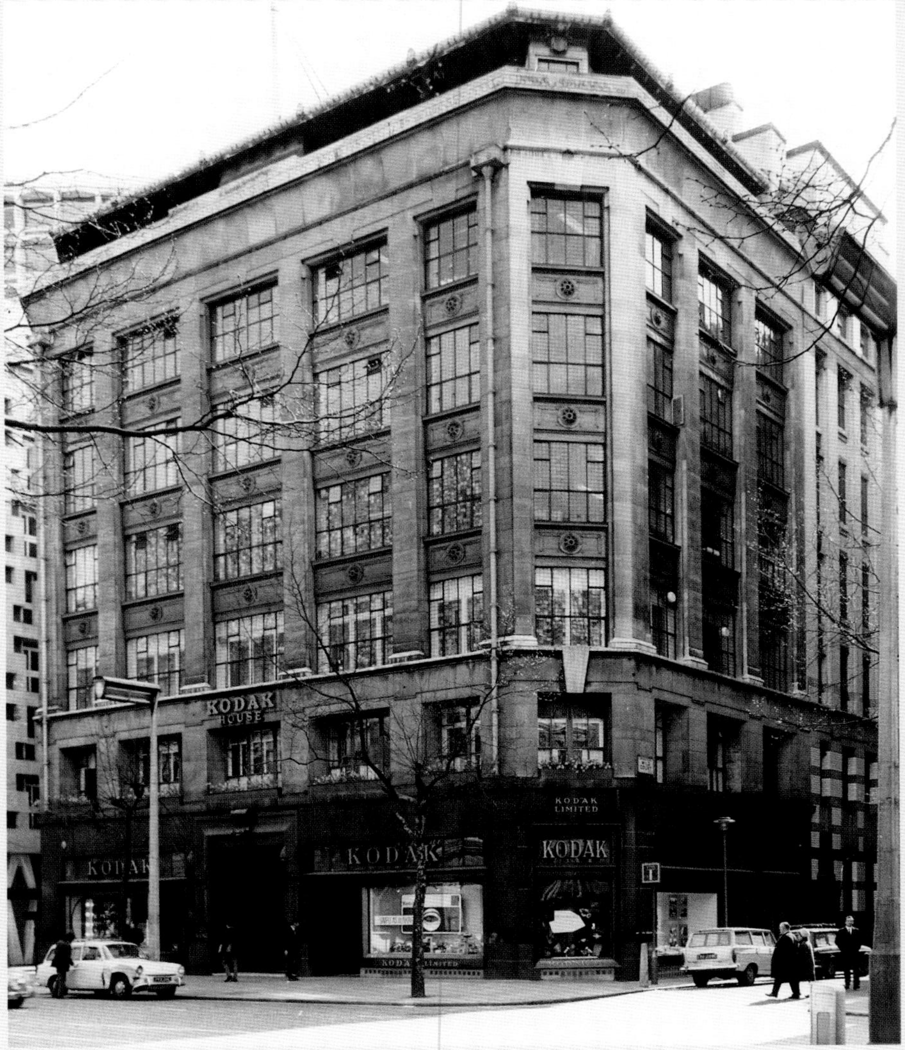

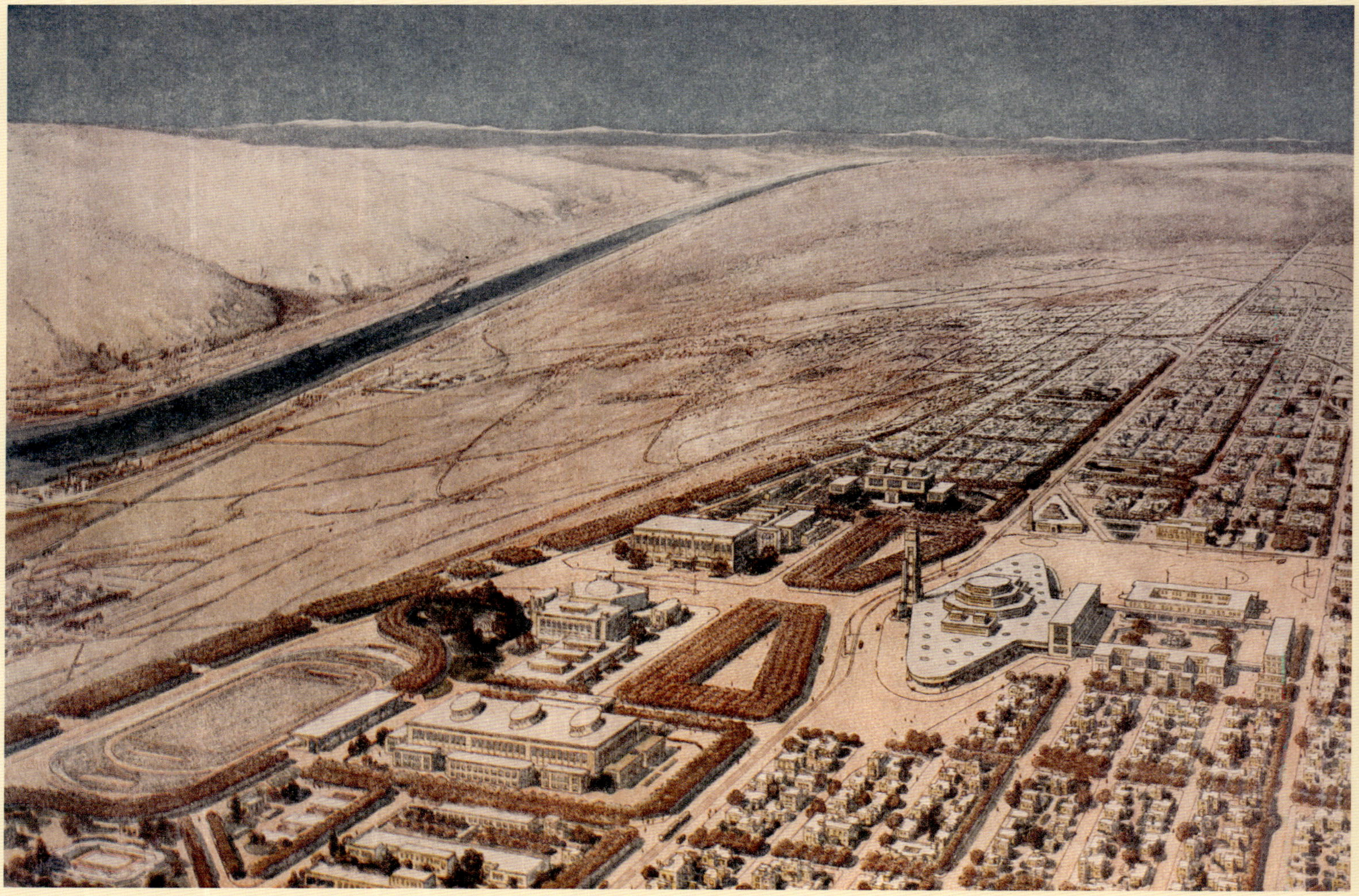

Figure 29
Tony Garnier; *Les Services Publics* (Public Services); from *Une cité industrielle: Étude pour la construction des villes* (An Industrial City: Study for the Construction of Cities; Paris: A. Vincent, 1918); The Art Institute of Chicago, Ryerson and Burnham Libraries

Germany might compete. Wagner sends Griffin the program translation on May 5, but with a criticism of paragraph 1.02, "Style": "Es ist [da]rin eine Entschuldigung enthalten, warum der Künstler die Formen [die] Tradition nicht anwenden sollen, statt dass gesagt worden wäre: '[Wir] erkennen die Berechtigung des Stiles unserer Zeit an und wünschen sich an der Konkurrenz nur wirkliche Künstler beteiligen, wirklich[e] Künstler *werden aber nie etwas kopieren*'" (There is a mistake in it about whether an artist might use traditional forms instead of declaring: "We recognize the necessity of the Style of our Time and wish only real artists participating as competitors: Real artists *never copy anything.*") (Wagner's emphasis).

Then a sidetrack: Griffin sends a telegram saying Poole will replace Sulman on the jury, but it is garbled and Wagner asks first the British Embassy to translate it (they say they can't), then L. H. Eisenmann. This was followed by the outbreak of the war, the cancellation of the competition in September 1914, and so finally a letter of December 29, 1914, from America in which Griffin's Chicago partner, Barry Byrne, asks whether the drawings have arrived from Paris—to which Wagner replies on January 21 in the negative.

Little is known about the Griffins' third national visit, London. They attended a dinner at the Royal Institute of British Architects, where they made contact with Reginald Blomfield, architect of the Regent's Street Quadrant and author of *The Mistress Arts* (1908), advocating monumental urban design in what he calls the "Grand Manner." They recruited John James Burnet (on the recommendation of Laloux) and must have visited his concrete-frame Kodak House on newly opened Kingsway (figure 28). They left Burnet with the French translation of the competition text, which he had edited by Eugène Bourdon, professor of architecture at the Glasgow School of Art, explaining this to the Australian authorities in a letter of July 15, 1914.[53] The Griffins must have tried to contact W. R. Lethaby, surveyor of Westminster Abbey. They had brought their box of twenty silk and five ink-line renderings, but there is no record of an exhibition and, when they were about to embark on their return to America, they sent the drawings to Bonnier in Paris.

What Was the Griffins' "Programm"?

What were the Griffins part of?—what was "unserem Programm," to quote Griffin to Wagner? In the case of Vienna, it was made clear by their friends declaring themselves a "Sezession" (Secession) from the traditionalist Akademie der Bildenden Künste in their publication *Hohe Warte*—the name of a hill constituting a fashionable Vienna suburb—and in Wagner's student Josef Olbrich's exhibition building with its program on the Ringstrasse. Bonnier's Paris parallel is less often cited or defined, but comes forward clearly with his presidency of the Société des Architectes Diplomés par le Gouvernement (Society of Architecture Graduates for the Government, or SADG)—which occasioned his nomination to the board of the Union Centrale—and in the founding in January 1906 of *L'Architecte* by the SADG along with Albert Lévy of the Librairie Centrale des Beaux-Arts. The new publication sets off with a declaration by the French architect Jean-Louis Pascal and ends its first year with a lengthy, illustrated appreciation of the work of Otto Wagner. The journal begins 1907 with an analysis of the competition projects for the city plan of Guayaquil, Ecuador; 1908 features the concrete-and-tile constructions of Auguste Perret, especially his apartment block at 25 bis Rue Franklin, and of the French architect Paul Guadet. In 1914, Albert Lévy was preparing to publish several of Marion Mahony Griffin's silks in color—before publication was suspended by the outbreak of the war.

What did the Griffins leave behind? The critic Paul Lafollye says that the students at the École des Beaux-Arts were already experimenting with Marion's rendering technique, but if they had indeed begun to do so—then at the very end of term—they went off to war before school began again in the fall.[54] Much more to the point, in 1916 the seminal *Gazette des Beaux-Arts* promoted the Griffins' concrete construction seen in the Canberra drawings (citing the display of house

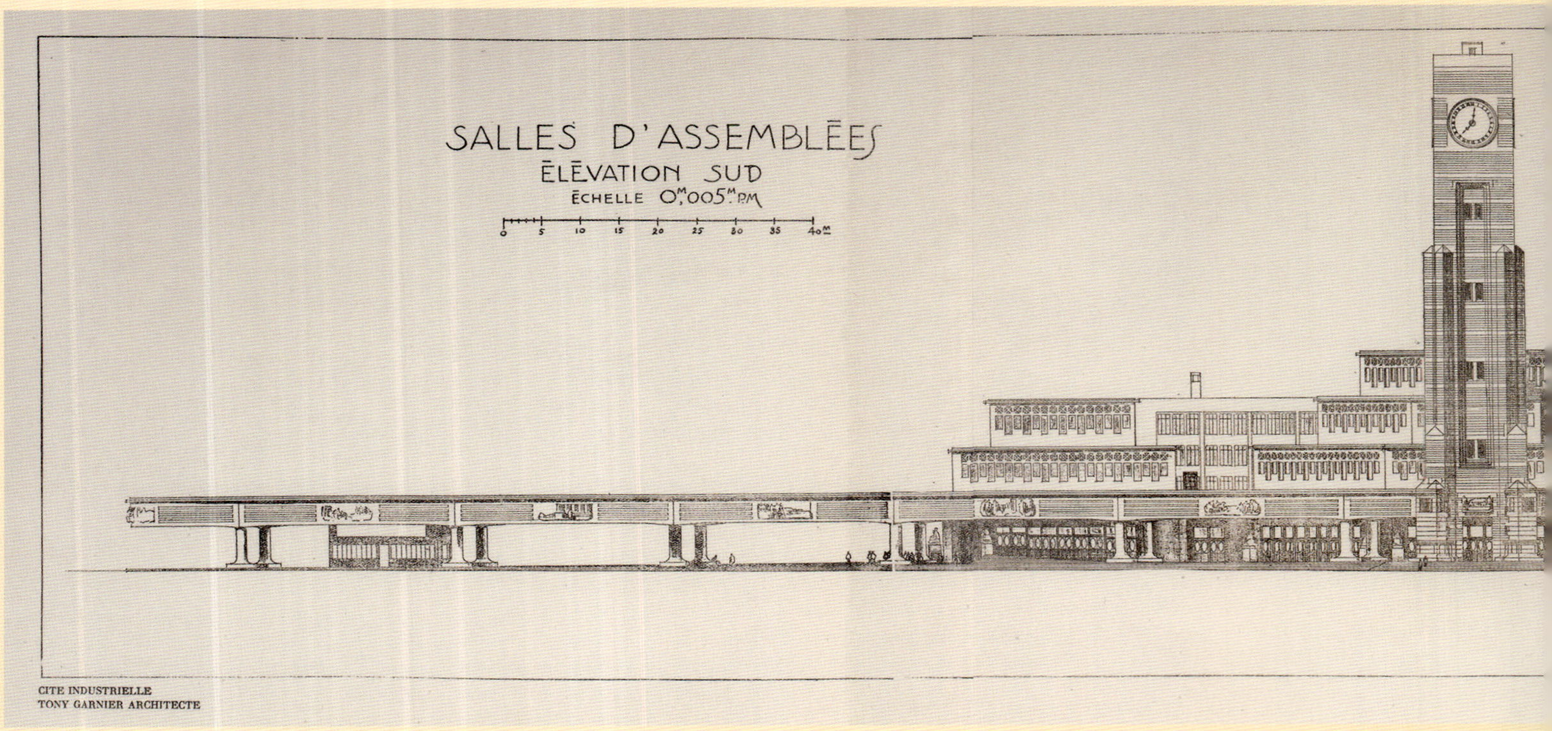

renderings at the Musée des Arts Décoratifs) as a model for a new architecture needed for the reconstruction of the cities and towns of northern France after the war.[55] Agache and his Société Française des Architectes Urbanistes also carried forward that project with *Nos cites détruites: notions d'urbanisme s'appliquant aux villes, bourgs et villages* (Our Destroyed Cities: Urban Planning Concepts That Apply to Cities, Towns, and Villages, 1915), resulting in another exhibition at the Musée des Arts Décoratifs.

But most important—if most fragilely linked—in 1917, Lyon saw the publication of Tony Garnier's utopian urban project *Une Cité Industrielle* (An Industrial City, figures 29 and 30).[56] The planned city in Garnier's proposal is about the same size as the Griffins' Canberra—twenty-five thousand to thirty-five thousand people—although far simpler in design; and its concrete architecture has Canberra's "look." Both plans provided large public areas. Walter advocated the teachings of the American economist Henry George, who called for land to be owned in common. In Garnier's Cité Industrielle, houses are surrounded with public parks and walks

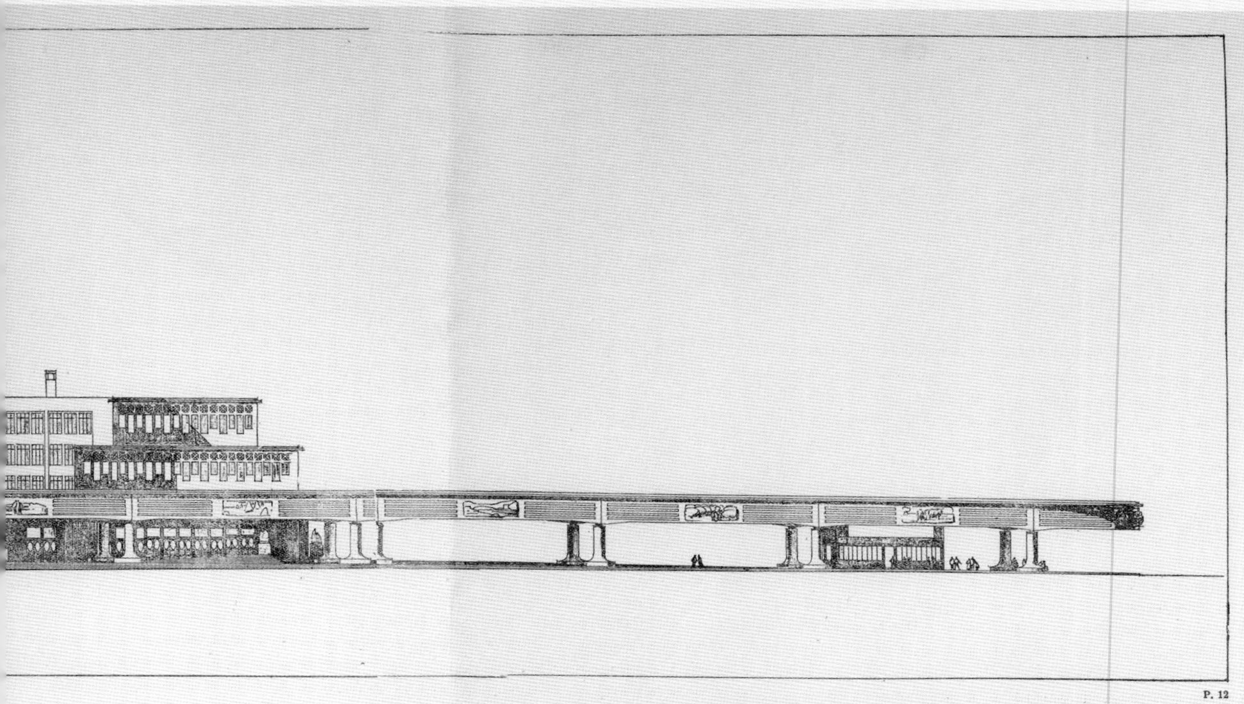

Figure 30
Tony Garnier; *Salles d'assemblées—Elevation Sud* (Assembly Rooms—South Elevation); from *Une cité industrielle: Étude pour la construction des villes* (An Industrial City: Study for the Construction of Cities; Paris: A. Vincent, 1918); The Art Institute of Chicago, Ryerson and Burnham Libraries

open to all residents. But what is most similar, intriguingly, is that both plans pivot on a large, open place of public assembly under a stack of octagonal concrete slabs piled up ziggurat-like. The two plans are distinct in actual function and social implications: Griffin's capitol building atop Capital Hill in Canberra was to be a ceremonial gathering place and repository of records and monuments between the prime minister's and governor general's mansions, at the intersection of the city's visual axes, to command the whole complex.[57] Garnier's Salles d'assemblées, although also in the middle of his planned city, stand on a flat plane without dramatic framing. The building consists of a broad, sheltered public space divided into meeting rooms (one for three thousand participants, one for one thousand, and two for five hundred) and six committee rooms (figure 30). It is the centerpiece of his democratic community which, as it gently implies by omission, functions without church, police station, or prison. The two designs reflect not quite the same idea of democracy, but they encapsulate it similarly in their two central structures.

Progressive Design Takes Shape

Progress Before Precedent

—MOTTO OF THE ARCHITECTURAL LEAGUE OF AMERICA

Progressive architecture in France and Austria teetered on the edge of achieving a new and consistent stylistic vocabulary just before the outbreak of the war, as technique—shaped by the geometry of an emerging concrete technology—combined with regularity of form. In France, Louis Bonnier's journal *L'Architecte* culminated in 1913 with extensive documentation of his own cast-concrete *groupe scolaire* (school complex) on the Rue Rouelle—presented as a general solution, "A propos d'une groupe scolaire"—set next to Auguste Perret's concrete Théâtre des Champs-Elysées. In Austria, something parallel emerged in Wagner's Postal Savings Bank (1903–12) and Steinhof hospital chapel (1903–7), in steel-cage construction barely concealed behind a thin coat of attached marble plaques. Tony Garnier nudged the two together in the structure, imagery, and evenness of his Cité Industrielle. It was eyes hoping to see this sort of architecture that received Wright's *Ausgeführte Bauten* and the Griffins' Canberra plans and silk renderings.

If this was the international "program" of architectural renovation the Griffins sought to mobilize for the Parliament House competition of 1914, what was the parallel progressive context from which they took off in Chicago?[58] Again, the outline is clear enough: There was a group of concerned activists, centered around the vigorous city planning advocate George E. Hooker and his friends the landscape architect Jens Jensen and the social scientist Charles Zueblin (professor of sociology at the recently founded University of Chicago), together with the public-minded architects Allen B. Pond and Dwight Heald Perkins. Perkins was Marion's first cousin and, in 1894–95, her first employer.[59] Initially the group met informally, constituting themselves as "The Committee on the Universe."

As Burnham's planning projects burgeoned from the McMillan Commission Plan for Washington (1901–2) to the Chicago Plan itself (1906–9), the members organized themselves as a more formal debate and advocacy group, the City Club of Chicago, founded in 1903. By 1909, the club had two thousand members, a building of their own conception in the Loop (figure 58, from the designs of Pond and Pond, the firm of the brothers Allen B. and Irving K. Pond), and a span of committees (including a City Planning Committee founded in 1908 with Frank Lloyd Wright among its members) sponsoring lectures, debates, and publications. The younger, more progressive architects of the city participated—the Pond brothers and Perkins of course, but also Wright, Hugh Garden, William Drummond and his partner Louis Guenzel, and finally Walter Burley Griffin, who by 1913 was chair of the City Planning Committee.

In 1911, Hendrik Petrus Berlage had visited Chicago at the invitation of the architect William Gray Purcell.[60] The City Club brought other prominent European architects and political leaders to Chicago. The club invited Albert Südekum and Werner Hegemann from Germany and Raymond Unwin, Thomas Mawson, and Henry Vivian from the United Kingdom to speak. The members displayed the Burnham Plan at the club for close discussion, then instituted, first, a competition to design an ideal residential quarter-section of the Chicago inner suburbs, then a competition to design a "neighborhood center" for it. Otto Wagner was sufficiently interested in the program from the second competition to translate it into German.[61] One of his students, Rudolph M. Schindler, completed a design, but only after he had himself settled in Chicago in February 1914 (see figure 70).[62] The projects submitted in the first competition were published under the editorship of Alfred Yeomans in 1916 as *City Residential Land Development* (see figures 62, 63, 64, and 65). The second competition is analyzed by Leslie Coburn in her essay in this catalog. Simultaneously the City Club patronized the public presentation of a series of plans for the reorganization of the rail access and terminals of the city, producing an illustrated book in 1913, *The Railway Terminal Problem of Chicago*. The National City Planning Conference was held in Chicago May 5 to 7, 1913, with the club's encouragement; the discussions were also published as a book.[63]

But developments were more complex than this, and there was a profound tension between fact and image that the Griffins had to manage in their Canberra "solution," striving to reconcile the competing visions exemplified by Burnham and Sullivan. Already in 1893 the triumphant classicism of Burnham's Court of Honor at the World's Columbian Exposition (figure 34) had been confronted by Louis Sullivan's unprecedented "natural" architecture in the Golden Door of his Transportation Building there. By the late 1890s, this confrontation had stiffened. Burnham's severe classical office building solution—in 1901 and 1902 elaborated into his McMillan Commission Plan for the completion of the monumental National Mall in Washington, D.C.—was opposed by the experiments of the younger members of the Chicago Architectural Club led by the progressives Dwight Perkins, the Pond brothers, and Frank Lloyd Wright. Sullivan (just then erecting his Carson Pirie Scott store on State Street) served as the Chicago Architectural Club's prophet and sage.[64] In 1899, this group joined other American architectural clubs to found the Architectural League of America with "Progress Before Precedent" as their motto. They met that year in Cleveland, and the next year in Chicago in the Auditorium Building, where they were addressed by both Wright and Sullivan. Griffin later remembered Sullivan's speech "The Young Man in Architecture" as inspiring his future ambitions. The 1901 publication of Nathan Ricker's English-language version of Otto Wagner's *Moderne Architektur* was "under the auspices of the Architectural League of America."[65]

In 1901 at the Philadelphia meeting of the Architectural League, there were efforts to conceptualize a new architecture, especially by Emil Lorch in his presentation of "pure design" developing the idea of the art educators Arthur Wesley Dow and Denman Ross.[66] Concurrently, Lorch was reshaping the architectural design program at the School of the Art Institute of Chicago—at that time calling itself the Chicago School of Architecture—working under

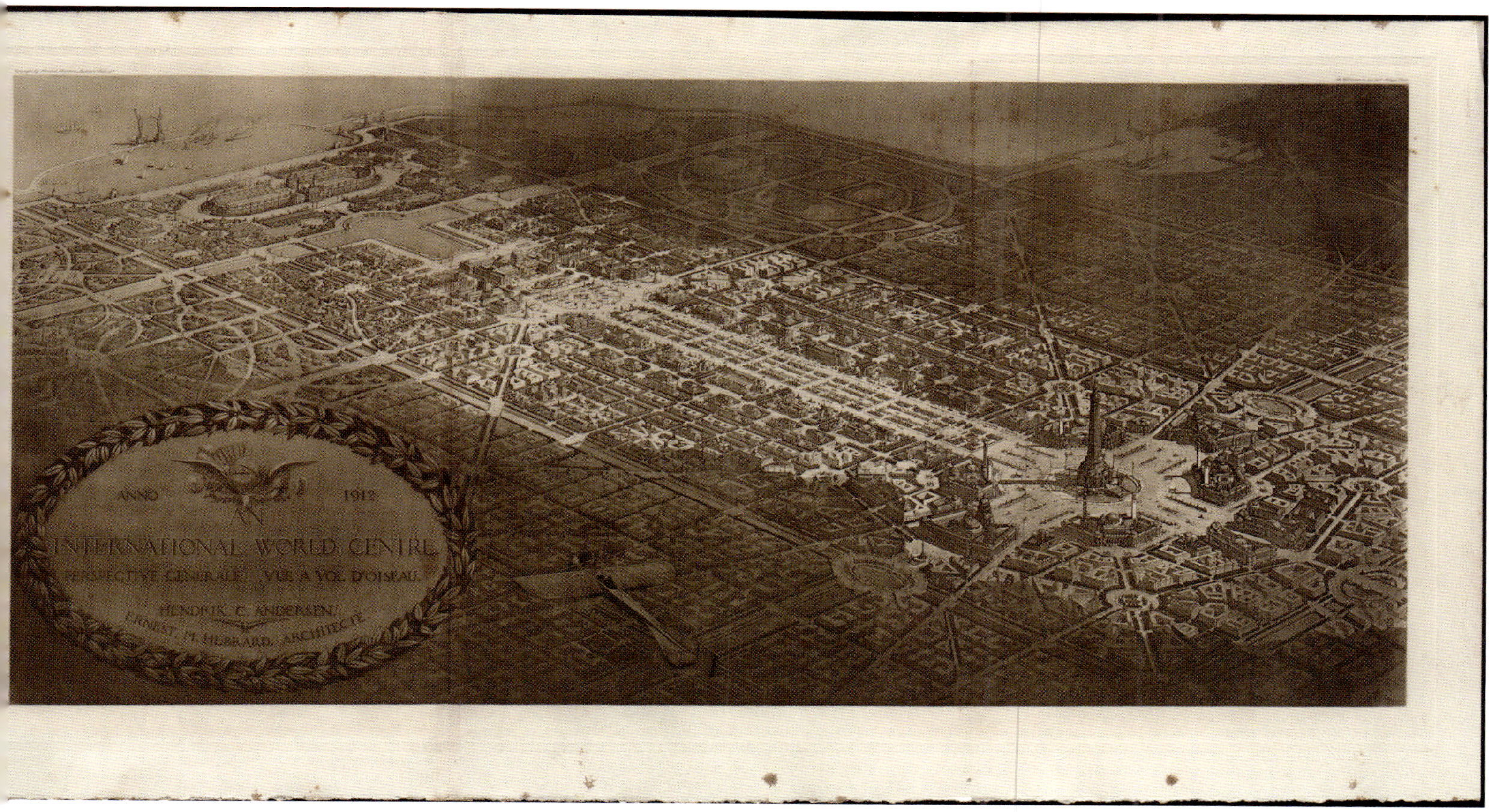

Figure 31
Hendrik Christian Andersen; *International World Centre, Perspective Generale vue a vol d'oiseau* (General Perspective from a Bird's-eye View); from *Creation of a World Centre of Communication* (Paris: n.p., 1913); 18 ½ × 34 ½ in.; Charles Deering McCormick Library of Special Collections, Northwestern University Library

its dean, Louis J. Millet, Sullivan's closest associate and the artist who executed Sullivan's Golden Door of 1893. In 1900 and 1901, the club sponsored a four-part competition to design "An American Embassy in a European Capital," provoking progressive designs by William Drummond (a Sullivanesque proposal) and Birch Burdette Long (a Japanese-inspired design).[67] The Chicago Architectural Club's journal for the year 1901 adopted the Architectural League of America's periodical name, *The Chicago Architectural Annual,* and published a special section devoted to Frank Lloyd Wright's work. In its June 1900 issue, the Boston *Architectural Review* had published a lengthy presentation of Wright by his friend Robert C. Spencer.[68]

Conservative reaction was swift—in 1902 a new organizing committee at the Chicago Architectural Club swung the annual exhibition (and its catalog) back to more conventional work. At the Art Institute, Lorch was fired and Millet shifted to direct the Normal Division, that is, to instructing art teachers rather than architects—women rather than men—which would have been considered a demotion.[69] Yet simultaneously, the City Club emerged with the Pond brothers and Perkins among the first members, and Wright, Griffin, and Drummond became involved soon after. More broadly, outside interventions (such as Berlage's visit and lectures of 1911 and the arrival of young European architects like Rudolph Schindler and Rob van 't Hoff, both in 1914) buttressed the progressive cause.[70] Increased recognition also buoyed the progressives, especially Wright's Wasmuth portfolio of 1910 and, most spectacularly, Griffin's 1912 victory in the Commonwealth of Australia Federal Capital Design Competition for Canberra to an explosion of media adulation, lecture invitations, and exhibitions of his plans.

This all came just after the Burnham Plan was presented with exemplary showmanship in the summer of 1909. The City Club sought to absorb it and nudge the resulting discussion from monumental order and transportation systems to housing texture with the two neighborhood projects organized by George Hooker from 1912 to 1914. Wright and Griffin both offered designs in the quarter-section competition, and Wilhelm Bernhard (from Dresden, and recently a collaborator of Olmsted's)[71] won it with a design in Griffin-like concrete (see figure 64). Hooker explained that his intention was to present "speculative" urbanism, exploring how real cities might be better laid out as totalities.[72] At the Fifth National City Planning Conference in Chicago, the landscape architect John Nolen presented a parallel body of housing quarters conceived in competition.

And what did this new progressive architecture look like? Not like what by the 1930s was understood to be Frank Lloyd Wright's brilliant breakthrough, baptized then the "International Style."[73] The architectural historian Neil Levine has analyzed Wright's quarter-section plan closely, folding it back on the pinwheel grouping of the site plan of Wright's groundbreaking *Ladies' Home Journal* "House on the Prairie" published in February 1901—itself derived from an Oak Park studio competition with Griffin (see figures 62 and 63).[74] Significantly, Marion Mahony in a later account of Wright's plan (including a small pencil diagram) missed Wright's whole point by straightening it up to omit the rotation.

Thomas Tallmadge coined the term the "Chicago School" in 1908 in an article of the same name in the *Architectural Review*. Tallmadge praised the group's objectives but found it heterogeneous in its stated intentions and efforts at theory. Yet progressive architecture was less about form and theory than about finding practical means to social ends—especially as these were projected in the discussion and publications of the City Club. Here Griffin's solution—modestly sketched in his 1911 "Solid Rock House," more boldly (if theoretically) presented in the cast concrete *staffage* of his wife's Canberra cross sections, and finally realized at Castlecrag—makes sense. The progressive architects take this new, cheap material—concrete—to build up a texture both respectful of the site and fantastic in its geometry.

In December 1914, the minutes of the Board of Directors of the Art Institute record the architect Howard Van Doren Shaw, one of their number, informing them that he had commitments from three leading American architects to divide the endowed annual Scammon lectures for early 1915 among them, with two lectures each by Ralph Adams Cram, Thomas Hastings, and Claude Bragdon.[75] These were duly delivered and promptly published (which was required, although Shaw was hesitant). Bragdon followed them up with a display of his explorations in architectural geometry at the May 1916 Chicago Architectural Club exhibition, also in the Art Institute. Clearly these three designers represented, to Shaw's professional eye, the architectural divisions of that moment at the outbreak of the world war: Arts and Crafts medievalism, academic classicism, and progressivism. Architectural historians might debate his last selection, preferring Bragdon over either the aged Sullivan, the now socially unacceptable Wright, or the absent Griffin. But perhaps he got it right: Bragdon pursued the theory Lorch and the others had failed to shape, one of geometric elaboration (figure 32), which Bragdon's admirer Buckminster Fuller finally transformed into a total architecture in the 1920s.[76]

Burnham's peculiar insistence on a historicist vocabulary rather than a "rationalist" approach seems antiprogressive until one acknowledges that "order" was exactly what the European progressives sought to achieve—and one of them, Werner Hegemann, was loud in his support of American classicism.[77] The progressives' variety of expression is disappointing until one acknowledges that they valued the process itself with the confidence that, once structure and form were clearly defined, a new natural order would necessarily appear.

What is puzzling is Wright.[78] He stands at the heart of these developments. His work has become the point of reference (especially as known from the *Ausgeführte Bauten* through Marion Mahony's renderings) for contemporaries and still for ourselves. His presence skews things. There is a difference

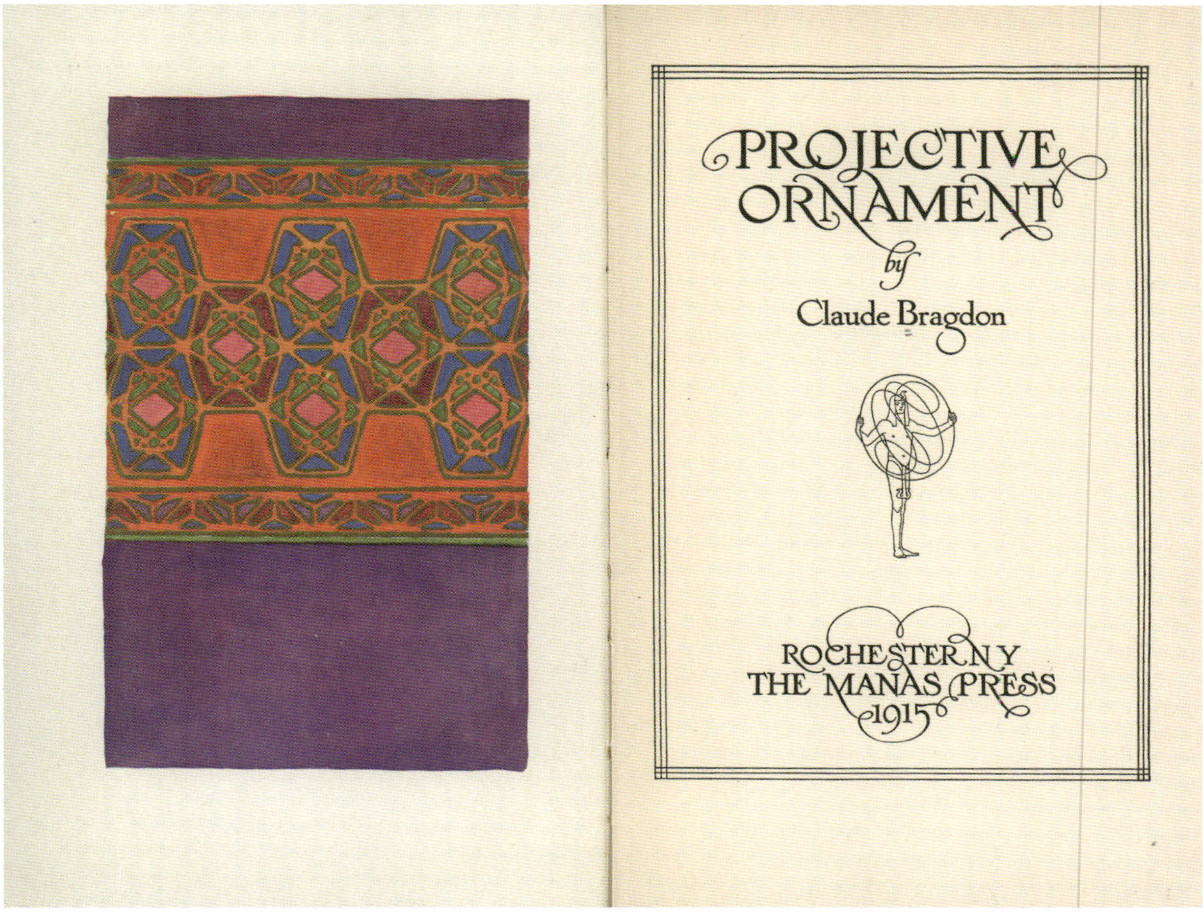

Figure 32
Claude Bragdon; facing page and frontispiece from *Projective Ornament* (Rochester, N.Y.: Manas Press, 1915); 8 ¾ × 11 ¼ in.; Charles Deering McCormick Library of Special Collections, Northwestern University Library

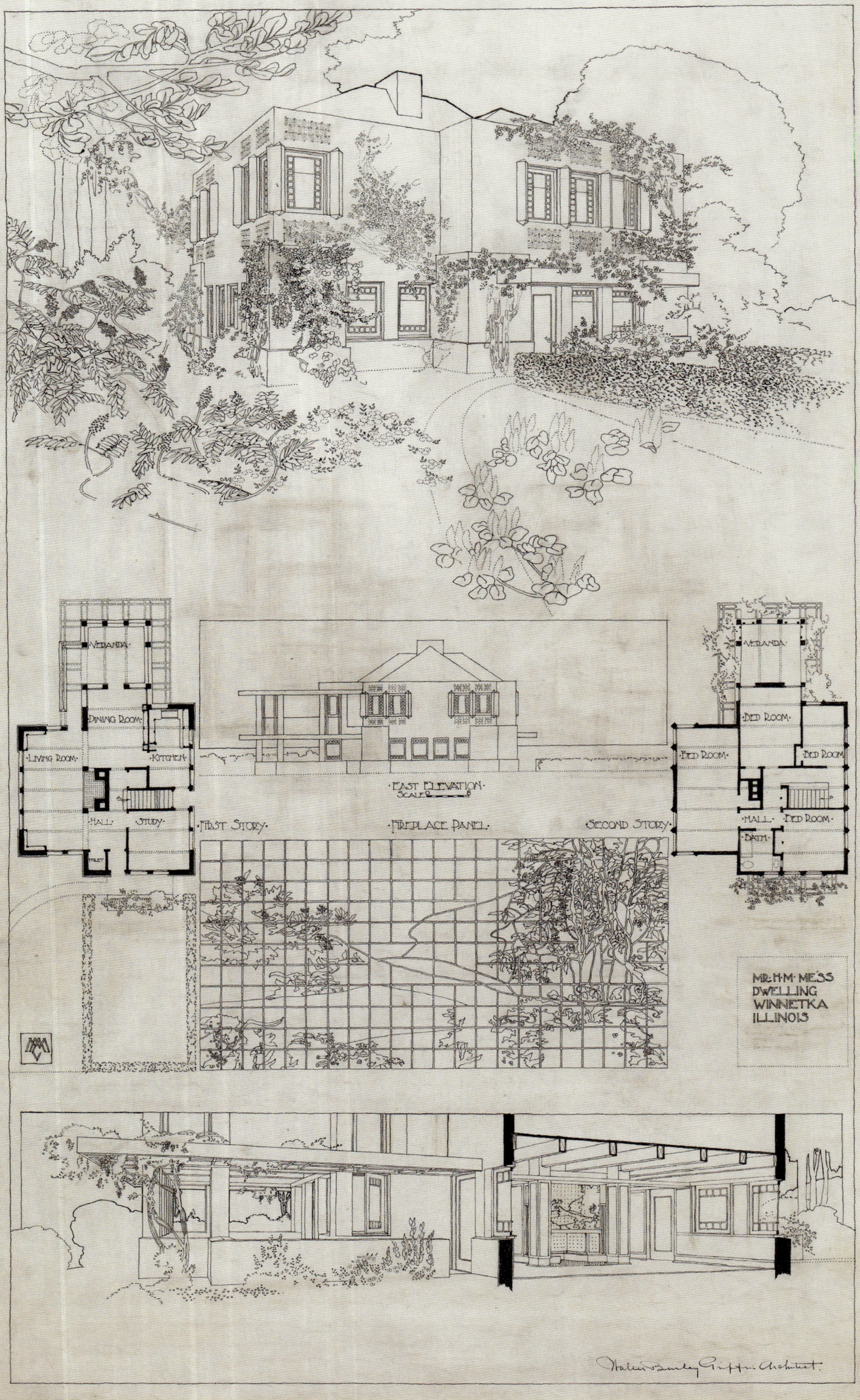

VERANDA
DINING ROOM
LIVING ROOM
KITCHEN
HALL
STUDY
FIRST STORY
EAST ELEVATION
FIREPLACE PANEL
SECOND STORY
VERANDA
BED ROOM
BED ROOM
BED ROOM
HALL
BED ROOM
BATH
MR. H. M. MESS
DWELLING
WINNETKA
ILLINOIS
Walter Burley Griffin Architect.

between a style as a state of mind and a mere vocabulary of forms or motifs, and no time was more aware of this difference than the moment before World War I, when the idea of style was most carefully framed. Neil Levine speculates that Wright's 90-degree pinwheeling rotation of each house in his Quadruple Block Plan of 1901, soon multiplied to become a broad city texture in his City Club quarter-section plan of 1912–16, presaged the experimental architecture of the years immediately after the war—that of Le Corbusier and Ludwig Mies van der Rohe. This postwar architecture was codified in the International Style strictures of 1932: volume, regularity (instead of symmetry), and unornamented surface. But Wright alone among the Chicago progressives treads here.[79] The Canberra plan is not an open, democratic field as in Wright's quarter-section scheme, but a fixed ordering of parts.

The "style" in the Griffins' work—beyond Marion's spectacular if sketchy *staffage* in the Canberra cross sections—lies in Walter's compact, geometricized houses, starting with the 1903 Lamp dwelling in Madison, Wisconsin, executed while still in Wright's office, through the 1906 Peters and 1907 Bovee houses, and extending to the "Solid Rock" and Mess dwellings of 1911–12 (figure 33 and page 83). This geometry is more like Bragdon's than Wright's. In Australia, this became the vocabulary of the one-story, concrete-roofed Castlecrag houses pushed into that rocky headland (figures 41, 42, 43, and 44). But this style was only a thread in a larger, more various production. It is original and socially and structurally consistent but lacks Wright's expansive spatial experiment.

Figure 33 *(facing page)* Walter Burley Griffin and Marion Mahony Griffin; *H. M. Mess Dwelling, Winnetka, Illinois*, 1912; pen and black ink over graphite on drafting linen; 38 × 23 ¼ in.; Mary and Leigh Block Museum of Art, Northwestern University, gift of Marion Mahony Griffin, 1985.1.109

Urban Planning and Utopian Visions

> *For the practice of architecture he [Daniel Burnham] did this: he made it known and respected by millions who had never heard of an architect in all their lives.*
>
> —PETER B. WIGHT

Walter and Marion Griffin matured as architects amid this back and forth between the monumental and the progressive. The Canberra problem—a national capital in an uneven upland landscape—brought the problem forward powerfully. The amazing thing is that in response Griffin produced something ceremonial, natural, and structured all at once—and still immediately legible.

The Canberra problem encouraged a magisterial imposition of mind that was characteristic of the time. It is important to understand that architecture as a profession—as a consistent way of thinking and acting—was new. American universities first offered architecture as a course of study in the 1870s. The entity "architect" had become a loaded term in the quarter century before 1914, involving in the educated mind the ideas of progress, rationalization, democratic politics, and world organization under European authority.[80]

In an early essay on "civic design" in the 1916 *Town Planning Review,* Lionel Budden (a graduate of the Liverpool School of Architecture and subsequently an instructor there) starts a list of planning desiderata with the placement of the project in an architect's hands—"No other profession can pretend to the requisite knowledge."[81] And what was this knowledge that only an architect had? Burnham wrote in a letter of 1901 to his friend Theodore Thomas telling him of his joy in setting to work with Charles McKim and Frederick Law Olmsted on the McMillan Commission Plan for the development of Washington, D.C.:

> Our happiness has at times seemed almost too full. When I come home [to Evanston, Ill.] I want you to spend Sunday with me and let me tell you of the dream visions. The parks, the roads, the great mall with its avenues, woods, fountains and statues, the distant vistas in the hills, the monumental bridges and arches, all of which we are allowed to play with for the nation, have brought back the day dreams of youth and we stop at nothing, developing our themes to ever nobler heights, each man raising the thoughts of the others, and altogether we have risen where I never hoped to tread in this existence.[82]

Burnham's Columbian Exposition, repeatedly cited by Griffin, was the key (figure 34). The writer William Dean Howells called himself an "Altrurian

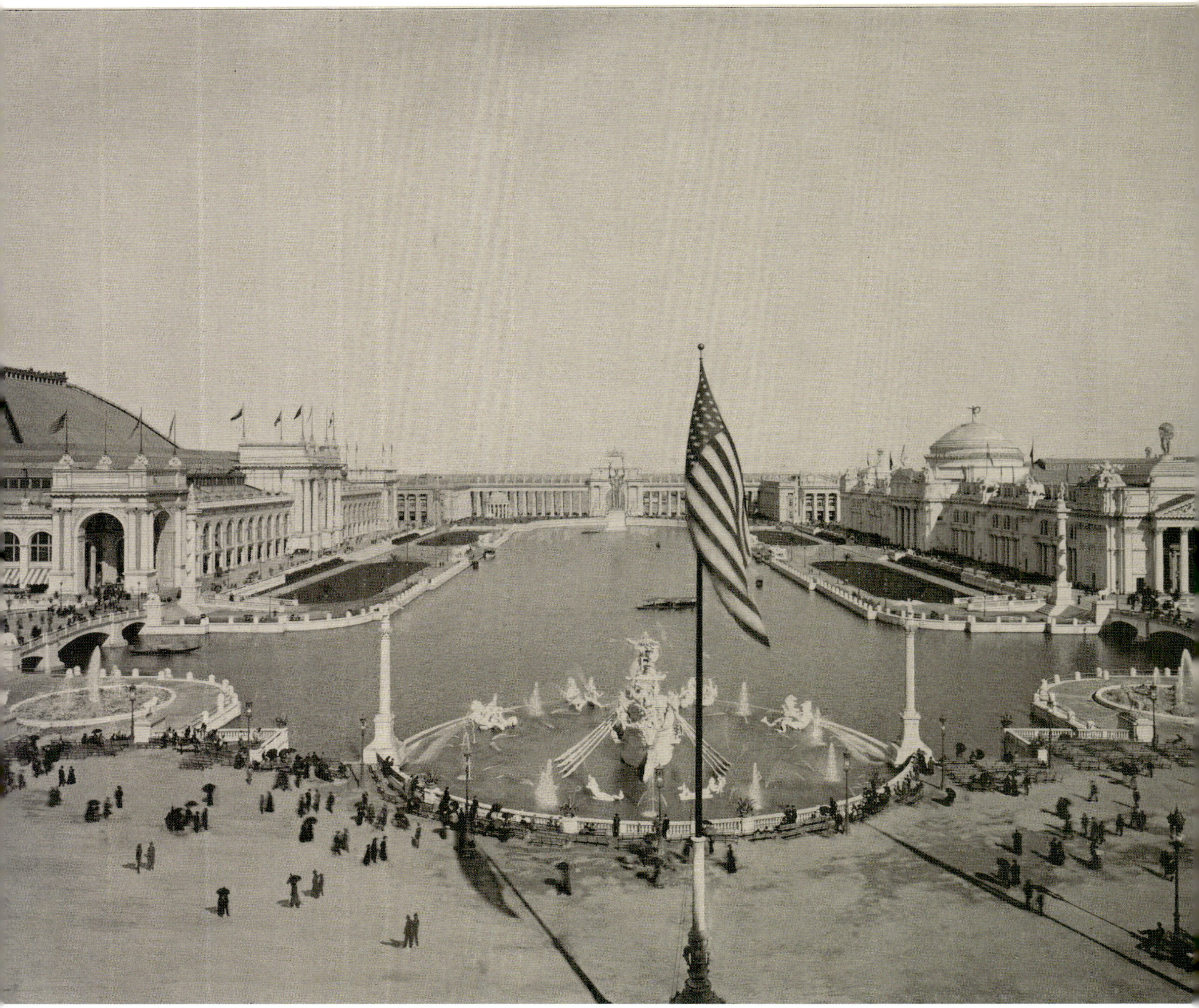

Figure 34
Daniel Hudson Burnham, architect; *Court of Honor, Looking East*; photograph by William Henry Jackson from *The White City: As It Was* (Chicago: White City Art Company, 1894); 15 × 19 in.; Charles Deering McCormick Library of Special Collections, Northwestern University Library

Traveller" in a series of magazine articles profiling American cities from 1892 to 1894 (also published in book form). Howells's text, *Letters of an Altrurian Traveller,* starts with a citizen of a fictional Altruria describing the architecture of the World's Columbian Exposition: "But the Fair City is a bit of Altruria: it is as if the capital of one of our Regions had set sail and landed somehow on the shores of the vast inland sea, where the Fair City lifts its domes and columns."[83] In 1915, this vision folded in on itself at the San Francisco Panama-Pacific International Exposition designed by Burnham's assistants Willis Polk and Jules Guerin plus one of the Griffins' fellow competitors in the Canberra competition, Bernard Maybeck. At the San Francisco exposition, the complex becomes a sequence of spaces, not masses—courts of "Abundance," "Flowers," "Palms," a "Tower of Jewels"—intensely colored in ochers and reds typical of Vuillard and Roussel, theatrically lit at night, making profligate use of the new electric technology.[84]

In popular literature, Clara Burnham's 1894 novel *Sweet Clover*—again citing the World's Columbian Exposition—gives the unnamed "architect" almost religious qualities. In the words of one character, "T'aint only the quiet and the grandeur o' those buildin's compared with the fantastic things you've left behind; I believe it's just the fact that the makers o' the Fair believed in God and put Him and their enlightenment from Him into what they did; and we feel it some like we'd feel an electric shock." Earlier, Clara—no relation to Daniel Burnham—writes that one of the novel's two heroes, Jack Van Tassel, "with reverence and a species of awe . . . gazed about him. The Court of Honor had given him his first approach to a realization of the possibilities of the Celestial City." At the end, the other hero, Clover, says she will take one last look at that space: "I shall see the peacock-blue lake through the columns of the Peristyle, look up into the Italian sky roofing all, and say my prayers or sing the doxology; then I shall come home and pack."[85]

The power of architecture becomes one of the character-building motifs of children's storybooks. For example, in the 1895 book *In Story-land* by Elizabeth Harrison, a Chicago educator (and collaborator with Jane Addams), the protagonist "Blessed Eyes," a doer of good with the power to see the best in anyone he meets, is counselor to the king. In succession, he puts an unemployed quarryman to work cutting blocks of marble, a deaf architect to assembling that marble into colonnades around a lake in the king's garden, a stammering painter to speaking in colors within those structures, a blind musician to leading a great orchestra there, and finally a bereaved mother to managing a great kindergarten in what Harrison by now is calling "The Court of Honor." The kingdom becomes happy and prosperous, and when the king dies, Blessed Eyes is proclaimed his successor, "and the nation became wise and great and powerful . . . For the little children grew up learning to love the beautiful and to see it everywhere, until at last there was a whole nation of blessed-eyes, and every city in the land became as beautiful as was the White City by the Lake."[86]

The importance of architecture also haunts an interesting Illinois text of 1915, Vachel Lindsay's *The Art of the Moving Picture.* The activist poet presents the medium as a tool for promoting good causes and, accepting that the Columbian Exposition presented a glimpse of utopia, proposes in a chapter "Architects as Crusaders" that the "photoplay" be used to persuade Americans to carry out a total architectural transformation of their country. "Why not erect our new America and move in?"[87] Cleveland's Frederic Howe verbalized this idea in his memoir *The Confessions of a Reformer* (1925):

> I had an architectonic vision of what a city might be. I saw it as a picture. It was not economy, efficiency, and business methods that interested me so much as a city planned, built, and conducted as a community enterprise. I *saw* the city as an architect sees a skyscraper, as a commission of experts plans a world's fair exposition [Howe's emphasis].[88]

This vision folds back on architecture in the "World Centre" project of 1913 by the society sculptor Hendrik Andersen (Norwegian by birth, American by citizenship, Italian by domicile, French by the draftsmen employed). The idea for a new city was displayed in huge drawings and published in a four-inch-thick folio volume (figure 31). Andersen's World Centre houses Olympic competitions, scientific cooperation, and a world government, and is meant to be dropped whole at one or another site around the world—Tervuren outside Brussels; Bern, Switzerland; The Hague in the Netherlands; the Forêt de Montmorency near Paris; Fréjus, France; Istanbul, Turkey; Ostia near Rome; and the New Jersey shore near Manasquan being illustrated as examples.[89]

What is important, however, is in the last sentence of Burnham's famous dictum "Make no little plans . . . ," namely: "Let your watch-word be order and your beacon beauty." This is exactly what the Griffins achieve in their Canberra competition plan—lucidity and fascination, but in a more original and concentrated configuration than Burnham could envision. Canberra was a better World's Columbian Exposition—built, habitable, and still there for us to admire today. This confidence in architecture's unlimited, beneficial power may explain Walter's intransigence in his last years as director at Canberra, when he refused to share his authority—which he declared was a personal trust from the minister for home affairs—and resigned when an oversight board was named.[90]

Subtexts

Perhaps here is the place to balance Burnham's letter to Theodore Thomas with one from Henry James of 1912 to his good friend Andersen:

> When you write to me that you are now lavishing time and money on a colossal ready-made City, I simply cover my head with my mantle and turn my face to the wall, and there, dearest Hendrik, just bitterly *weep* for you . . . The unutterable Waste of it all makes me retire into my room and lock the door to howl!. . . Cities are *living* organisms, that grow from within and by experience and piece by piece; they are not bought all hanging together, in *any* inspired studio anywhere whatsoever, and to attempt to plank [*sic*—for plunk?] one down on its area prepared, as even just merely projected, for use is to—well, it's to go forth into the deadly Desert and talk to the winds [James's emphasis].[91]

The understanding of "architecture" implicit in Burnham's Court of Honor (figure 34) activated multiple mentalities coalescing at that moment. To start with, there was the notion of the world's fair itself, emerging during the second half of the century into what in 1889 in Paris became the triumphal celebration of technology symbolized by the Eiffel Tower. In addition, the Paris exhibition pivoted on the huge Galerie des Machines, a cage of painted steel glazed with colored glass. Both the tower and the Galerie des Machines were illuminated at night by the new technology of electric lighting (electric power also moved the scampering, noiseless elevators of the tower).[92] The idea was less to create a new architecture (as in the Paris Exposition Universelle of 1878) than a *new world*—weightless in the case of the tower. There was a proposal to reproduce it for the World's Columbian Exposition in Chicago,[93] a project that ultimately became the Ferris Wheel. Interestingly, *The American Architect and Building News* proposed a more overt international model for Chicago's just-awarded world's fair, a model suggested for the Berlin Trade Exhibition of 1896: a created landscape around a lake, with a village to one side and mountains to the other; industrial machine exhibits in the cavernous interiors of these fake mountains; a crescent of exhibition pavilions around; and the whole woven together by an electric tram system.[94] In this context, what seems exaggerated enthusiasm in American comparisons of the 1893 exposition—Howells likening it to utopia, Clara Burnham to heaven—may be on the mark with the creation of a picture, not just of an architectural composition but of a whole new world, just when the assumption of "Progress" gave confidence in the realization of such things.

The white colonnaded images of William Dean Howells, Clara Burnham, and Elizabeth Harrison were not the only ones possible. In 1914, the German fantasy writer Paul Scheerbart wrote *Das graue Tuch und zehn Prozent Weiß* (The Gray Cloth and Ten Percent White) about a Chicago architect. The novel starts with a description of the architect's world's fair structure just erected on the shore of Lake Michigan, but the writer imagines it in steel and glass, blazing with color and illuminated by electric lights, blending 1889 and 1893 to produce a fantasy parallel to Marion Mahony's Canberra cross sections in concrete of three years before. It is important to realize that industrial America was struggling to emerge in the international public mind as the world contemplated Burnham's Court of Honor from the vantage point of the "gray" skyscraper city of the Loop, which foreign architects such as Jacques Hermant described with wonder (in that case through the lens of Sullivan's Schiller Building). These visitors had arrived in America through New York Harbor, with the Brooklyn Bridge (opened in 1884) to their right, the Statue of Liberty (dedicated in 1886) to their left, the skyscrapers of Manhattan straight before them—a whole tableau like the 1899 Exposition Universelle, but actually realized and inhabited.[95] Fact and fantasy pushed and pulled constantly in this experience.

This thrust, when shaped as Burnham achieved it in the world's fair in 1893, shifted from triumphalist to utopian, which in the literature of the years just before it was taking strong if conflicted form. The new architectural world of 1890 vacillated between white classicism and multicolored nature—both enabled by engineering that architects sought to make humane. Indeed, the Columbian Exposition, beyond the Court of Honor, modulated into Olmsted's Wooded Island and its surrounding lagoon, dominated by Sullivan's brilliantly polychrome Transportation Building which, when visiting in Paris in September and October of 1893, Sullivan described as an experience in nature.[96]

Burnham saw his reorganization of Washington, D.C., with Olmsted beside him, nestled in a larger nature, as he says in his letter to Theodore Thomas of 1901 and shows in the extraordinary aerial renderings he had prepared for the presentation of the plan. Walter and Marion Griffin saw nature first, in the sense of Ebenezer Howard's *To-Morrow* (1898) answering William Morris's *News from Nowhere* (1890) answering Edward Bellamy's *Looking Backward*. Griffin worked to find a place for the required monumental masses and axes within the site itself, literally nestled between unencumbered hills. He took Howard's dispersed Garden City (figure 21) network and pressed it into the Australian topography, divided and drawn together as a city. In Marion's cross sections, this vision of the city makes itself felt as a cast concrete fantasyland in which this elastic, cheap new technology enables a spreading built utopia.[97]

Everything in Its Place

Yet within these "architects' worlds" so gladly accepted on the eve of the Great War there lay frightening assumptions of race and class. Race first of all, the historian Robert Rydell has argued in *All the World's a Fair*, was entwined in the idea of progress, which was not just an advance of technology but also of "scientific" eugenics, justifying world dominance and exploitation by Northern European populations.[98] Twenty years ago, the architectural historian Gwendolyn Wright and the anthropologist Paul Rabinow, in parallel studies, explored early-twentieth-century French colonial urbanism as a hygienic "laboratory" whose discoveries were later exported back to France—that laboratory being convenient because of a subject population obliged to submit to these experiments.[99] The revolution Australia represented was thus taken a step farther in the near-extinction of the local population and the extension of the European homeland beyond North America to the far side of the Pacific Ocean, an expansion intimated in Burnham's Philippine projects (recently studied in Warwick Anderson's *Colonial Pathologies*).[100] Order (to use Burnham's word) was the desideratum, as the urban historian Christine Boyer has emphasized. A new architecture in the context of this "Art of Darkness," the art historian Debora Silverman suggests, is embracing and subsuming the imagery of the appropriated territories—in the case of Belgium, which she studies, one internalizing the jungle and its fauna as the structure for a progressive architectural and decorative vocabulary.[101] The Griffins used the architectural forms of the Angkor Wat temple complex in Cambodia in their original and gratifying design for the capitol—finally realizing the lookout at the lagoon end of the Columbian Exposition sketch of 1891 (figure 34). Their design is a more modest conception: neither functional nor abstract but instead a new "global" eclecticism far broader-reaching and

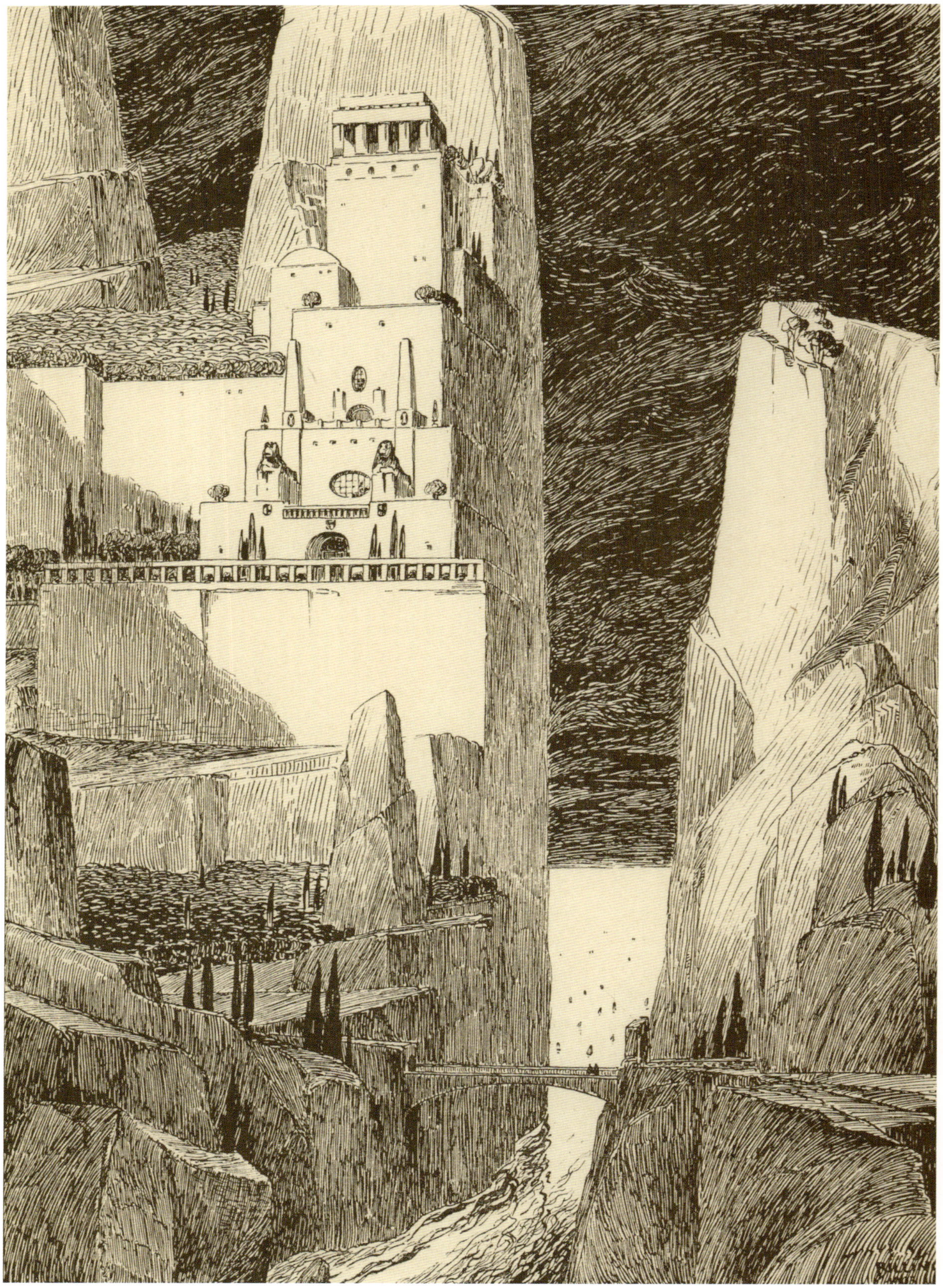

Figure 35
Hermann Billing; plate from *Architektur Skizzen* (Stuttgart: Julius Hoffmann, 1904); 11 × 8 in.; private collection

more politically loaded than the mere manipulation of Gothic, classic, and Renaissance styles.

This chilling nuance of that admirable monument in the Canberra project makes one aware of the systematic class-coding of its otherwise Howardian pattern—the elite suburb on the slope isolated to the west of Capital Hill; the workers' zone intertwined with railroad yards to the north along the main road to Sydney; the multiple middle-class quarters to the east of Capital Hill across the Molonglo floodplain to Fyshwick (figure 20)—each unit in panoptic geometry suggesting both outward growth and unimpeded sight lines. This is precisely the opposite of what Howard thought his Garden City network would enable, namely a series of intimate classless communities floated across a smiling and productive nature. At Canberra, that diagram enables enclaves; nature becomes a spacer isolating them. Like a Beaux-Arts plan diagram, the Canberra design is all about distinction and hierarchy. In Germany, this was the moment of the theory of zoning of dividing the city into distinct functional (and class) districts and reassembling them as a field of separate, if interwoven, parts.[102]

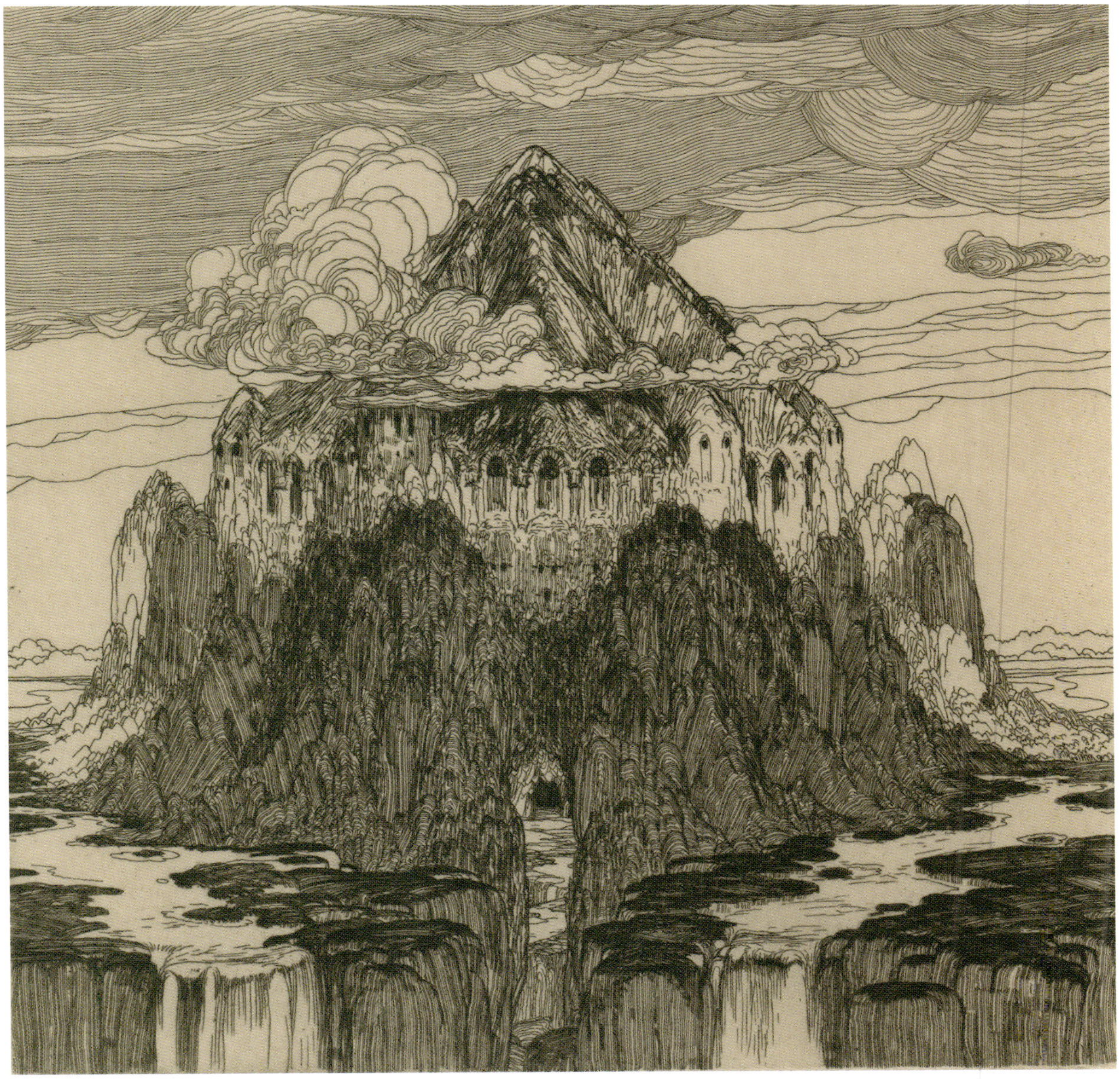

Figure 36
Wenzel Hablik; plate from *Schaffende Kräfte* (Creative Forces; Itzehoe, Germany: n.p., 1909), second edition, 1942; etching on paper; 12 × 12 in.; Charles Deering McCormick Library of Special Collections, Northwestern University Library

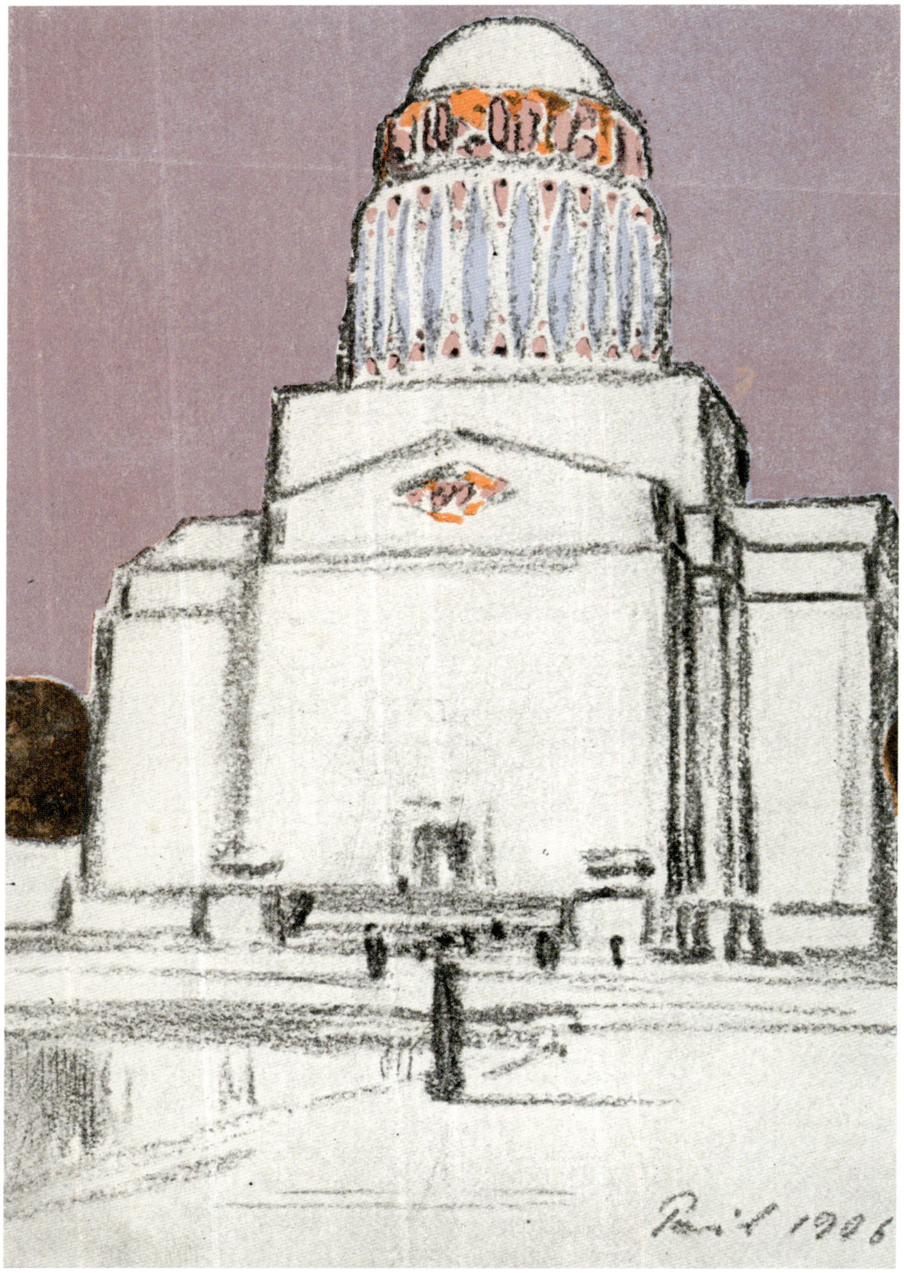

Figure 37
Otto Kohtz; untitled plate from *Gedanken über Architektur* (Thoughts on Architecture; Berlin: Otto Baumgärtel, 1909); 9 × 7 ½ in.; Charles Deering McCormick Library of Special Collections, Northwestern University Library

Picture Cities

Pulling Griffin's unitary, lucid gestalt apart, however, leads one away from that thing Canberra shares most decisively with the Columbian Exposition, namely the theatrical tableau looking south across the lagoons which Griffin describes with such eloquence in 1913—and by 1920 had staked out. This new architecture of 1890 to 1914 made a peculiar swerve in its methods, especially in the newly self-confident German architectural conceptualization moving away from the French polytechnic and Beaux-Arts diagramming to an exploration of effects. Architectural cogitation dissolved into the exploration, in small sketches instead of great plan sheets, of intriguing environments, parallel to but much more embracing than Paul Scheerbart or Belgian art nouveau. This new urban task, instead of pushing architecture into statistical problems and solutions, settled into phantasmagorical images.

This new architecture is reflected in a series of publications, from the classical fantasies of Otto Rieth in *Architektur Skizzen* (Architecture Sketches, 1891) to the academic exercises of Hermann Billing given to fine artists at the Karlsruhe Akademie der Bildenden Künste and published in his *Architektur Skizzen* in 1904 (figure 35). The new style also appears in the wonderful etchings of the painter Wenzel Hablik published as his collection *Schaffende Kräfte* (Creative Forces, figure 36) and in the bold experiments of Otto Kohtz in his *Gedanken über Architektur* (Thoughts on Architecture, figure 37), both published in 1909. Kohtz's *Gedanken* took off from the most experimental of Josef Olbrich's renderings published in the massive Wasmuth folios over the years 1901 to 1914 (continued, the art historian Paul Kruty suggests, in the Wasmuth publication of Wright's *Ausgeführte Bauten*). After the war, this tradition exploded in the utopian musings of Bruno Taut and the drawings made by his "Gläserne Kette" (Crystal Chain, a series of letters exchanged by architects that formed a basis of the expressionist architectural movement in Germany), especially Taut's *Alpine Architektur* (1917–19, figure 38) and *Die*

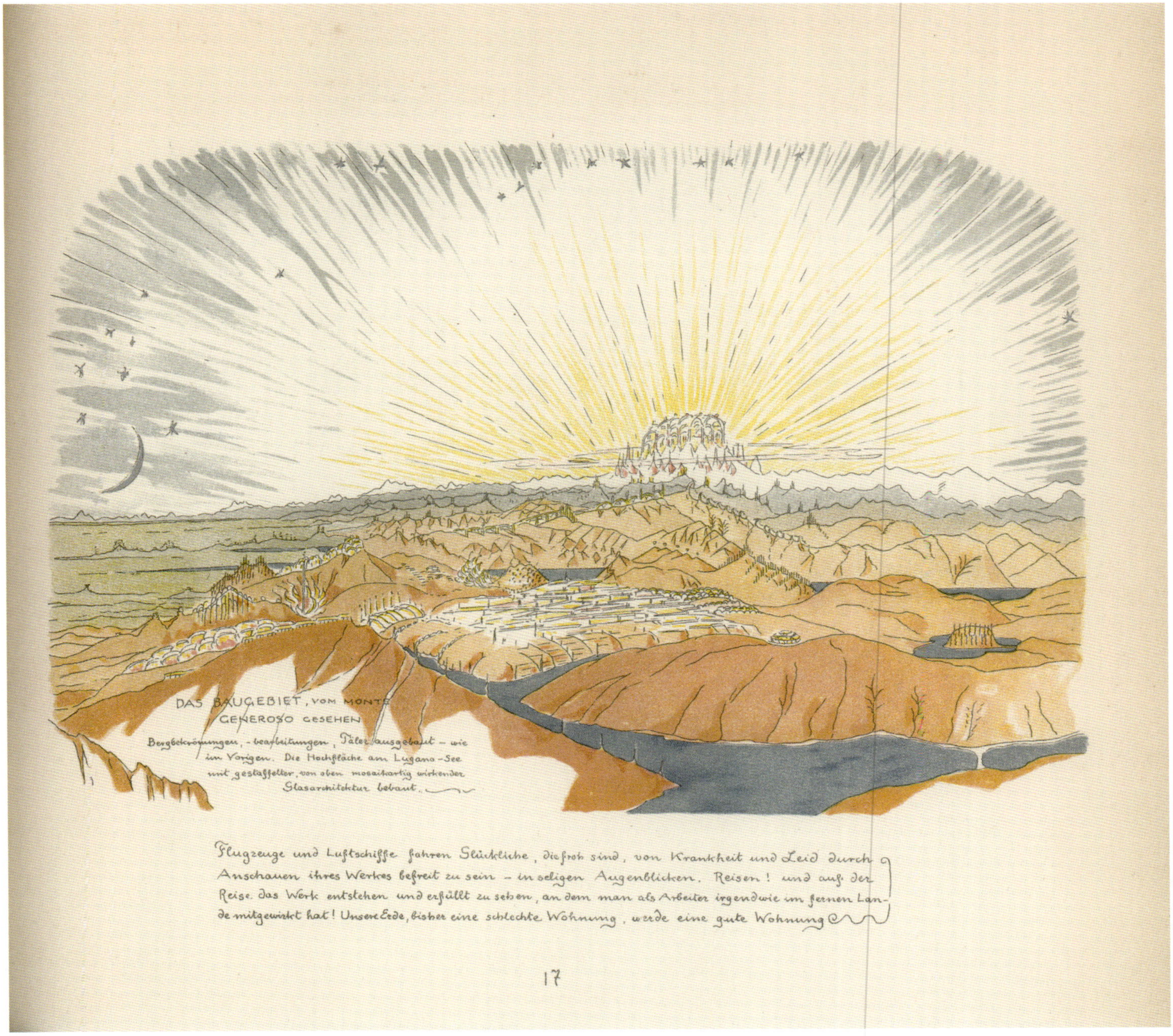

Figure 38
Bruno Taut; *Das Baugebiet vom Monte Generoso Gesehen* (The Building Area Seen from Monte Generoso); from *Alpine Architektur* (Hagen, Germany: Folkwang, 1919); 16 × 13 in.; Charles Deering McCormick Library of Special Collections, Northwestern University Library

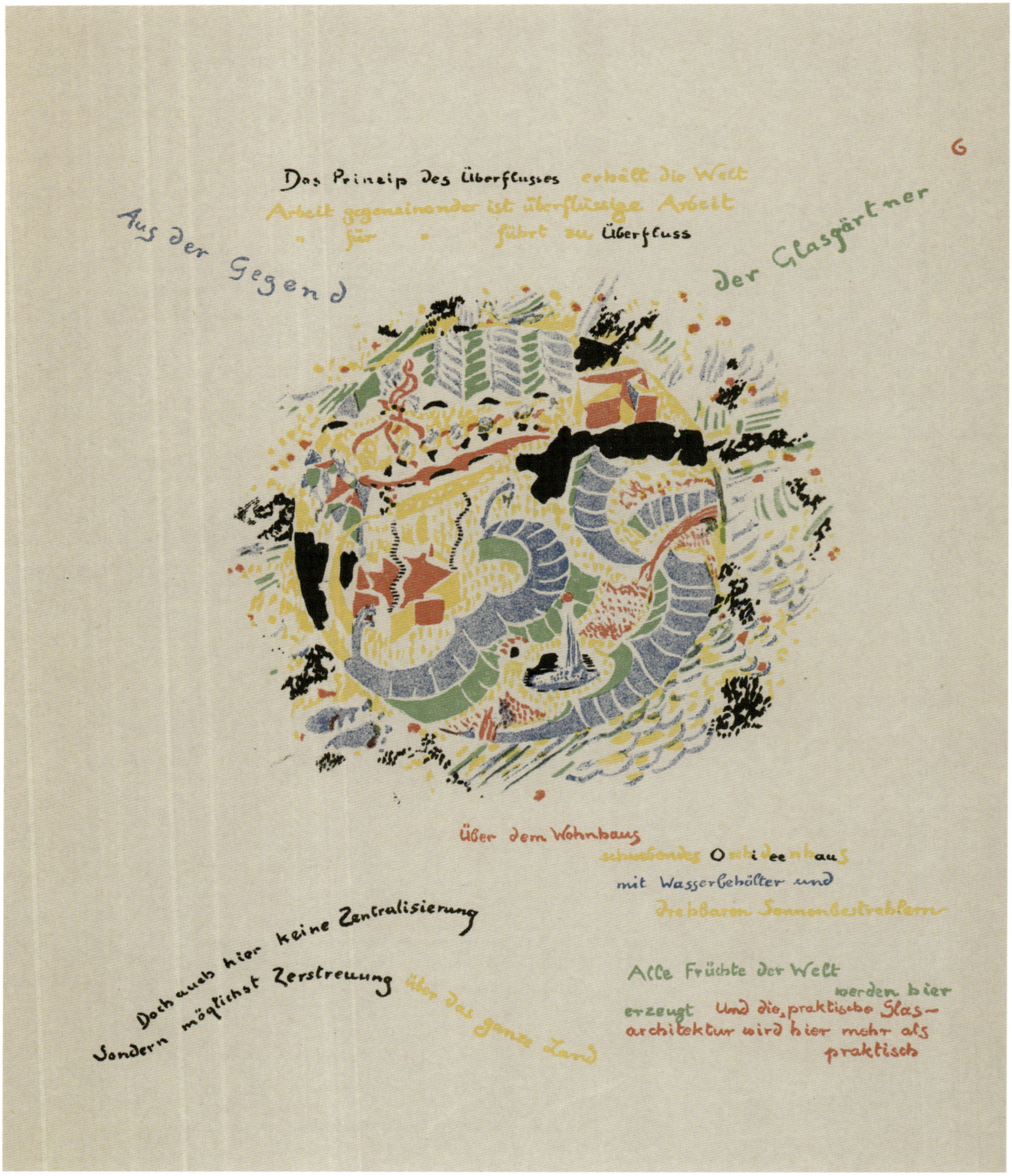

Figure 39
Bruno Taut; *Das Prinzip des Überflusses* (The Principle of Abundance); from *Die Auflösung der Städte* (The Dissolution of the Cities; Hagen, Germany: Folkwang, 1920); 11 × 8 ½ in.; Charles Deering McCormick Library of Special Collections, Northwestern University Library

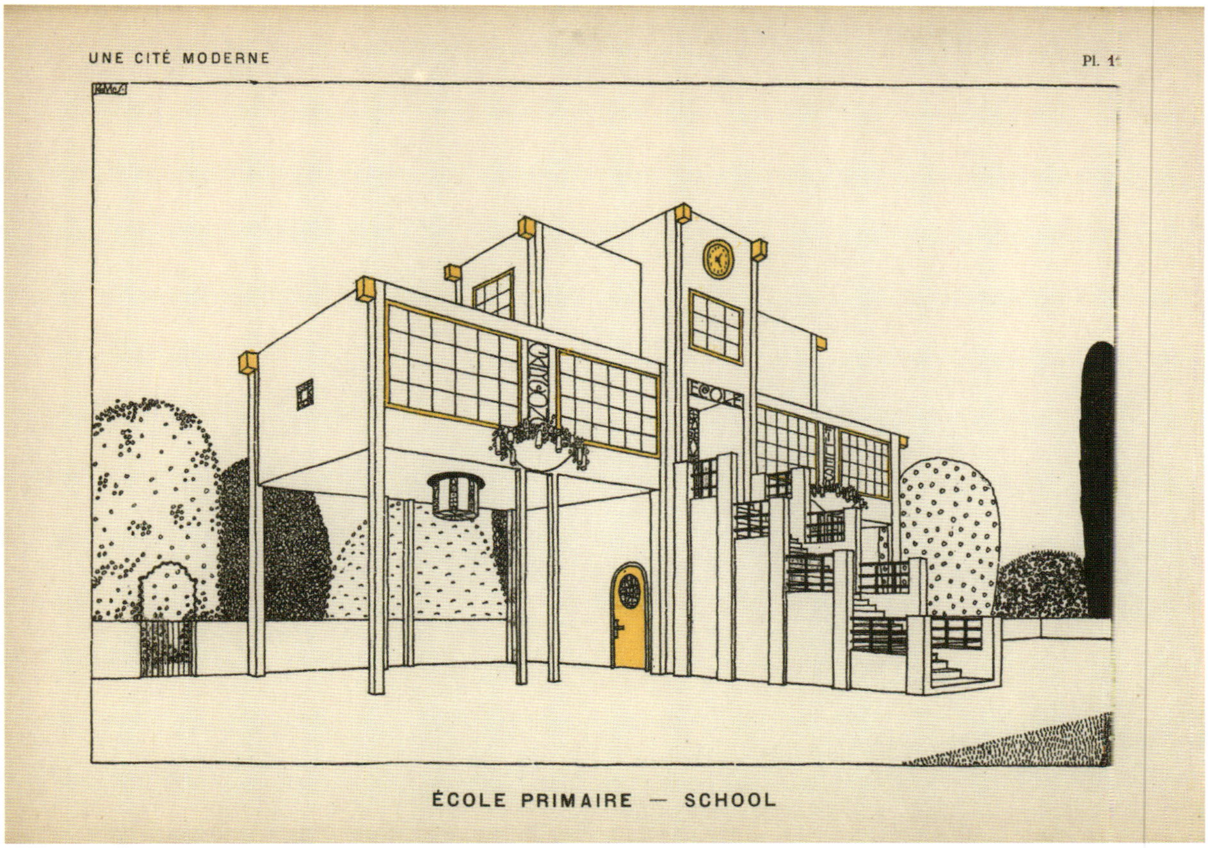

Figure 40
Robert Mallet-Stevens; *Ecole Primaire—School*; from *Une cité moderne: Dessins* (Paris: Massin, 1921); 9 ½ × 13 in.; Charles Deering McCormick Library of Special Collections, Northwestern University Library

Auflösung der Städte (The Dissolution of the Cities, 1920, figure 39).[103]

The architectural historian Iain Boyd Whyte's study of the work of Otto Wagner's students Emil Hoppe, Marcel Kammerer, and Otto Schönthal reveals something of Wagner's revolutionary teaching methods.[104] Wagner started students with simple, practical design assignments—such as an apartment house—the opposite of the Beaux-Arts foundation in spreading, abstract institutional arrangements. But by the third and last year, this practical foundation was meant to enable the student's work to blossom into a bold release of imaginative power in some huge configuration, drawing in dramatic perspective on a hillside or a Mediterranean island—all in the steel frames and smooth surfaces with which Wagner had been experimenting since his Vienna Stadtbahn stations of the late 1890s and his competition projects, like that for the Hague Palais de la Paix of 1906.

It would require a study of the spread of the Wagnerschule (Wagner school) across south-central Europe during the years just before World War I to understand (with Otto Antonia Graf and Esther da Costa Meyer) how the Italian architect Antonio Sant'Elia developed it into his extraordinary drawings ultimately displayed in 1914 as his *Città Nuova* (New City) or (helped by Pierre Vaisse and Dominique Bertin) the debt that Tony Garnier owed as well.[105] Again, it was in this context that Wright's *Ausgeführte Bauten* was received in 1911 and that Walter Burley Griffin was received soon afterward. Wagner presented Wright's work to his students, Graf has found, with the words "Er kennt mehr wie ich" (he knows more than I), echoing what Domenico Ghirlandaio supposedly said about his apprentice Michelangelo.[106] It is likewise illuminating to note, amid the bombast of the Wagnerschule projects and the Sant'Elia drawings, the contrasting lyricism of Garnier's Cité—and, moving parallel Robert Mallet-Stevens's playful, even childlike "Cité Moderne," published in the 1920s but evidently in process during (and even just before) the war (figure 40).

Castlecrag

In 1887, an odd book had appeared, W. H. Hudson's novel *A Crystal Age*, republished to some interest in 1906 and 1913. Utopian, like the later novels *Looking Backward* and *News from Nowhere, A Crystal Age* tells the story of a man of our time who suffers an accident and awakes hundreds of years in the future—in this case a totally bucolic future of open love amid glorious nature. Reminiscent of the Griffins' effort to nuance the colors of the foliage on the Canberra hilltops is Hudson's account of a unique flower, the "rainbow lily":

> Yoletta had told me that they gave a beauty to the earth which could not be described or imagined. The flowers were all undoubtedly of one species, having the same shape and perfume, although varying greatly in size, according to the nature of the soil on which they grew. But in different situations they varied in color, one color blending with, or passing by degrees into another, wherever the soil altered its character. Along the valleys, where they first began to bloom, and in all moist situations, the hue was yellow, varying, according to the amount of moisture in different places, from pale primrose to deep orange, this passing again into vivid scarlet and reds of many shades. On the plains the reds prevailed, changing into various purples on the hills and mountain slopes; but high on the mountains the color was blue; and this also had many gradations, from the lower deep cornflower blue to a delicate azure on the summits, resembling that of the forget-me-not or the hairbell [harebell].[107]

As the air thins and the situation lightens, the "rainbow lily" darkens in concatenation, from yellow in the narrow valleys to blue on the mountaintops—as in Japanese prints or Marion's Canberra renderings.

Equally striking is Hudson's delineation of this new world's architecture, broad communal structures on rock ledges:

> The house had been raised on the natural foundation of one of these rocks standing a little above the river . . . The stone was gray, tinged with red, and the whole rock, covering an acre or so of ground, had been worn or hewn down to form a vast platform which stood about a dozen feet above the surrounding green level . . . Broad, shallow steps led up to the house, which was all of the same material—reddish-gray stone; and the main entrance was beneath a lofty portico, the sculptured entablature of which was supported by sixteen huge caryatides, standing on round massive pedestals . . . [It] resembled a ruin to my eyes because of the extreme antiquity of its appearance, the weather-worn condition and massiveness of the sculptured surfaces, and the masses of ancient ivy covering it in places. On the central portion of the building rested a great dome-shaped roof, resembling ground glass of a pale reddish tint, producing the effect of a cloud resting on the stony summit of a hill.[108]

This does not seem a matter of Hudson's influencing Marion or Walter, but a coincidence of mind-set. What they share is a dream of the earth itself becoming architectural—that is, the brightly colored but incidental foliage assuming an even gradation articulating relief (like the sponged lightening of the heights in Marion's rendered Canberra plan sheet), while buildings become merely an upheaval of the bedrock underneath.

The Great War erased this quarter century of confidence in the architect as world planner from the twentieth-century mind, although it lived on in a chastened, beneficent shadow in the Weimar Republic and the Congrès Internationaux d'Architecture Moderne (International Congresses of Modern Architecture, or CIAM), a series of architecture and urban planning meetings from 1928 to 1959.

What remains today? To a degree, what survives is sketched in the galleries of this exhibition: books of images (whether city plans or fantasy projections of the urban texture of the future) and accounts of conferences, photographs, and memories of elaborately imagistic exhibitions. The Griffins' Canberra plan balances the architectural with the natural utopia, even extending to "painting" the hills by controlling their foliage. Their great accomplishment, coming just as Walter was forced out of his government position in 1920–21, was the creation just then of the Sydney suburb of Castlecrag on a bald headland in the city's Middle Harbour (figures 41, 42, 43, and 44).[109] The suburb grew to be a col-

Figure 41 *(facing page)*
Walter Burley Griffin and Marion Mahony Griffin; *J. and J. Wearne and E. Finlay Dwelling,* Castlecrag, Sydney, 1925; architectural photoreproduction (blueprint); 30 × 22 ¼ in.; Mary and Leigh Block Museum of Art, Northwestern University, gift of Marion Mahony Griffin, 2009.6.86

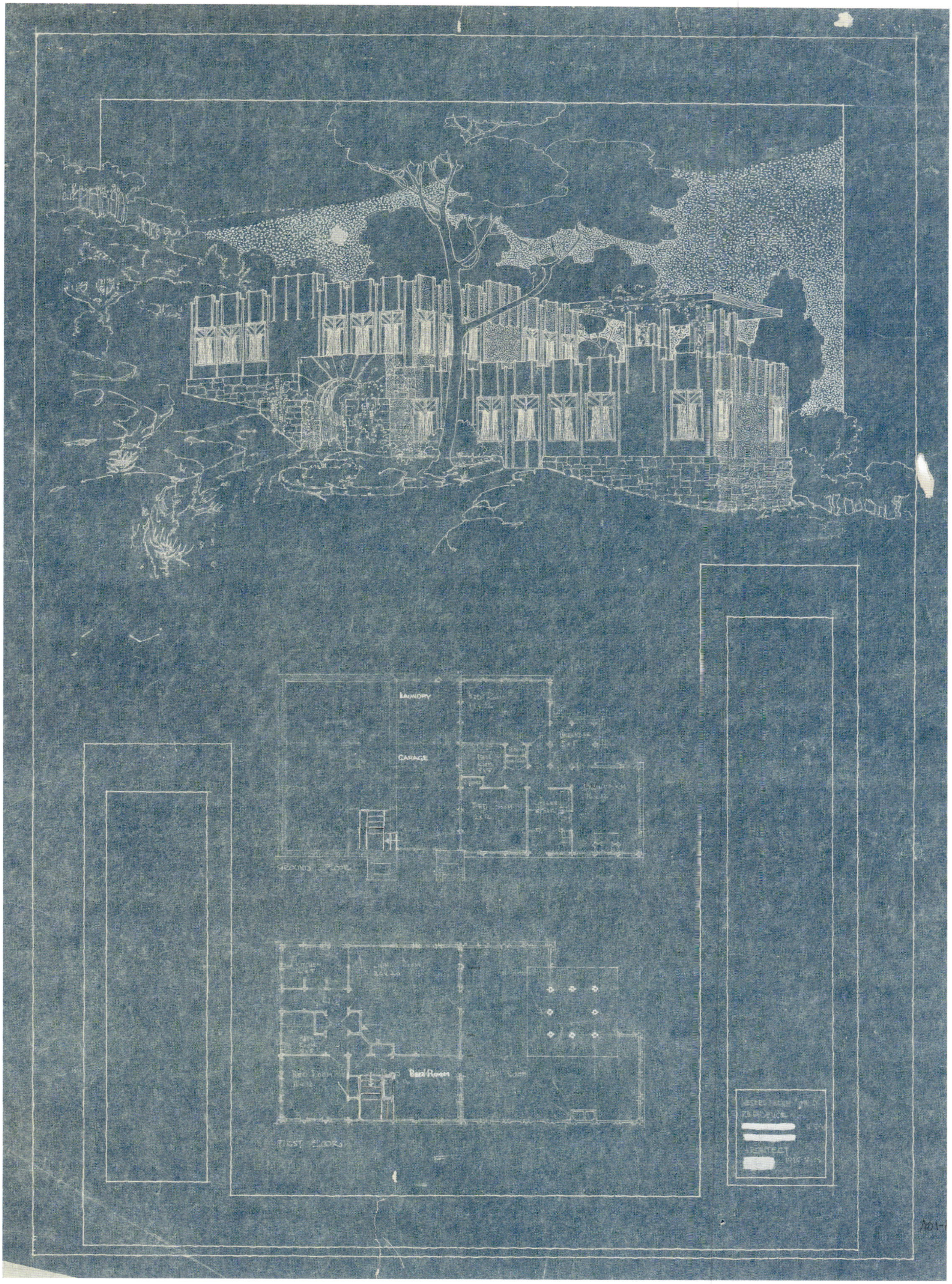

LAUNDRY
GARAGE
GROUND FLOOR
BED ROOM
FIRST FLOOR

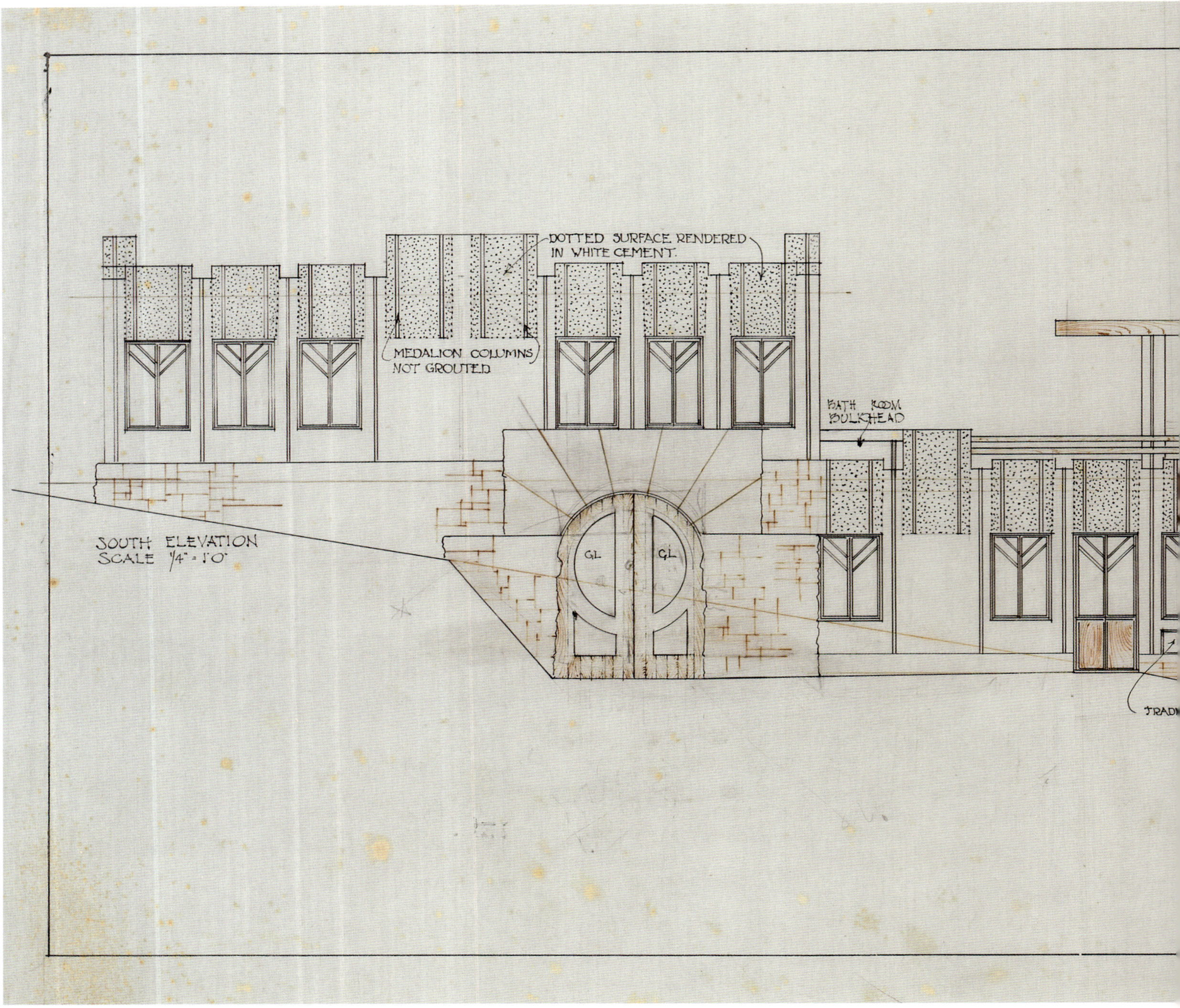
DOTTED SURFACE RENDERED
IN WHITE CEMENT.
MEDALION COLUMNS
NOT GROUTED.
BATH ROOM
BULKHEAD
SOUTH ELEVATION
SCALE 1/4" = 1'0"
GL
GL

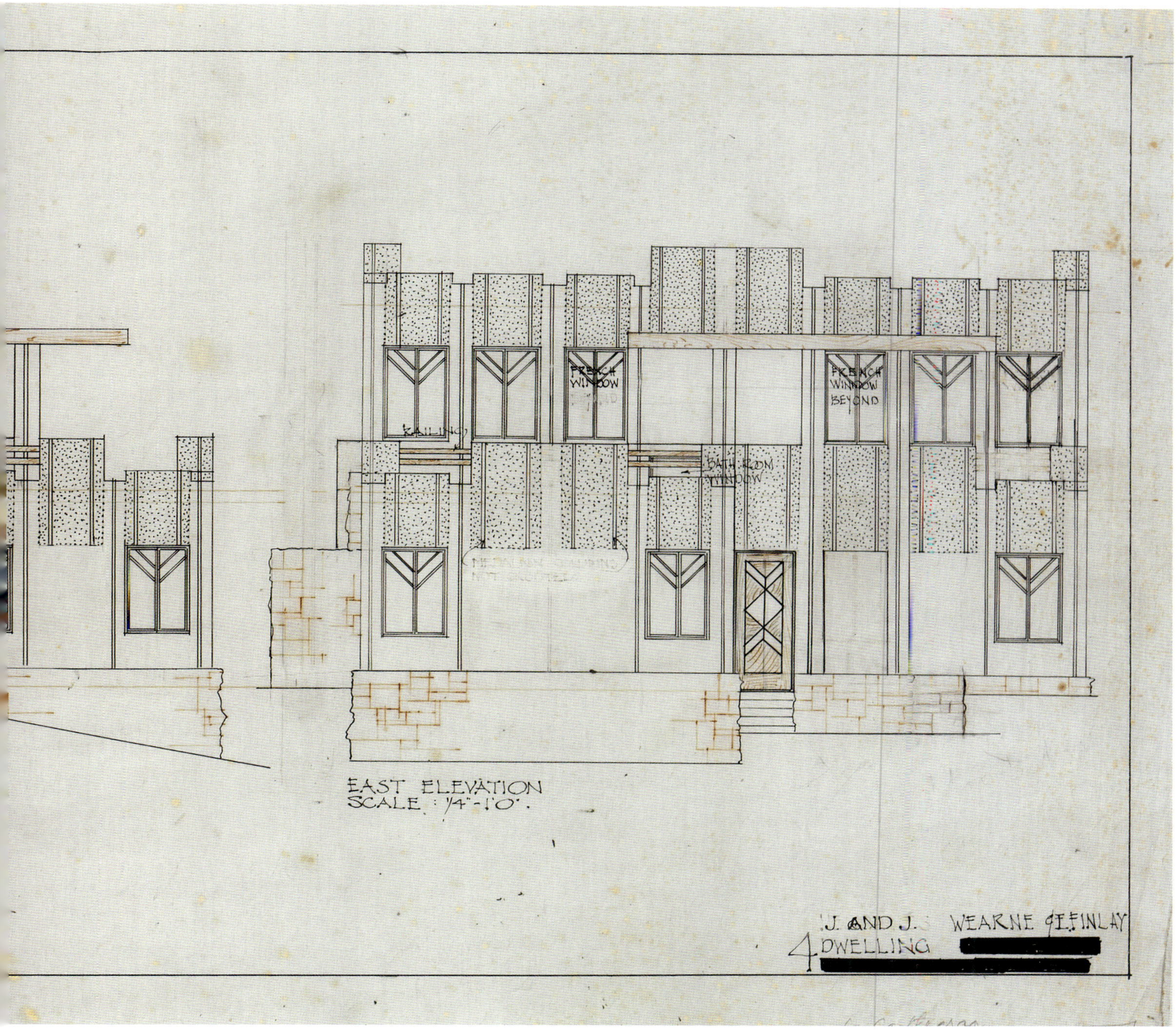

Figure 42
Walter Burley Griffin and Marion Mahony Griffin; *J. and J. Wearne and E. Finlay Dwelling,* Castlecrag, Sydney, 1925; ink and pigment on drafting linen; 13 ¼ × 30 ½ in.; Mary and Leigh Block Museum of Art, Northwestern University, gift of Marion Mahony Griffin, 1985.1.77

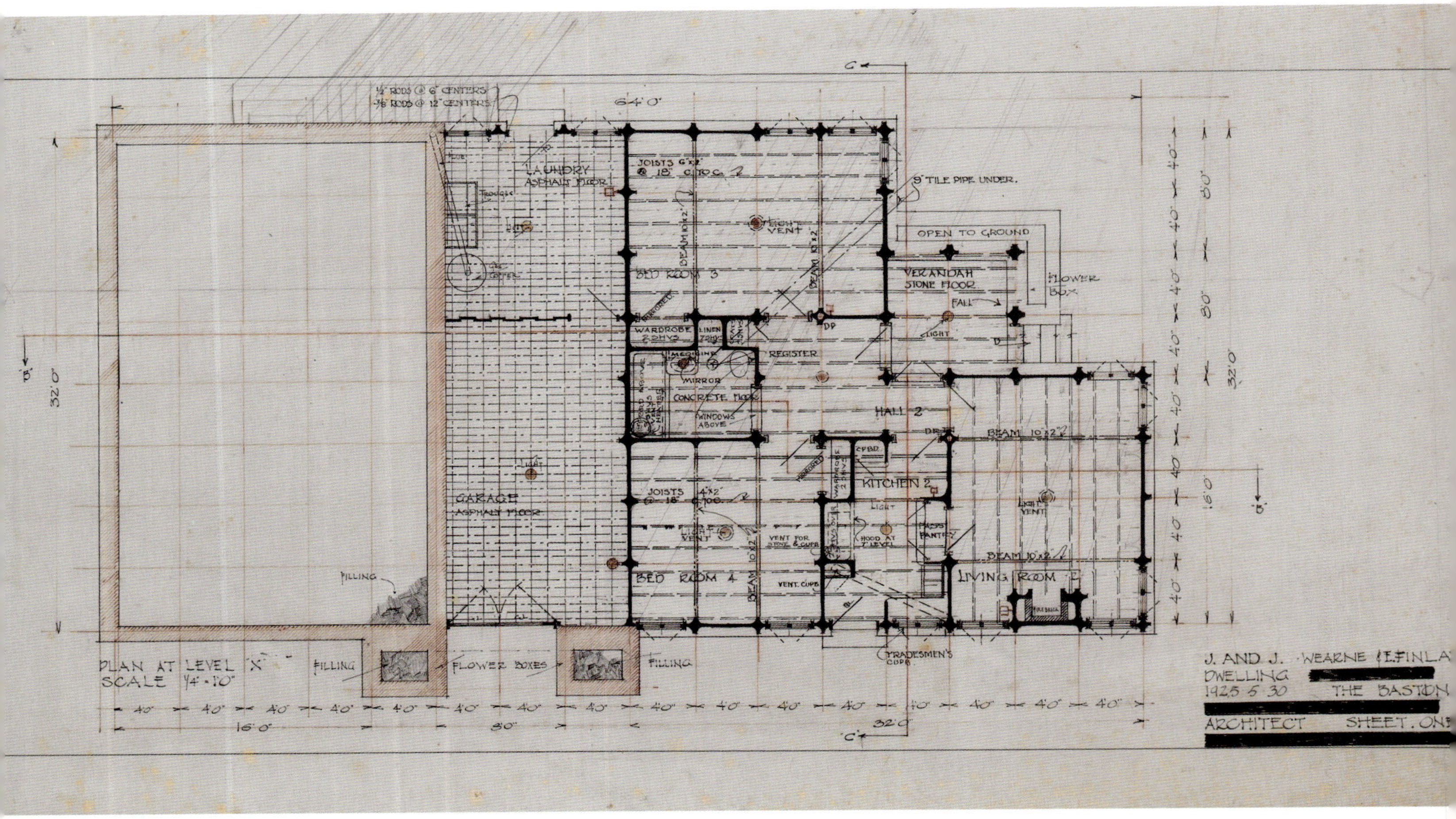

Figure 43
Walter Burley Griffin and Marion Mahony Griffin; *J. and J. Wearne and E. Finlay Dwelling* (detail), Castlecrag, Sydney, 1925; ink and pigment on drafting linen; 13 ½ × 30 ½ in.; Mary and Leigh Block Museum of Art, Northwestern University, gift of Marion Mahony Griffin, 1985.1.76

lection of efficient one-story concrete houses amid a warren of rock outcrops and backyard paths, among which the extravagant local flora was encouraged to flourish. In a sharp gulley at one end, Marion and the friends who purchased houses there built an open theater with stone seats on the slope under a canopy of trees with views past the stage out into the harbor.

Chicago planning has left us extraordinary gifts. The matrices of certain cities filled out unsteadily over the next hundred years: Washington recentered on the National Mall and pushed out into the Potomac marshes anchored there by the new Lincoln and Jefferson memorials; Chicago's lakefront kept open and clear; and Canberra's central triangle focused on what now is called Lake Burley Griffin. Through the efforts of two urban planners, Peter Harrison of Australia and William Holford of England, the Griffins' plan for Canberra was finally carried to completion only in the 1960s with the Italian-born architect Romaldo Giurgola's new Parliament House replacing Walter's capitol at the apex in 1988.

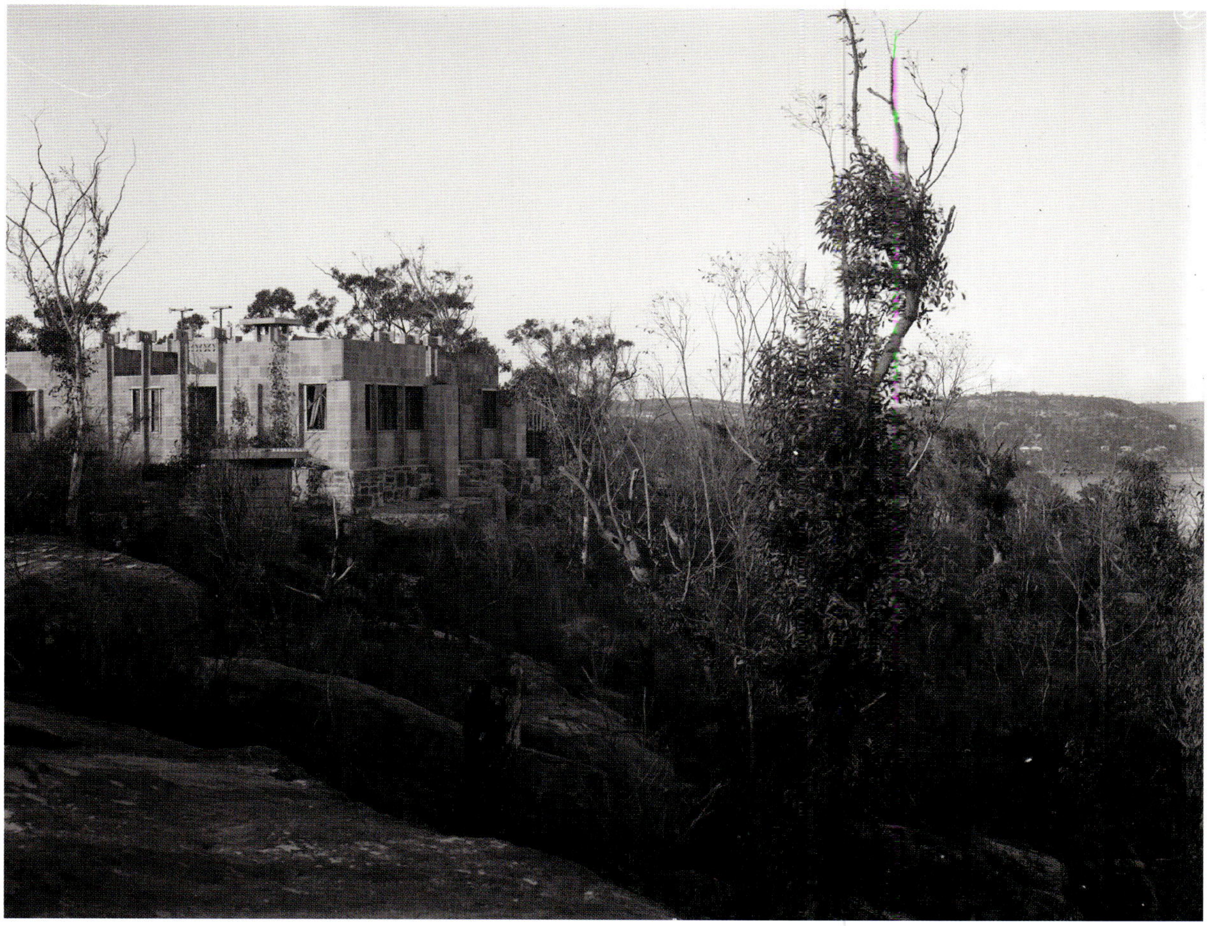

Figure 44
Walter Burley Griffin; Creswick House, 4 The Barbette, Lot 196, Castlecrag, Sydney, 1926–27; modular concrete blocks; Eric Milton Nicholls Collection, National Library of Australia

Notes

1. The most recent and closest studies of this part of their careers include: Paul Kruty, *Walter Burley Griffin in America* (Urbana: University of Illinois Press, 1996); Paul Kruty and Paul E. Sprague, *Marion Mahony and Millikin Place* (St. Louis: Walter Burley Griffin Society of America, 2007); Paul Kruty, "Graphic Depictions: The Evolution of Marion Mahony's Architectural Renderings," in *Marion Mahony Reconsidered,* ed. David Van Zanten (Chicago: University of Chicago Press, 2011), 51–93.

2. These events are carefully documented in John W. Reps, *Canberra 1912: Plans and Planners of the Australian Capital Competition* (Melbourne: Melbourne University Press, 1997); Paul Reid, *Canberra Following Griffin: A Design History of Australia's National Capital* (Canberra: National Archives of Australia, 2002); and Alasdair McGregor, *Grand Obsessions: The Life and Work of Walter Burley Griffin and Marion Mahony Griffin* (Camberwell, Australia: Lantern [Penguin Books], 2009).

3. I am deeply obliged to David Headon and Ian Batterham for arranging a visit to see these extraordinary works at the National Archives annex outside Canberra. The best color reproductions are in Reid, *Canberra Following Griffin,* chapter 4, but even here the metallic gouache skies flatten to a single muddy band. It is explained that the metallic content of the paint frustrates digital reproduction.

4. Debora Wood has studied Marion Mahony Griffin's technique: "Introduction: Drawing the Form of Nature," in Debora Wood, ed., *Marion Mahony Griffin: Drawing the Form of Nature* (Evanston, Ill.: Northwestern University Press and Block Museum of Art, 2005), viii–xii.

5. Reproduced in Wood, *Marion Mahony Griffin,* 30–31. Compare with *Olbrich Architektur,* 4 vols. (Berlin: Wasmuth, 1901–14).

6. Reps, *Canberra 1912,* reproduces all the surviving images of various competition drawings. Reid, *Canberra Following Griffin,* reproduces one sheet each of Saarinen's and Agache's drawings in color, 94–95.

7. Glenda Korporaal reminds me that the panorama formed part of the competition materials, reproduced in color in Reid, 30–31, and Reps, 56.

8. Mark Alan Hewitt, *Jules Guerin: Master Delineator* (Houston: Rice University Press, 1983).

9. Published in Dustin Griffin, ed., *The Writings of Walter Burley Griffin* (Cambridge: Cambridge University Press, 2008), 2–20, especially 9.

10. Jill Roe, *Her Brilliant Career: The Life of Stella Miles Franklin* (Cambridge, Mass.: Harvard University Press, 2009), 162. Roe also collects a number of letters between Marion Mahony and Miles Franklin in *My Congenials: Miles Franklin and Friends in Letters* (Sydney: Angus and Robertson, 2010).

11. *The Federal Capital: Report Explanatory of the Preliminary General Plan,* 3; reproduced in Griffin, *The Writings of Walter Burley Griffin,* 46 and following pages, especially 50.

12. In Daniel Burnham's *Plan of Chicago* (Chicago: Commercial Club, 1909), plate lxxxvii.

13. Kruty, "Graphic Depictions."

14. The format first appears in Griffin's design for the Dickinson House, Hollister, California; Block Museum of Art, Northwestern University, 1985.1.116.

15. Louise Lightfoot reminiscences gathered by Donald Leslie Johnson and kindly lent to me by Glenda Korporaal. See Meredith Walker, Adrienne Kabos, and James Weirick, *Building for Nature: Walter Burley Griffin and Castlecrag* (Castlecrag: Walter Burley Griffin Society, 1940), 32.

16. Carl J. Smith, "Promotion," *The Plan of Chicago* (Chicago: University of Chicago Press, 1906), 111–29, especially 116.

17. It is interesting to compare Burnham's successful presentation events for the McMillan and Chicago plans to others, such as the display of the University of California campus plan competition drawings in 1899 (*The International Competition for the Phoebe Hearst Architectural Plan for the University of California* [San Francisco: Trustees of the Phoebe A. Hearst Architectural Plan for the University of California, 1899], 42–43) or the gallery photographs in Werner Hegemann's two-volume catalog for the Berlin/Düsseldorf Städtebau (urban planning) exhibition of 1911, *Städtebau nach der Ergebnissen der Allgemeinen Städtebau Ausstellung* [Urban Planning According to the Results of the General Urban Planning Exhibition] (Berlin: Wasmuth, 1913).

18. H. P. Berlage, *Amerikaansche Reisherinneringen* [American Travel Recollections] (Rotterdam, Netherlands: W. L. and J. Brusse, 1913), 27. He compares Canberra to Karel de Bazel's 1905 plan for a world center near The Hague.

19. Berlage, *Amerikaansche Reisherinneringen,* 36; "Neue Amerikanische Architektur," *Schweizerische Bauzeitung* [Swiss Building Journal] 60, no. 11 (September 14, 1912): 148–51, especially 150; Paul Venable Turner, "Frank Lloyd Wright and the Young Le Corbusier," *Journal of the Society of Architectural Historians* 42, no.4 (December 1983): 350–59, especially 359.

20. I explain this further in "Just What Was Beaux-Arts Architectural Composition?" in *Chinese Architecture and the Beaux-Arts,* eds. Jeffrey W. Cody, Nancy S. Steinhardt, and Tony Atkin (Honolulu: University of Hawai'i Press, 2011), 23–37.

21. Raymond Unwin lectured in Chicago in 1911, then published *Nothing Gained by Overcrowding! How the Garden City Type of Development May Benefit Both Owner and Occupier* (London: P. S. King, 1912) with his draftsman Alfred Mottram's "Garden City Principle Applied to Suburbs" as its frontispiece.

22. Concrete building is a large topic, covered generally in Peter Collins, *Concrete: The Vision of a New Architecture,* 2nd ed. (Montreal: McGill-Queens University Press, 2004); Reyner Banham, *A Concrete Atlantis* (Cambridge, Mass.: MIT Press, 1986). About enthusiasm for concrete building in the 1920s, see Julius Vischer and Ludwig Hilberseimer, *Beton als Gestalter* [Concrete as a Shaper] (Stuttgart: Julius Hoffmann, 1928); Sigfried Giedion, *Bauen in Frankreich: Eisen, Eisenbeton* [Building in France: Iron, Reinforced Concrete] (Berlin: Klinkhardt and Biermann, 1928). About concrete as a utopian material, see Laurent Baridon, "Béton et utopie avant 1914: architecture et 'moule social'" [Concrete and Utopia Before 1914: Architecture and the "Social Mold"], *Revue d'art canadienne/Canadian Art Review* 31, nos. 1–2 (2006): 7–11. About concrete and the "Prairie" architects, see Andrew Saint, *Architect and Engineer: A Study in Sibling Rivalry* (New Haven, Conn.: Yale University Press, 2007), 207–79, especially 249 and following pages.

23. *Construction News* (Chicago) (July 9, 1911): 11.

24. William Storer, *The Frank Lloyd Wright Companion* (Chicago: University of Chicago Press, 1993), S.063 (1903) and S.163 (1910). The Griffin/Mahony Avery Library drawings include an undated rendering for a pavilion labeled "Universal Portland Cement State Fair Exhibition Building."

25. Published by the company: *Plans for Concrete Residences* (Chicago, 1909).

26. *American Architect* 91, no. 1636 (May 4, 1907): 161 and following pages.

27. See Andrew Saint's article on Wright's work with the concrete engineer Paul Mueller, "Frank Lloyd Wright and Paul Mueller: The Architect and His Builder of Choice," *Architectural Research Quarterly* 7, no. 2 (2003): 157–67. Also Paul Kruty, *Frank Lloyd Wright and Midway Gardens* (Urbana: University of Illinois Press, 1998).

28. Charles du Bus, "Deux aspects de l'art urbain" [Two Aspects of Urban Art], *Gazette des Beaux-Arts* 12 (1916): 368–90, especially 279. I owe this reference to Christopher Vernon.

29. F. Rudolf Vogel, *Das amerikanische Haus* (Berlin: Wasmuth, 1910), 264; *Schweizerische Bauzeitung* 60, no. 12 (September 21, 1911): 167.

30. Again a large topic. On this specifically, see Dominique Bertin and Pierre Vaisse, "Tony Garnier en contexte (1899–1914)," *L'esprit d'un siècle: Lyon 1800–1914* [The Spirit of a Century: Lyon 1800–1914] (Lyon: Musée des Beaux-Arts, 2007), 92–101; Pierre Vaisse, "Entre utopie et publicité: Les ambiguités d'une cité industrielle" [Between Utopia and Advertising: The Ambiguities of *Une Cité industrielle*] in Philippe Dufieux, *Tony Garnier, la cité industrielle et l'Europe: Actes du colloque international Tony Garnier* [Tony Garnier, the Industrial City, and Europe: Proceedings of the International Symposium on Tony Garnier] (Lyon: Conseil d'Architecture, d'Urbanisme et de l'Environnement du Rhône, 2008), 91–103. Also see *Tony Garnier: l'Œuvre complète* (Paris: Centre Pompidou, 1989).

31. Walter summarizes his trip in a letter of June 9, 1914, to the minister for home affairs, reproduced in parliamentary paper 153-F8489, 1914–15, *The Parliament of the Commonwealth of Australia: Federal Capital*, 37–39. Of his American presentations, he writes, "I . . . prepared slides and delivered addresses—some fifteen in all—to the local Real Estate Boards and Associations of Commerce, and the City Clubs of St. Louis, Milwaukee and Chicago, being obliged for lack of time to refuse similar requests from Louisville, Des Moines, Cleveland, and San Francisco, and from many lesser organizations."

The subject of Wright's architecture and Europe is a large one, summarized in Anthony Alofsin, *Frank Lloyd Wright—The Lost Years, 1910–1922: A Study of Influence* (Chicago: University of Chicago Press, 1993), and Anthony Alofsin, ed., *Frank Lloyd Wright: Europe and Beyond* (Berkeley: University of California Press, 1999). See also Heidi Kief-Niederwöhrmeier, *Frank Lloyd Wright und Europa* (Stuttgart: Krämer, 1983).

32. National Archives of Australia, series A2911, undated.

33. National Library of Australia, Nicholls Collection, box 6, folder 27: "Federal Parliament House Competition," n.d. The printed text is the application of Griffin's original statement of principles:

> My work has been previously best known in connexion with the development in this country of a type of architecture that is independent of classic, Gothic, or any other historical or academic basis, and also free from effort to be original, eccentric or striking, further than results from the contrast between the borrowed finery of applied academic architecture and a straightforward adaptation of present day labour-saving economic constructive methods and materials to the essential, but often new, functions of our more complex activities. This, in other words, is to treat architecture as a democratic language of everyday life . . .

This statement appears in a letter of January 21, 1913, to Minister for Home Affairs King O'Malley, with which Griffin began his campaign to be named to execute his plan. The letter is quoted in Dustin Griffin, ed., *The Writings of Walter Burley Griffin*, 35–39.

34. National Archives of Australia, A110, FC 1916/340, documenting the aborted 1916 competition.

35. Compiled by Christopher Vernon building off Walter's letter of January 1913, confirmed by the Griffins' Paris hotel bill and Wagner's note on their meeting. A receipt for currency exchange indicates that on March 11, 1914, the Griffins were in Venice, presumably having taken the train round-trip from Vienna. Gergely Baics kindly found their return trip in the National Archives New York Passenger Lists.

36. Letter of June 9, 1914, previously cited.

37. National Library of Australia, Eric Nicholls Collection, box 5, folder 25 letters and notes relating to the European trip.

38. Archives Municipales, Lyon, 781 WP 5. Fullerton is cited as "Commissaire Américain" (American Commissioner). On Hérriot trying to meet Walter: letter "Maire de Lyon" to Walter, April 17, 1914. On Fullerton: Marion Mainwaring, *The Mysteries of Paris: The Quest for Morton Fullerton* (Hanover, N.H.: University Press of New England, 2001). Reviewed tellingly by Hermione Lee, *London Review of Books* 23, no. 5 (March 8, 2001), 3–6.

39. Chicago History Museum, Research Center, Manuscript 414C, box 2, minutes of City Club Board of Directors, October 30, 1913.

40. Elizabeth Grossman, *The Civic Architecture of Paul Cret* (Cambridge: Cambridge University Press, 1996), 19, 26, and following pages.

41. Frédéric Seitz, *L'École Special d'Architecture, 1865–1930* (Paris: Picard, 1995).

42. Announced in *Der Städtebau* 7, no. 5 (May 5, 1910): 60.

43. Or, to give his entire title as written in the Bottin (Paris city directory) for 1913: "Directeur, Direction Administrative des Services d'Architecture et des Promenades et Plantations de la Voirie et du Plan de Paris" (Director, Administrative Services Branch of Architecture and the Promenades and Plantations, Highways, and the Plan of Paris)—in fact, head simultaneously of three fundamental administrations in the city government.

44. "L'art à l'Exposition de Chicago," *Gazette des Beaux-Arts* 10 (1893): 237–50 (especially 246), 416–25, 441–61; *Gazette des Beaux-Arts* 11 (1894): 149–69.

45. Checking in the 1913 Bottin, all these addresses are confirmed—perhaps because Walter was using the Bottin to begin with.

46. On Agache and the Société Française des Architectes Urbanistes established in 1911: Paul Rabinow, *French Modern: Norms and Forms of the Social Environment* (Cambridge, Mass.: MIT Press, 1989), 211 and following pages.

47. Marie-Laure Crosnier-Leconte, *Victor Laloux, 1850–1937: L'architecte de la gare d'Orsay* (Paris: Musée d'Orsay, 1987).

48. On the French architectural press about 1900: Jean-Michel Leniaud and Béatrice Bouvier, *Les périodiques d'architecture* [Architectural Periodicals] (Paris: École des Chartes, 2001); Hélène Jannière, *Politiques editorials et architecture 'moderne': L'émergence de nouvelles revues en France et en Italie (1923–1939)* [Editorial Politics and "Modern" Architecture: The Emergence of New Journals in France and Italy (1923–1939)] (Paris: Editions Arguments, 2002); Béatrice Bouvier, *Edition d'architecture à Paris au XIXe siècle: Les maisons Bance et Morel et la presse architecturale* [Architecture Publishing in Paris in the Nineteenth Century: The Bance and Morel Houses and the Architectural Press] (Geneva: Droz, 2004).

49. The Griffins' Paris hotel bill survives in the Nicholls papers, documenting them at the hotel March 3–7.

50. On Ricker: Mark Peisch, *The Chicago School of Architecture* (New York: Random House, 1964), 7–12. Excerpts of Ricker's translation appeared in "Modern Architecture," *The Brickbuilder* 10, nos. 6–8 (June–August 1901): 124–28, 143–47, 165–71. There is a huge literature on Viennese Secession architecture, most recently and exhaustively in the 2011 exhibition at the Österreichische Galerie Belvedere, *Gustav Klimt and Josef Hoffmann: Pioneers of Modernism,* and the 2010 exhibition at the Mathildenhöhe Darmstadt, *Josef Maria Olbrich.* See Eduard Sekler's model *Josef Hoffmann: The Architectural Work* (Princeton, N.J.: Princeton University Press, 1985) and Carl Schorske's *Fin-de-siècle Vienna: Politics and Culture* (New York: Alfred A. Knopf, 1980).

51. In a subsequent letter of April 10, 1914, Griffin describes Lethaby to Wagner as "gründlich beschlagen in den fundierenden Prinzipien der Architektur" [thoroughly grounded in the basic principles of architecture]. See Godfrey Rubens, *William Richard Lethaby: His Life and Work, 1857–1931* (London: Architectural Press, 1986).

52. Christopher Vernon believes Marion Mahony knew German. In the 1960s, Walter's sister Genevieve told me that Walter did not.

53. National Archives of Australia, 2911 664/1914.

54. Paul Lafollye, "Exposition d'esquisses d'architecture de l'architecte américain Walter-Burley Griffin" [Exhibition of Architectural Drawings of the American Architect Walter Burley Griffin], *Architecture* 27, no. 29 (July 18, 1914): 247. Ashley Dunn presents this bibliography more completely in her essay here.

55. Charles du Bus, "Deux aspects de l'art urbain," 368–90, especially 379: ". . . ce magnifique ciment armé dont M. Walter Griffin édifiera demain la métropole de Yash [*sic*] Canberra . . . " [(With) this magnificent reinforced concrete, Mr. Walter Griffin will build tomorrow the metropolis of Yash Canberra . . .]. I owe this citation to Christopher Vernon.

56. Tony Garnier, *Une Cité Industrielle* (Paris: Vincent, 1917); 2nd ed. (Paris: Massin, 1939). See, in addition to the Vaisse articles cited previously, Tony Vidler's seminal "The New Industrial World: The Reconstruction of Urban Utopia in Late Nineteenth Century France," *Perspecta* 13–14 (1971): 242–56.

57. Walter explained in his October 1913 *Report Explanatory of the Preliminary General Plan* (5): "Centrally located, the Capitol is focussed in an extensive hill park, and at that has a limited function, either as a general administration structure for popular reception and ceremonials, or for housing archives and commemorating Australian achievements rather than for deliberation or counsel; at any rate representing the sentimental and spiritual head, if not the actual working mechanism of the Government of the Federation."

58. The history of a progressive "Chicago" or "Prairie" school starts with the books of Mark Peisch, *The Chicago School of Architecture,* and H. Allen Brooks, *The Prairie School: Frank Lloyd Wright and His Midwest Contemporaries* (Toronto: University of Toronto Press, 1972) and has most recently produced—beyond the lengthening Griffin/Mahony bibliography—Wilbert Hasbrouck's *Chicago Architectural Club: Prelude to the Modern* (New York: Monacelli, 2005) and a number of anthologies, such as Charles Waldheim and Katrina Rüedi Ray's *Chicago Architecture: Histories, Revisions, Alternatives* (Chicago: University of Chicago Press, 2005). The contemporary participant Thomas Tallmadge already identified it in his "The 'Chicago School,'" *Architectural Review* (Boston) 15, no. 4 (April 1908): 69–74 and his chapter "Louis Sullivan and the Lost Cause" in his *Story of Architecture in America* (New York: W. W. Norton, 1927)—a chapter he revised in his second edition of 1937.

59. The club's archive is preserved at the Chicago History Museum. It published the *City Club Bulletin* chronicling its activities from 1907. Its interaction with the "Prairie School" is examined by Donald Leslie Johnson, "Frank Lloyd Wright's Community Planning," *Journal of Planning History* 3 (February 2004), and Neil Levine, "The Quadruple Block Plan and Frank Lloyd Wright's Obsession with the Grid," *Enseignement architecture ville* 11 (2005/2006): 62–84.

60. *Construction News* (November 25, 1911): 7.

61. Neil Levine is working on a book about Frank Lloyd Wright's planning that focuses on the first of these competitions.

62. David Gebhard, *The Architectural Drawings of R. M. Schindler,* 4 vols. (New York: Garland, 1993), nos. 2363–66.

63. Publishing their *Proceedings of the Fifth National Conference on City Planning* (Cambridge, Mass.: University Press, 1913).

64. Hasbrouck, *Chicago Architectural Club,* 251 and following pages.

65. The significance of the Architectural League of America needs to be clarified—Sherman Paul brought it to attention in his 1962 *Louis Sullivan: An Architect in American Thought* (Englewood Cliffs, N.J.: Prentice-Hall, 1962); Marie Frank extends this analysis in her 1996 University of Virginia dissertation "The Theory of Pure Design and American Architectural Education in the Early Twentieth Century," chapter 4. I touch on it in *Sullivan's City: The Meaning of Ornament for Louis Sullivan* (New York: W. W. Norton, 2000), chapter 3. The organization published *The Architectural Annual* 1900–1, 1906–8 under the editorship of Albert Kelsey in Philadelphia.

66. See Marie Frank, "Theory of Pure Design."

67. I review this with illustrations in *Sullivan's City*, chapter 3.

68. Robert C. Spencer Jr., "The Work of Frank Lloyd Wright," *Architectural Review* (Boston), (1901): 61–72.

69. I treat this interesting but overlooked incident—largely from archival sources—in *Sullivan's City*, 77–79.

70. Dolf Broekhuizen, ed., *Robert van 't Hoff: Architect of a New Society* (Otterloo, Netherlands: Kröller-Müller Museum, 2010).

71. I owe this information to Neil Levine and William Whitaker.

72. City Club records, box 11, letter from George Hooker to Jens Jensen as chair of the City Planning Committee, April 27, 1910.

73. The effort to define Wright's work as a "style" in the strict German sense starts with Hermann de Fries, *Frank Lloyd Wright: Aus dem Lebenswerk* [Frank Lloyd Wright: From the Life's Work] (Berlin: Ernst Pollak, 1926); Curt Behrendt, *Modern Building: Its Nature, Problems and Forms* (New York: Harcourt Brace, 1937); and Sigfried Giedion, *Space, Time and Architecture* (Cambridge, Mass.: Harvard University Press, 1941)—although there were several premonitions, especially in Holland: Berlage's lecture in Zurich in 1912; continuing with Jan Wils, "De Nieuwe Boukunst: bij het Werk van Frank Lloyd Wright" [The New Architecture: In the Work of Frank Lloyd Wright], *Levende Kunst* [Living Art] 1, no. 11 (November 1918): 209–19; and culminating with J. J. P. Oud's essay in his *Holländische Architektur* (Munich: Langen, 1926), 77–83.

74. So Marion recounts in a penciled reminiscence in the Nicholls papers, National Library of Australia, box 3, folder 17.

75. I thank Bart Ryckbosch, archivist of the Art Institute, for letting me examine the directors' minutes and the relevant letter file here. The lectures were published as *Six Lectures on Architecture* (Chicago: University of Chicago Press for the Art Institute of Chicago, 1916).

76. Jonathan Massey, *Crystal and Arabesque: Claude Bragdon, Ornament and Modern Architecture* (Pittsburgh: University of Pittsburgh Press, 2009).

77. The late Manfredo Tafuri found Burnham's classicism entirely logical: *Architecture and Utopia: Design and Capitalist Development* (Cambridge, Mass.: MIT Press, 1976), 34–36. See also Christiane Crasemann Collins, *Werner Hegemann and the Search for Universal Urbanism* (New York: W. W. Norton, 2005).

78. The difficulty appears in an angry attack by Wright himself on unnamed imitators, "In the Cause of Architecture: Second Paper," *Architectural Record* 35 (May 1914), 405–13.

79. The concept of style animates Sigfried Giedion's *Space, Time and Architecture*, which he evolved as a student of Heinrich Wölfflin, himself a student of Jakob Burckhardt. It is conscientiously explored in Giedion's first book, *Spätbarocker und romantischer Klassizismus* [Late Baroque and Romantic Classicism] (Munich: Bruckmann, 1922). At that moment, it was simply accepted as a "fact" underpinning, for example, Henry-Russell Hitchcock and Philip Johnson's seminal Museum of Modern Art exhibition of 1932, and their book *The International Style*, accompanying it. See Michael Podro, *The Critical Historians of Art* (New Haven, Conn.: Yale University Press, 1982).

80. There is a literature on the architect as an emerging professional: Barrington Kaye, *The Development of the Architectural Profession in Britain* (London: Allen and Unwin, 1960); Spiro Kostof, ed., *The Architect: Chapters in the History of the Profession* (New York: Oxford University Press, 1977); Mark Crinson and Jules Lubbock, *Architecture: Art or Profession* (Manchester, U.K.: Manchester University Press, 1994); as an image (Andrew Saint, *The Image of the Architect* [New Haven, Conn.: Yale University Press, 1983]); in comparison to the engineer (Andrew Saint, *Architect and Engineer*); Mary Woods, *From Craft to Profession: The Practice of Architecture in Nineteenth-Century America* (Berkeley: University of California Press, 1999); but less as an ideology (Manfredo Tafuri, *Architecture and Utopia;* James Holston, *The Modernist City* [Chicago: University of Chicago Press, 1989]).

81. Lionel Budden, "The Relation of Exposition Planning to Civic Design," *Town Planning Review* 6, no. 3 (January 1916): 153–62. This after citing the Place de la Concorde, Versailles, and the Columbian Exposition as models.

82. Theodore Thomas Papers, Newberry Library: Burnham to Thomas, October 26, 1901. Historians rarely deal with Burnham's Swedenborgianism (exception: Kristen Schaffer, *Daniel H. Burnham: Visionary Architect and Planner* [New York: Rizzoli, 2003], especially 19), although Sullivan would write in his *Autobiography of an Idea* that he was "a sentimentalist, a dreamer . . . a mystic—a Swedenborgian—a man who readily opened his heart if one were sympathetic" (286). "Burnham had said to Louis: 'It is not good policy to go much above the general level of intelligence.' Burnham had also said: 'See! Louis, how beautiful the moon is, now, how tender. Something in her beauty suggests tears to me' " (316).

83. Published originally in *The Cosmopolitan*, republished in Clara M. Kirk and Rudolf Kirk, eds., *Letters of an Altrurian Traveller* (1893–94) by William Dean Howells (Gainesville, Fla.: Scholars' Facsimiles and Reprints, 1961), 21.

84. Two books produced by the fair authorities to explain and evoke its qualities: Eugen Neuhaus, *The Art of the Exposition* (San Francisco: Paul Elder and Co., 1915), and Louis Christian Mullgardt, *The Architecture and Landscape Gardening of the Exposition* (San Francisco: Paul Elder and Co., 1915).

85. Clara Burnham, *Sweet Clover: A Romance of the White City* (Boston: Houghton Mifflin, 1895), 202, 181, 332.

86. Elizabeth Harrison, *In Story-Land* (Chicago: Sigma, 1895), 65–77, especially 77.

87. Vachel Lindsay, *The Art of the Moving Picture* (New York: MacMillan, 1915; republished New York: Liveright, 1970), 272–79, especially 279.

88. Frederic C. Howe, *The Confessions of a Reformer* (New York: Charles Scribner's Sons, 1925), 113–14.

89. Hendrik C. Andersen, *Creation of a World Centre of Communication* (Paris: Hendrik C. Andersen, 1913); *"Conscience mondiale": Société internationale pour favoriser la creation d'un centre mondial* ["Global Conscience": International Society to Promote the Creation of a World Center] (Rome: Hendrik C. Andersen, 1913).

90. National Archives of Australia A199 FC1921/76, especially letter from Prime Minster Billy Hughes to Walter Burley Griffin of January 27, 1921.

91. Leon Edel, ed., *Henry James: Letters 1895–1916*, vol. 4 (Cambridge, Mass.: Belknap Press, 1984), 611–13, letter of April 14, 1912. James expresses his distress in several other letters as well.

92. Eugène Hénard, *Le palais des machines* [The Palace of Machines] (Paris: Imprimeries Réunies, 1891), especially section 1, "L'art de fer" [The Art of Iron], 1–9.

93. A letter from Eiffel to William Le Baron Jenney of August 31, 1889, in the Art Institute microfilm collection refuses to authorize this reproduction.

94. *The American Architect and Building News* 41 (November 15, 1893), p. 93.

95. There is a huge if disorganized literature of New York as a wonder city: Marvin Trachtenberg perhaps most carefully in his *Statue of Liberty* (New York: Viking, 1976), Jean-Louis Cohen, *Scènes de la vie future* [Scenes of the Future Life] (Paris: Flammarion, 1995), and Rem Koolhaas most imaginatively in his *Delirious New York* (New York: Oxford University Press, 1978).

96. His text in French survives in the libraries of the Chicago Art Institute. I have published it: "Louis Sullivan: Etude sur inspiration," *Enseignement architecture ville* 12 (2006/2007): 46–51.

97. There is a smaller, parallel literature of urban utopianism, for example, H.G. Wells's *Anticipations* (London: Chapman and Hall, 1902), Lewis Mumford's *Story of Utopias* (New York: Boni and Liveright, 1922), and W. H. G. Armytage's *Yesterday's Tomorrows: A Historical Survey of Future Societies* (London: Routledge, 1968). Also Jean Dethier and Alain Guiheux, *La Ville* (Paris: Editions Centre Pompidou, 1994). For concrete as a building material, see Laurent Baridon, "Béton et utopie avant 1914."

98. Robert W. Rydell, *All the World's a Fair: Visions of Empire at American International Expositions, 1876–1916* (Chicago: University of Chicago Press, 1984).

99. Paul Rabinow, *French Modern;* Gwendolyn Wright, *The Politics of Design in French Colonial Urbanism* (Chicago: University of Chicago Press, 1991).

100. Warwick Anderson, *Colonial Pathologies: American Tropical Medicine, Race and Hygiene in the Philippines* (Durham, N.C.: Duke University Press, 2006).

101. Debora Silverman, "Art Nouveau, Art of Darkness: African Lineages of Belgian Modernism, part I," *West 86th* 18, no. 2 (Fall/Winter 2011): 139–81.

102. On zoning: Brian Ladd, *Urban Planning and Civic Order in Germany, 1860–1914* (Cambridge, Mass.: Harvard University Press, 1990); more popular and evocative: Karl Scheffler, *Der Architektur der Großstadt* (Berlin: Bruno Cassirer, 1913).

103. These pedagogical exercises fall between utopian city vision, surveyed by Jean Dethier and Alain Guiheux, *La Ville*, and expressionist architectural fantasies (Timothy O. Benson, ed., *Expressionist Utopias: Paradise, Metropolis, Architectural Fantasy* [Los Angeles: Los Angeles County Museum of Art, 1994]), and have not been studied as a body of material in themselves. Exhibitions: *Hermann Billing: Architekt zwischen Historismus, Jugendstil und Neuem Bauen* [Hermann Billing: Architect Between Historicism, Art Nouveau, and Modernism], Städtische Galerie Karlsruhe im PrinzMaxPalais, 1997; *Farbenhäuser und Lichtgewächse: Wenzel Hablik, Paul Scheerbart, Bruno Taut* [Colored Houses and Light Flowers: Wenzel Hablik, Paul Scheerbart, Bruno Taut], Universität für angewandte Kunst, Vienna, 2005.

104. Iain Boyd Whyte, *Emil Hoppe, Marcel Kammerer, Otto Schönthal: Three Architects from the Master Class of Otto Wagner* (Cambridge, Mass.: MIT Press, 1989); Otto Antonia Graf, *Die vergessene Wagnerschule* [The Forgotten Wagner School] (Vienna: Jugend und Volk, 1969), 27. The Chicago equivalent was Emil Lorch's exercises in "Pure Design"—Marie Frank, "Theory of Pure Design."

105. Esther da Costa Meyer, *The Work of Sant'Elia* (New Haven, Conn.: Yale University Press, 1995), especially chapter 3, "The Impact of Vienna."

106. I owe this anecdote information to Otto Antonia Graf.

107. W. H. Hudson, *A Crystal Age* (New York: E. P. Dutton, 1917), 208–9.

108. Ibid., 35–36.

109. See Meredith Walker, Adrienne Kabos, and James Weirick, *Building for Nature.*

Louis Bonnier; *Buvette pour Saint-Tropez Quinquina, Exposition Universelle de Paris, 1900* (Refreshment Area for Saint-Tropez Quinquina, Paris Universal Exposition, 1900), 1899; Fonds Louis Bonnier. SIAF/Cité de l'architecture et du patrimoine/Archives d'architecture du XXe siècle. See also page 69.

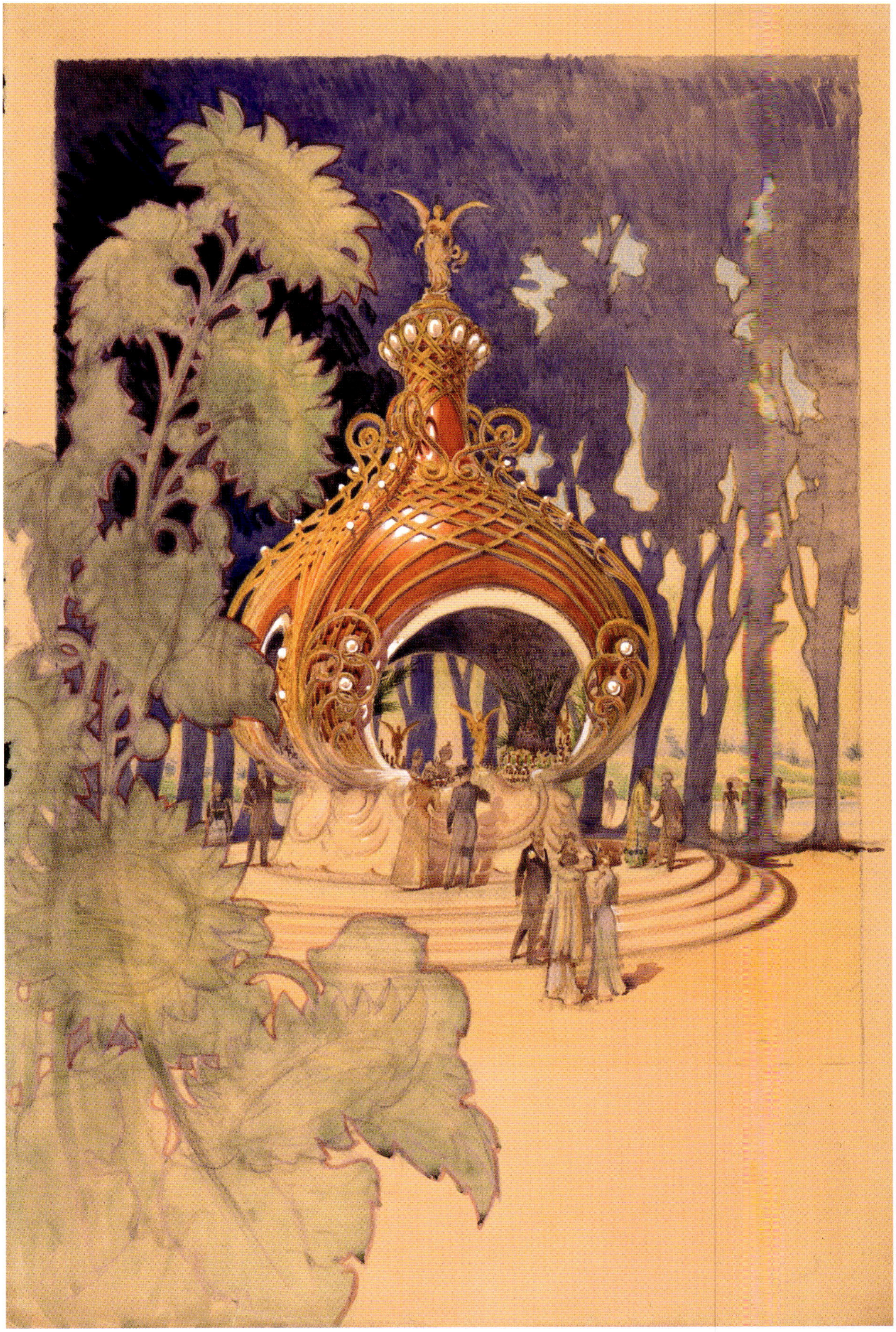

The Musée des Arts of Modern

In 1914, the Musée des Arts Décoratifs in Paris served as an important site for the translation and migration of ideas about city planning and modern architecture from Chicago to Europe. Its exhibition Esquisses d'architecture de l'architecte américain Walter-Burley Griffin (Architectural Sketches of the American Architect Walter Burley Griffin), which silently encompassed the work of Marion Mahony Griffin as renderer of the presentation drawings, was the museum's first to feature contemporary architecture. On view for just over three weeks from June 20 until July 13, the exhibition upheld the institution's mission "to keep alive in France the culture of the arts which seek to make useful things beautiful."[1] It was also one of the first occasions that the Chicago school of progressive architecture—embodied by Marion Mahony Griffin's presentation style—was put on display for European audiences.[2] Coinciding with the annual convention of the Société Française des Architectes, the exhibition's visibility among the professional community was no doubt significant; however, lasting recognition of its importance was severely hindered by the outbreak of World War I the following month.

The potential impact of the Griffins' work in France was doubled by the concurrent exhibition of their work at the Exposition Internationale Urbaine in Lyon, curated by the French architect Tony Garnier. Garnier's early interest in the Griffins is especially intriguing when one considers that the next presentation of work by a contemporary architect at the Musée des Arts Décoratifs was none other than that of Garnier himself in 1925. If a museum's exhibition programming speaks to its institutional

Ashley Elizabeth Dunn

DÉCORATIFS AND THE PRESENTATION ARCHITECTURE IN PARIS

goals, the Musée des Arts Décoratifs's selection of the Griffins and Garnier distinguishes these architects as especially conducive to the objective of unity among the arts that the museum, and its umbrella organization, the Union Centrale des Arts Décoratifs (UCAD), sought to promote.

In choosing the Griffins and Garnier as the subjects of the only solo exhibitions devoted to contemporary architects during the first twenty years of its history, the museum conveyed a distinct interest in two pioneers of twentieth-century city planning; however, a survey of the literature surrounding the exhibitions reveals that instead of stressing this aspect of the architects' careers, the museum featured works that highlighted their particularly creative practices of rendering architectural forms. Tony Garnier's and Marion Mahony Griffin's innovations through drawing, and the creation of an overall decorative effect by the skillful integration of nature into their designs, unite their efforts.

Intervening in this narrative is the violent interruption of World War I, which impelled the fantasy architecture of the city of the future to become an urgent reality. The Musée des Arts Décoratifs's engagement with city planning intensified during the war as it took an active role in the discourse of rebuilding the devastated cities of northern France by offering its space for exhibitions. After an unrealized effort to mount an exhibition on the subject of reconstruction in 1915, the museum displayed the results of a competition for the reconstruction of rural habitations in 1918 and loaned galleries to the Société de la Renaissance des Cités (Society for the Revival of Cities), a mutual aid organization tasked with spearheading rebuilding efforts, to exhibit city plans and projects in 1919. In facing the very real need to build from scratch and in turning its space over to other organizations, the Musée des Arts Décoratifs compromised on its prescription for what the modern architect should accomplish, relaxing its restrictions on referencing styles of the past.

This essay seeks to understand the position of architecture within the Musée des Arts Décoratifs during the first two decades of its history, particularly the kind of practice the museum advocated for the twentieth-century architect through the two cases of the Griffins and Garnier, and how it was complicated by the war. The museum emerges as an important locus in the dissemination of ideas about modern architecture and city planning, invested not only in the practical problems of building the city of the future but also in the expressive potential of architectural drawings as works of art.[3]

To situate these temporary exhibitions within the permanent display at the Musée des Arts Décoratifs, one may turn to descriptions of architecture within the museum's collection when it opened to the public in 1905. After more than two decades of searching for a permanent home, UCAD opened its museum in the Pavillon de Marsan, the northwest wing of the Louvre. The official guidebook of 1905 mentions architectural drawings only once, highlighting studies by Antoine Vaudoyer, a French architect active in the late eighteenth and early nineteenth centuries.[4] As a nod to the extensive holdings of the museum, the critic and art historian Paul Vitry in his review in *Art et Décoration* mentions that "L'architecture même y est représentée parfois de façon tout à fait intéressante" (Even architecture is represented here at times in a manner that is quite interesting), citing a series of seventeenth-century drawings by Charles Le Brun for the facades of the Château de Marly as an example.[5] Vitry particularly appreciated the value of the original drawings on view at the museum, which he believed revealed the ingenuity and taste of French *architectes-décorateurs*.[6] This conjunction of terms may in fact speak precisely to the conception of the architect put forward by the museum.

A more extensive guidebook from 1923 includes an index listing the architects whose work is cited therein; most often, architects are referred to simply in connection with sites of an object's provenance. When works by an architect are on display, they are commonly fragments—balconies, banisters, doors—or designs for ornament or the decoration of interiors. There are a few instances in which entire projects or plans appear to be on view and most date from the seventeenth or eighteenth centuries.[7] Although another Chicagoan, Louis Sullivan, had offered to donate models of his architectural ornament in earlier stages of planning the museum, by 1905 it seems the reconstruction of Georges Hoentschel's pavilion designed for UCAD to display at the Exposition Universelle of 1900 stood as the sole representation of contemporary architecture.[8] Hoentschel offers a prime example of an individual working within this fluid categorization of architect-decorator, even designating space within the pavilion for the display of his own ceramic work. Vitry recognized the Hoentschel pavilion as a promising example of the art and architecture of the present moment; in providing examples of such superior artistic creations, he credited the museum with working toward an overall unity among the arts and the innovation of a new style for the modern era.[9]

As a result of the outbreak of war weeks after the Griffins' exhibition, very little published critical response exists. One must turn to the framework of the individuals responsible for realizing the exhibition to reconstruct the potential interest in, and impact of, the Griffins' work. From correspondence, and a brief pamphlet published for the occasion of the exhibition, Louis Bonnier, architect of the city of Paris, emerges as a key organizer.[10] The Griffins met Bonnier during their visit to Paris earlier that spring, on a stop made during European travels to promote their recent prizewinning plan for Canberra, the new capital of Australia, and to gather jurors for a competition to design the Parliament House there, as discussed in greater detail by David Van Zanten in this volume. Bonnier would likely have had a keen interest in the city-planning aspect of the Griffins' work because of his role as inspector general of technical services and aesthetics for the extension of Paris. He designed his own plan for the extension of the French capital in 1912 and was preparing to launch a competition for others in 1914, when his plans were postponed due to the war (figure 45).

In describing his arrangement with Bonnier in early June 1914, Griffin wrote, "As a measure of further propaganda for our Australian ideas I complied with the request of Monsieur Bonnier, City Architect of Paris, and President of the Societe [*sic*] Centrale des Architectes de France, to leave samples of work with him for purposes of a special salon and architectural exhibit at the Ecole des Beaux-Arts . . . "[11] Griffin's assumption that the exhibition would take place at the École des Beaux-Arts is curious, and it is unclear whether it was a simple misunderstanding or if it had been Bonnier's intention at one time. In any case, it seems that Bonnier, through his professional relationship with François Carnot, then president of UCAD, arranged instead to display the Griffins' renderings at the Musée des Art Décoratifs. Notably, the following year, Bonnier was elected to the administrative council of UCAD, perhaps indicating a desire to continue the alliance with architectural interests initiated by the Griffins' exhibition.

Carnot and Bonnier most certainly knew each other from their work on the Exposition Internationale des Arts Décoratifs et Industriels Modernes, an event that ultimately became a landmark in announcing the new International Style represented by Charles-Édouard Jeanneret (Le Corbusier), among others. Although the exhibition did not take place until 1925, as early as 1911, Bonnier and Carnot were working on the project with the aim of realizing it in 1915. Along with representatives from seven artists' societies—Carnot in his capacity as president of UCAD, and Bonnier likely in association with his involvement in the Société d'Encouragement à l'Art et à l'Industrie—both signed a report jointly announcing their support of an international decorative arts exposition.[12]

Bonnier's insertion into the world of decorative arts reform was likely thanks to Siegfried Bing, a German-born Parisian art dealer and impresario of art nouveau, who hired the young architect to redesign and renovate his gallery, the Maison de l'Art Nouveau, in 1895. Gabriel Weisberg suggests that as a collector of Japanese art, Bonnier was in fact a client of Bing's.[13] Bonnier's knowledge of Japanese forms led him to comment that the Griffins' panels of silk "évoquent inévitablement le souvenir de l'art japonais" (inevitably evoke the recollection of Japanese art).[14] Visitors to the Griffins' exhibition could easily have established this visual connection themselves with the availability of the museum's Japanese collection and a concurrent series of exhibitions featuring Japanese art that ran from 1909 to 1914.

Marion Mahony Griffin's technique borrowed formal and material qualities from Japanese decorative arts; on a silk support she employed a variety of lines and embellished with colored ink washes to create a flat, decorative effect. By foregrounding nature in her compositions, she integrated the architectural design into a landscape (figure 46).[15] In the only extant review of the Griffins' exhibition, critic Paul Lafollye calls attention to these aspects: "Le grand intérêt de l'œuvre de M. Walter Griffin réside presque entièrement dans la présentation élégante de ses projets; joliment dessinés sur soie, ils ont tout à fait l'aspect de Kakemonos japonais (peintures suspendues), l'architecture n'occupe qu'une place secondaire, mais le paysage, les arbres, les fleurs, prennent le développement d'un brillant entourage." (The great interest in the work of Mr. Walter Griffin resides almost entirely in the elegant presentation of his projects; prettily drawn on silk,

Figure 45
Louis Bonnier, *Boulevard à deux niveaux de circulation, Paris* (Boulevard with Two Levels of Circulation, Paris), undated; graphite with white gouache on tracing paper mounted to board, 13 ¼ × 18 ¼ in.; Fonds Louis Bonnier. SIAF/Cité de l'architecture et du patrimoine/Archives d'architecture du XXe siècle.

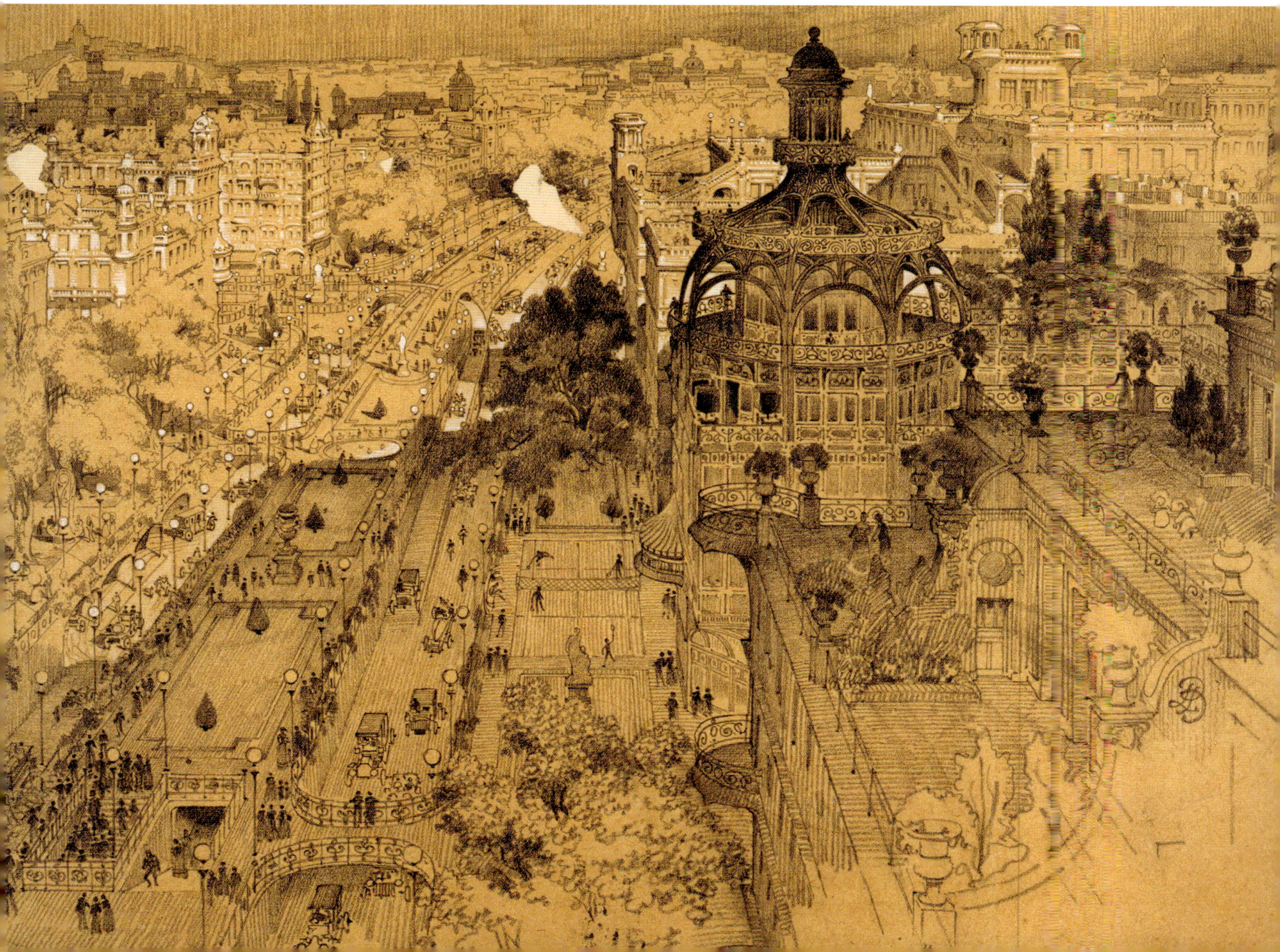

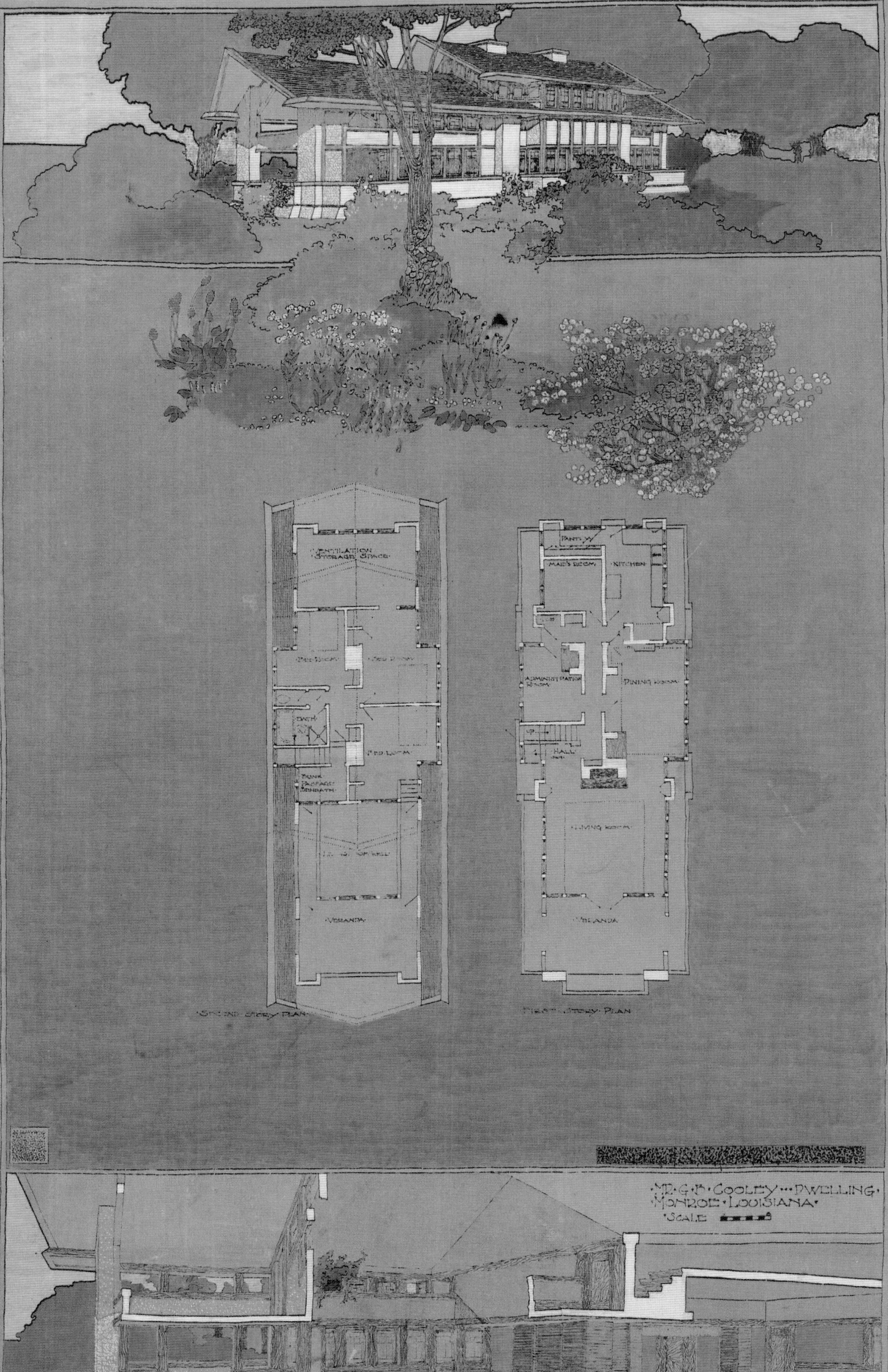
VENTILATION STORAGE SPACE
BATH
VERANDA
SECOND STORY PLAN
PANTRY
MAID'S ROOM
KITCHEN
ADMINISTRATION ROOM
DINING ROOM
HALL
LIVING ROOM
VERANDA
FIRST STORY PLAN
MR. G. B. COOLEY DWELLING
MONROE LOUISIANA
SCALE

they have entirely the look of Japanese kakemonos [hanging scroll paintings], architecture only occupies a secondary place, but the landscape, the trees, the flowers, develop into a beautiful surrounding frame).[16]

Bonnier also privileges the decorative over the practical in his promotion of the Griffins' work. Although he begins his exhibition pamphlet by outlining the parameters of the Canberra competition, emphasizing that participants were invited to show in their designs "all the recent developments in the science of laying out the city," rather than elaborating on this facet of the Griffins' architectural practice, Bonnier admits he is most intrigued and enchanted by its rendering: "Mais ce qui en fait le charme principal et ce qui nous a le plus engagés à les mettre sous les yeux du public parisien . . . c'est l'extraordinaire habilité de la présentation" (What constitutes their principal charm and what motivated us to put them before the eyes of the Parisian public . . . was the extraordinary power of the presentation).[17] Bonnier was interested in these works—"petits ensembles excessivement curieux de couleur et d'expression artistique" (excessively curious little ensembles of color and artistic expression)—primarily as drawings, and his language encouraged viewers to look at the renderings as works of art in themselves, exceeding their assumed function of conveying architecture to a patron or the public. Bonnier's own designs for pavilions at the 1900 Exposition Universelle in Paris reveal a similar strategy to Marion's, both in their colorful graphic representation and in embedding the architecture in its setting, "encadrées de verdure" (framed in greenery) (figures 47 and 48).[18]

Bonnier credits Walter Burley Griffin with painterly talents (though of course it is Marion who deserves the credit). Color is key: "M. W.-B. Griffin révèle un temperament de peintre—ou plutôt d'un architecte qui ne possède pas seulement le senti-

Figure 48 *(below)*
Louis Bonnier; *Kiosque pour "Le Figaro," Exposition Universelle de Paris*, 1900 (Kiosk for *Le Figaro*, Paris Universal Exposition, 1900), 1899; watercolor and gouache on paper mounted on canvas; 40 × 27 in.; Fonds Louis Bonnier. SIAF/Cité de l'architecture et du patrimoine/Archives d'architecture du XXe siècle

Figure 47 *(right)*
Louis Bonnier; *Buvette pour Saint-Tropez Quinquina, Exposition Universelle de Paris*, 1900 (Refreshment Area for Saint-Tropez Quinquina, Paris Universal Exposition, 1900), 1899; watercolor and gouache on paper; 38 × 24 ½ in.; Fonds Louis Bonnier. SIAF/Cité de l'architecture et du patrimoine/Archives d'architecture du XXe siècle

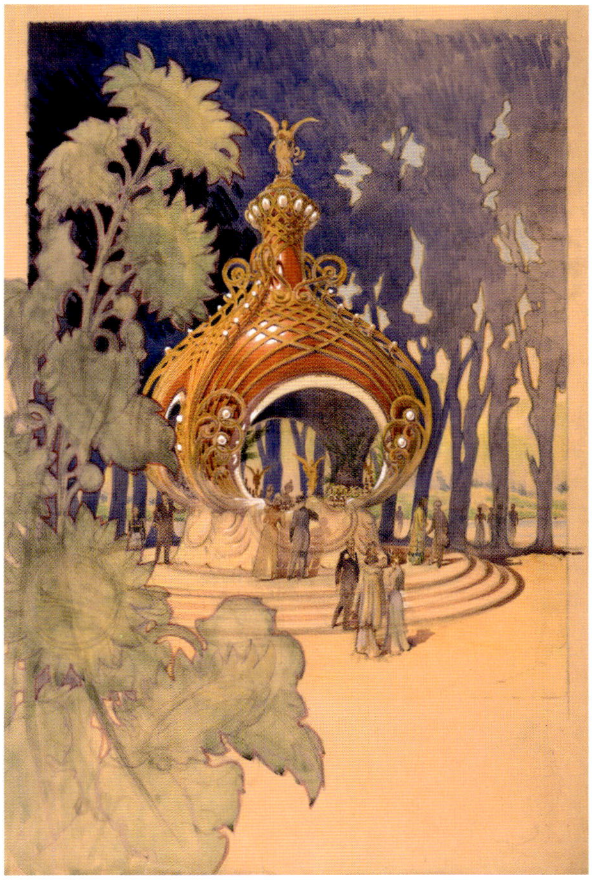

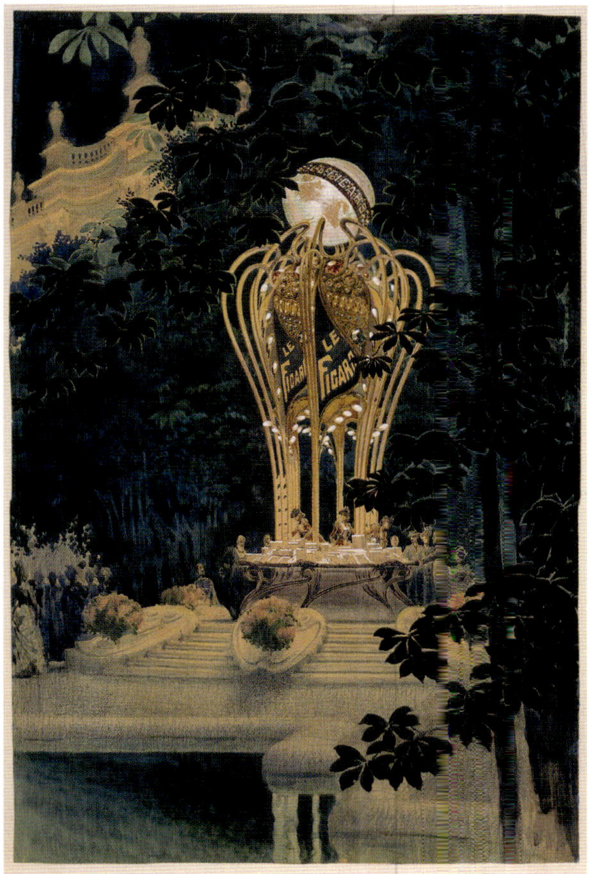

Figure 46 *(facing page)*
Walter Burley Griffin and Marion Mahony Griffin; *G. B. Cooley Dwelling, Monroe, Louisiana*, 1910; pen and black and brown ink over graphite with brush and colored ink, dyes, and white gouache on beige silk; approximately 36 × 24 ¾ in.; Mary and Leigh Block Museum of Art, Northwestern University, gift of Marion Mahony Griffin, 1985.1.112

ment plastique de son art, mais qui sent tout le prix d'une coloration juste, forte et harmonieuse" (Griffin reveals the temperament of a painter or rather an architect who not only possesses the plastic feeling of his art, but senses the value of just, strong, and harmonious color).[19] Lafollye also noted, "Le choix délicat du ton des soirs, des encres employées, des coloris des paysage; tout cela est si nouveau, si délicieux . . ." (The delicate choice of the tone of silks, the inks employed, and the shades of the landscapes; all of it is so new and so delightful . . .).[20] The critic for *L'Architecture* was so enamored by the novelty and vibrancy of Marion's renderings that he intended to try to print color reproductions in a subsequent issue.[21] This would have been the first use of color printing technology by the journal, but it was not realized due to suspension of publication during the war.

Following the Griffins' exhibition, the Musée des Arts Décoratifs turned to the impending question of rebuilding. In 1915, under the leadership of Louis Bonnier, the museum solicited plans from the nation's architects for an exhibition devoted to the reconstruction of destroyed cities and villages. The museum conceptualized its role as "initiating the wider public to the questions of urbanism."[22] The effort was severely encumbered by the fact that so many architects were already mobilized in the war. Letters from the front conserved in the UCAD archive convey their strong desire to participate, but the frustrating impossibility of doing so from afar. Conscious of this challenge, the museum invited the submission of city plans designed for international competitions of the recent past: Barcelona, Antwerp, Bucharest, Buenos Aires, and Casablanca, for example. A few architects did submit past work—Alfred Agache offered his plan for the extension of Dunkerque, France, and his third-place Canberra plan—but most were prevented by the circumstances of war.

A number of architects objected to the guidelines set forth by the exhibition prospectus, which stated, "Tous les projets devront être conçus dans un esprit moderne, sans aucune réminiscence des styles passés" (All projects must be conceived in a modern spirit without any reminiscence of past styles). A letter on behalf of an anonymous group of architects protested that architecture was impossible without referencing the past.[23] The architect-decorator's relationship to forms of the past was a particular concern for UCAD as the organization posited the role of its collections in the education of the artisan. Discouraging direct copying and pastiche, UCAD promoted instead the recognition of the "imperative of stylistic evolution."[24] Vitry wrote that the ultimate lesson to be learned from the Musée des Arts Décoratifs is that "transformation est la loi nécessaire de tout art vivant, que tout arrêt dans une formule est un danger de mort, que toute reproduction textuelle d'une forme ancienne est une faute contre nature" (transformation is the necessary law for all vibrant art, that any pause in a formula is a risk of death, that any reproduction of an ancient form is a misdeed against nature).[25]

This issue of stylistic evolution came into heightened relief during the war as UCAD tried to strike a balance between its institutional imperative of innovation and the importance of respecting the regional traditions in devastated areas. Though repetition of historical forms was strictly off-limits, the museum did encourage consideration of the local conditions and materials available in the region. Its exhibition prospectus says, "Nous ne saurions douter qu'en s'inspirant des traditions locales, les Architectes appelés à reconstruire les villes . . . n'arrivent à élever les bâtiments de goût véritablement français et d'inspiration moderne" (We do not doubt that in drawing on local traditions, the architects called upon to reconstruct the cities . . . will raise buildings of true French taste and modern inspiration).[26]

The emphasis placed on regionalism was even stronger in the exhibitions that did eventually take place, the results of the competitions organized by the undersecretary of state for fine arts in 1918 and by the Société de la Renaissance des Cités in 1919. Architectural historian Jean-Claude Vigato goes so far as to describe the 1918 exhibition as a "treatise of regionalist architecture."[27] It is safe to assume that Bonnier again had a hand in bringing these exhibitions to the museum, particularly the 1919 exhibition, as president of the Société de la Renaissance des Cités's Theoretical and Technical Commission.

It is noteworthy that even during this immediate postwar period, when one might assume the practical applicability of a plan might outweigh the aesthetic qualities of its rendering, museum curator Louis Metman cannot help but comment that "les projets étaient pour la plupart présentés avec infiniment de goût, attestant chez leurs auteurs des qualités de dessin et de couleur qui ne nuisaient en rien à l'étude très serrée du détail des constructions" (the projects were for the most part presented with infinite taste, attesting to the qualities of drawing and color in their authors without hindering in any way the close study of construction details).[28]

The museum's negotiation with regionalism and architecture of the past continued in commentaries surrounding the exhibition featuring Tony Garnier, on view from February 26 to March 26, 1925. Garnier showed one hundred three objects in total, including photographs, encompassing an assortment of projects realized in Lyon (the abattoir, hospital, and stadium), more recent or current projects (most prominently a variety of monuments to the dead), alongside his intriguing fantasy drawings (figures 49 and 50).[29] The architect was most excited to show this latter category of work, which came out of his daily practice of sketching.[30] His graphic preoccupation allowed for imaginative architectural invention that often had little to do with projects intended for construction; see for example his *Escalier dans un parc* (Staircase in a Park, figure 51).[31]

In a letter to Léon Deshairs, the curator of the Bibliothèque des Arts Décoratifs, who invited Garnier to exhibit at the museum, the architect referred to his recent drawings as "des perspectives conçues dans un esprit décoratif d'architecture" (perspectives conceived in a decorative spirit of

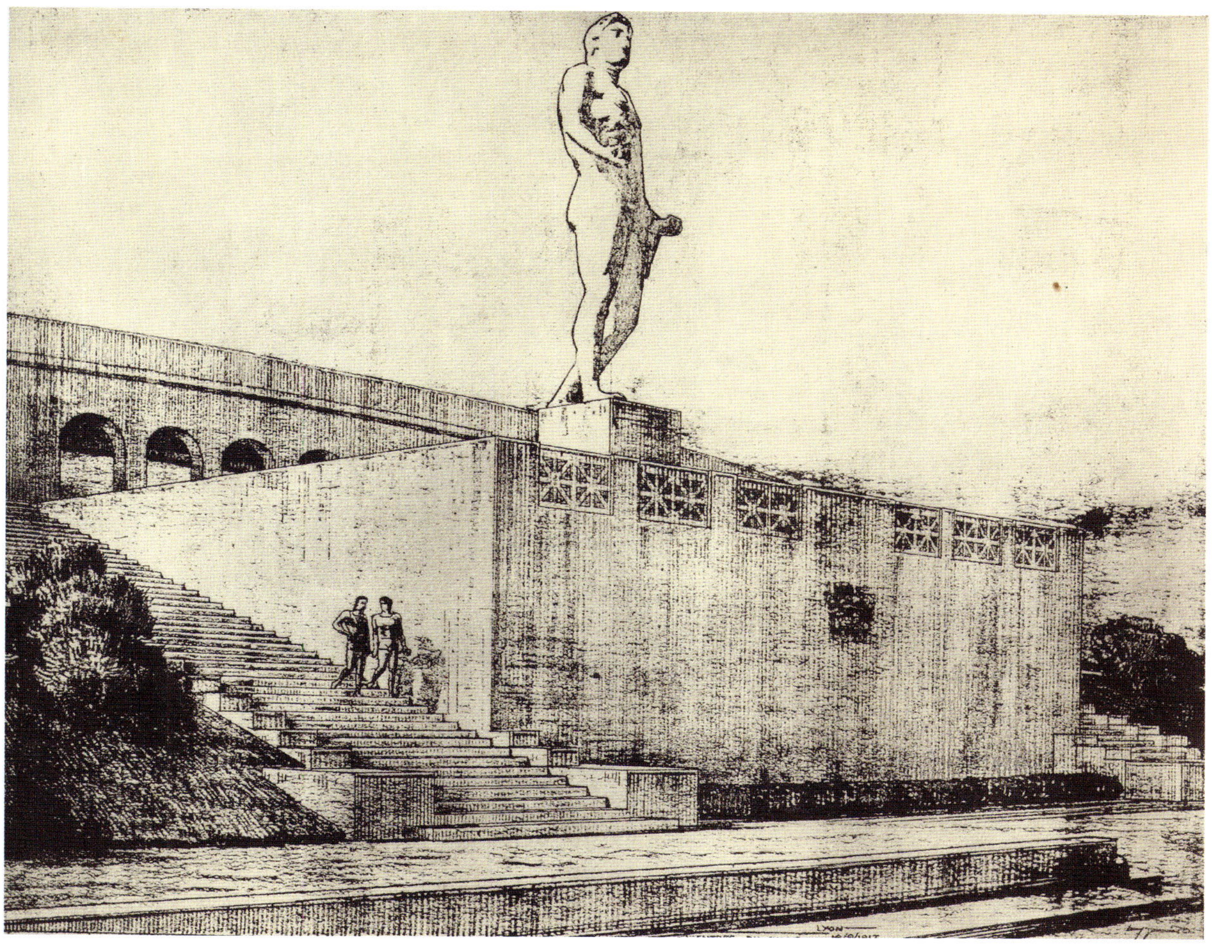

Figure 49
Tony Garnier, *Stade pour les sports athlétiques—Entrée, avenue Leclère* from *Les grands travaux de la ville de Lyon: Études, projets et travaux exécutés* (The Public Works of the City of Lyon: Studies, Projects, and Works Carried Out; Paris: Massin, 1923); 13 × 18 in.; Charles Deering McCormick Library of Special Collections, Northwestern University Library

TONY GARNIER - GRANDS TRAVAUX DE LA VILLE DE LYON. PL. 52

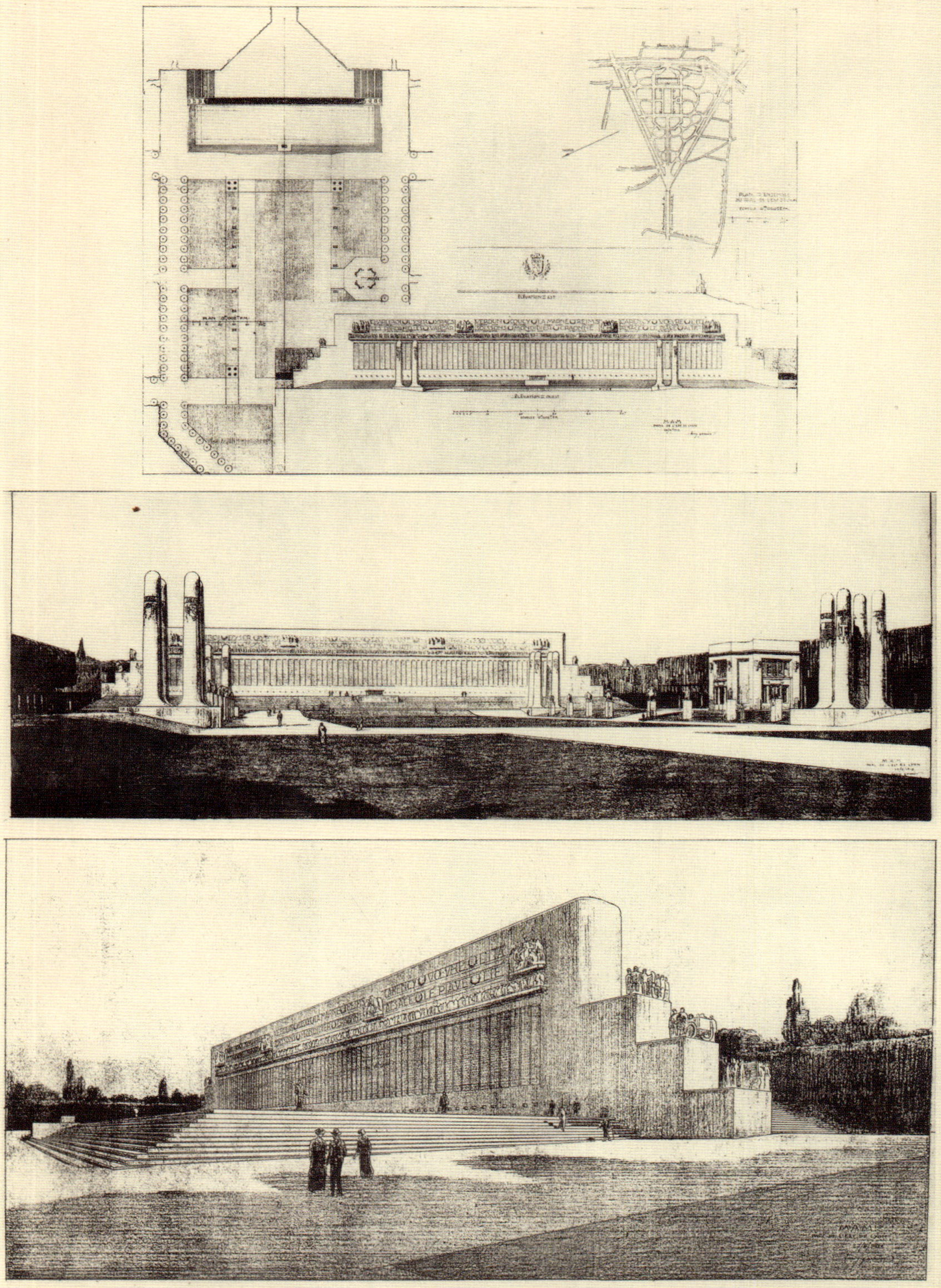

Monument aux Morts dans le parc de l'est de Lyon (2e projet)
Plan et vues perspectives

Hélio. Faucheux, Chelles Ch. Massin, édit. Paris

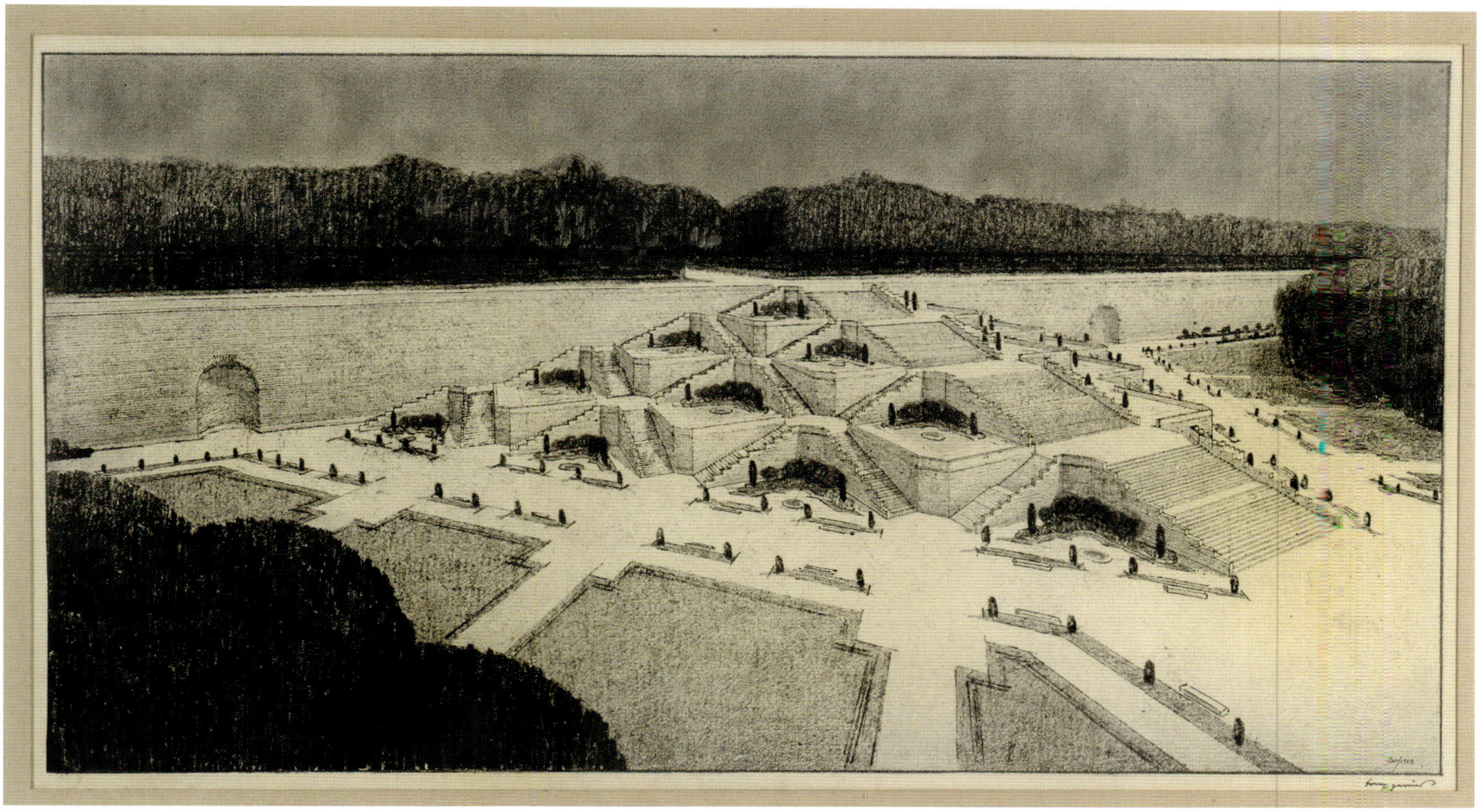

Figure 51 *(above)*
Tony Garnier; *Escalier dans un parc* (Staircase in a Park), 1923; charcoal drawing on paper; 27 ¾ × 46 ½ in.; Musée des Beaux-Arts de Lyon, 1952–79. Copyright © Lyon MBA. Photograph Alain Basset.

Figure 50 *(facing page)*
Tony Garnier; *Monument aux Morts dans le parc de l'est de Lyon (2e projet)* (Monument to the Dead in the Park in East Lyon [Second Project]); from *Les grands travaux de la ville de Lyon: Études, projets et travaux exécutés* (The Public Works of the City of Lyon: Studies, Projects, and Works Carried Out; Paris: Massin, 1923); 18 × 13 in.; Charles Deering McCormick Library of Special Collections, Northwestern University Library

Figure 52
Tony Garnier; *Villa de l'architecte à Saint-Rambert, étude pour la chiminée de la chambre à coucher* (Villa of the Architect in Saint-Rambert, Study for the Bedroom Chimney), 1922; graphite and charcoal on tracing paper; 27 ½ × 35 ½ in.; Musée des Beaux-Arts de Lyon, 1970–66.

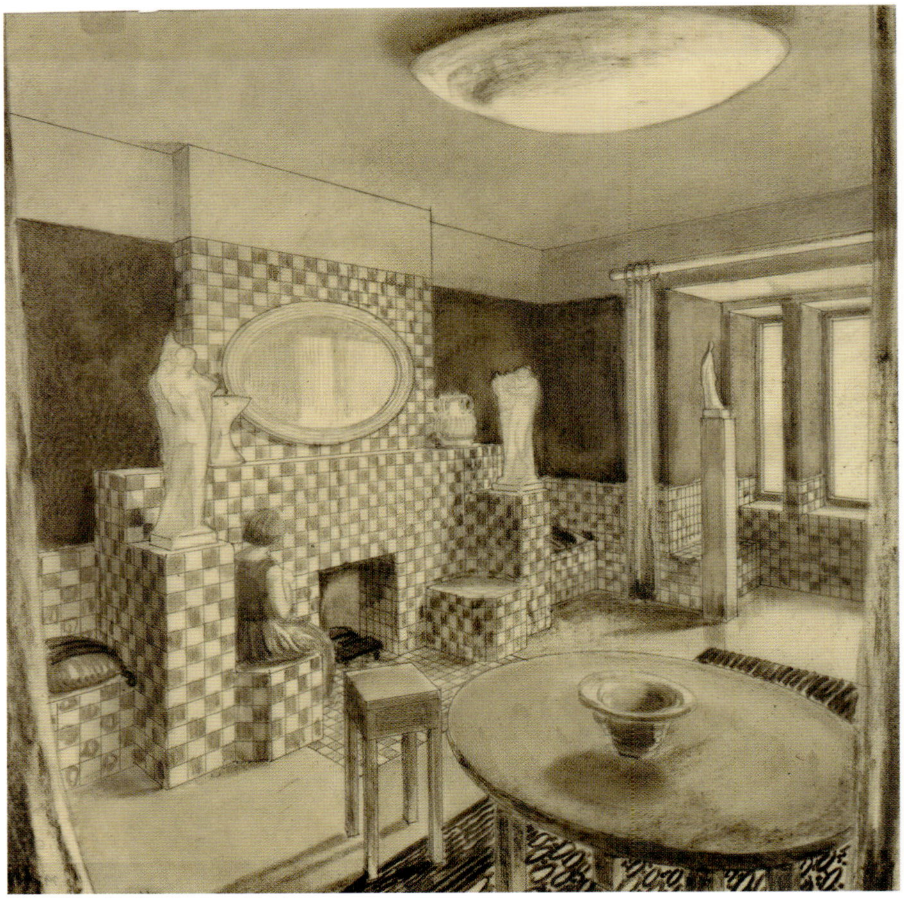

Figure 53
Tony Garnier; *Ville de Lyon—Sanitorium Franco-Américain;* from *Les grands travaux de la ville de Lyon* (The Public Works of the City of Lyon); (Paris: Massin, 1923); 13 × 18 in.; Charles Deering McCormick Library of Special Collections, Northwestern University Library

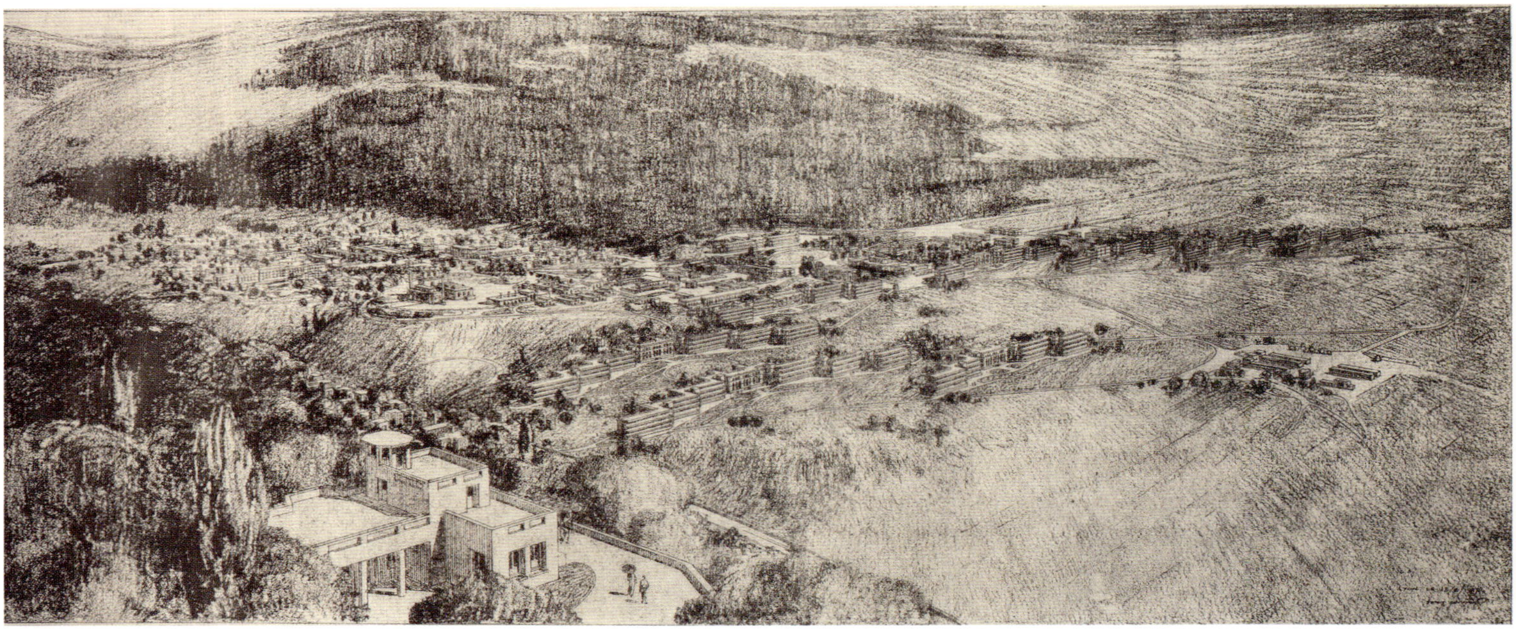

architecture).[32] Precisely what he meant by this is difficult to determine; however, the museum evidently saw something of the decorative in Garnier's work. It was displayed as part of a larger group exhibition of decorative artists, which seemed to preempt, on a much smaller scale, the massive Exposition Internationale des Arts Décoratifs et Industriels Modernes that opened only two months later. Louis Metman expressed his desire to show contemporary works at the museum early in the year before they were all committed to the international exhibition.[33] Perhaps he saw this exhibition as an opportunity to show UCAD's particular "school" of decorative artists before they were absorbed into the larger national narrative of the international exhibition. The Musée des Arts Décoratifs' exhibition included retrospectives of two silversmiths, Charles Rivaud and Jules Brateau, whose metalwork Metman considered "une des première manifestations du renouveau de l'art décoratif" (one of the first manifestations of the renewal of decorative art); and an ironworker, Émile Robert, who had collaborated with Hoentschel on the 1900 UCAD pavilion.[34] The other three bodies of work included were from living artists: designs on silk from the Cheney Brothers silk mill of Connecticut, inspired by the ironwork of Edgar Brandt; furniture by Eugène Gaillard, the oldest surviving collaborator of Siegfried Bing's art nouveau; and lastly, architect Tony Garnier's series of sketches, never before shown in Paris.[35] Maurice Brincourt's review in *L'Architecture* focuses mainly on Garnier but mentions a few of the other artists toward the end; he closes by stating simply, "Les décorateurs ne manquent pas de fantaisies" (The decorators are not lacking for fantasies).[36] Garnier appears to be equally included under the label of decorator; below the concluding statement, one of his drawings of an interior punctuates the article (figure 52).

At first glance, the group of artists featured in the exhibition seems an odd assortment; however, a constant search for the new emerges as a tentative common thread. For instance, Frantz Jourdain describes jeweler Charles Rivaud as "esprit indépendant, novateur audacieux, chercheur assoiffé de nouveau, ennemi d'une routine dévirilisante, partisan résolu de l'évolution" (an independent spirit, an audacious innovator, an unquenchable seeker of the new, an enemy of debilitating routine, and a resolute partisan of change).[37] In attempting to identify a doctrine that emerges from ironworker Émile Robert's diverse work, Thilda Harlor writes, "C'est que l'ardente recherche vers le nouveaux est d'autant plus fructueuse que le respect demeure à l'égard de certaines grandes traditions" (It is that ardent research into the new is more fruitful than respecting certain great traditions).[38] Brincourt, too, is struck by Garnier's consistent effort to escape the influence of the classical, particularly in his "means of expression," referring, one presumes, to his "decorative" sketches.

Yet in his exhibition pamphlet on Garnier, Deshairs firmly roots the Lyonnais architect in his Roman heritage, calling him "a son of Claudius and Caracalla."[39] Like Garnier, these two Roman emperors were born in Lyon. According to Deshairs, like these ancient orchestrators of public works, Garnier wanted above all to be useful. "Comme eux, il est d'abord 'urbaniste' . . . L'accord des murs avec le sol, l'orientation des façades, la soumission exacte du plan à la destination de l'édifice, voilà ses soucis premiers" (Like them, he is foremost an 'urbanist' . . . The accord of the walls with the ground, the orientation of facades, the precise submission of the plan to the destination of the building, these are his primary concerns).[40] It is evident from Deshairs's emphasis on Garnier's realized projects that he likely composed his essay before the architect's most recent sketches had arrived at the museum, perhaps referencing the album *Les grands travaux de la ville de Lyon: Études, projets et travaux exécutés par Tony Garnier* (The Public Works of the City of Lyon: Studies, Projects, and Works Carried Out by Tony Garnier), published in Paris in 1923 and cited at the close of the pamphlet (figures 49, 50, and 53). Had Deshairs seen Garnier's latest work, the imaginative drawings in black and white that so intrigued exhibition critics, the curator's assessment of the architect could not have been as straightforward. As if to make up for this omission, Deshairs wrote an article published in *Art et Décoration* the following year devoted to the fantasy sketches, which had clearly made an indelible impression. He writes, "Ses dessins nous rappellent que les vrais créateurs sont d'abord des hommes d'imagination" (These drawings remind us that true creators are first of all men of imagination).[41]

Reminiscent of the Griffins' exhibition almost ten years prior, reviewers most frequently commented upon Garnier's imaginative integration of architecture into nature and the highly artistic quality of its presentation. Brincourt wrote, "M. Tony Garnier sait admirablement user de l'effet décoratif naturel des plantes, et ses terrasses, ses pergolas, ses architectures de jardin évoquent d'antiques visions odorantes et fleuries" (Mr. Tony Garnier admirably knows how to use the natural decorative effect of plants; his terraces, his pergolas, and his garden architecture evoke ancient visions, fragrant and full of flowers).[42] Garnier's assimilation of nature seems to stimulate the senses in a way that perhaps pure architectural drawings might not. His skillful use of the natural environment is evident in his project for the expansion of his Villa de Cassis, in which the trees on the terrace receive more attention than the villa itself, relegated to the background (figure

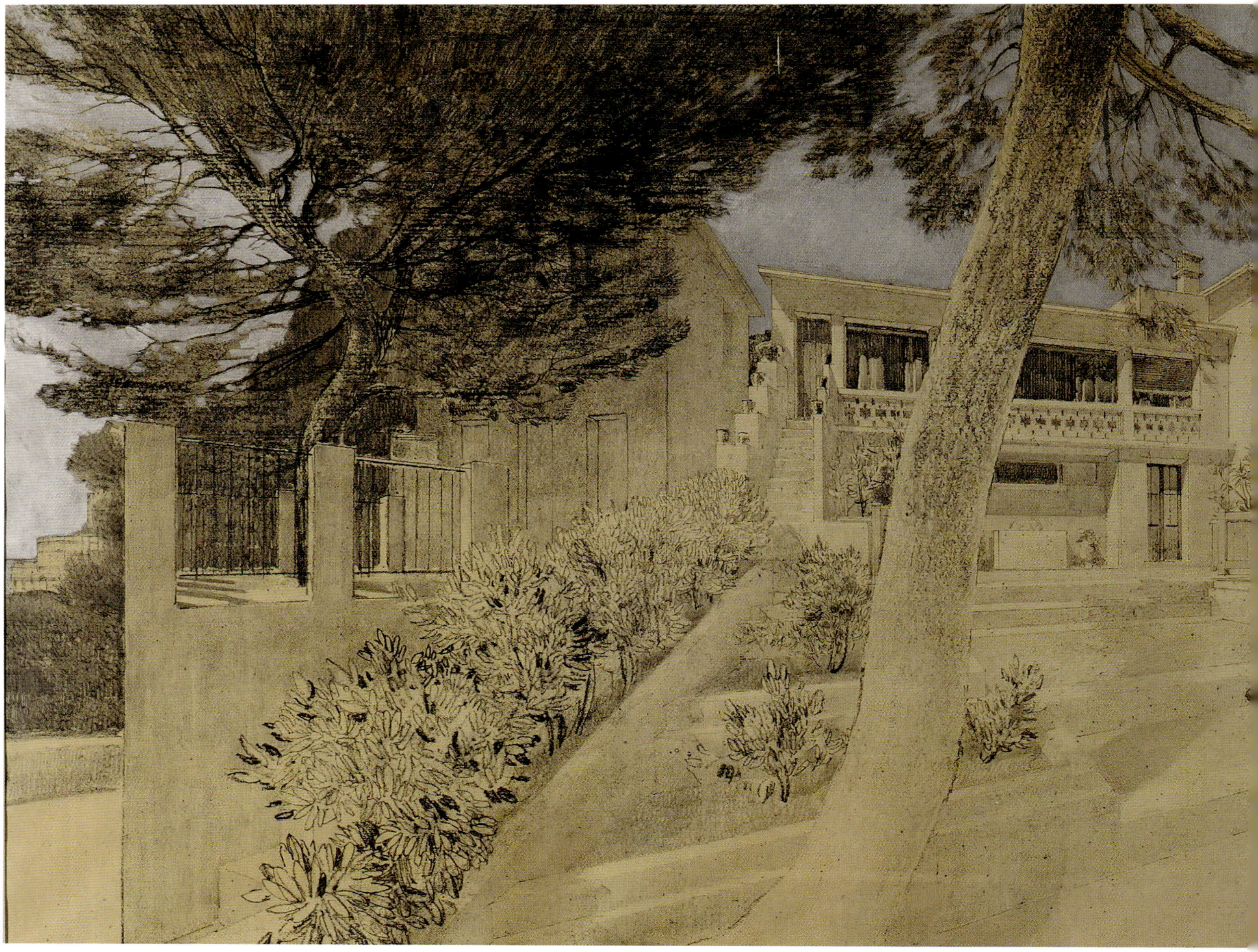

54). In a work such as *Thalassa,* Garnier goes so far as to bring nature indoors, enlivening the geometry of the space with the organic forms (figure 55). This design for an entry to a bathhouse straddles the realm of fantasy drawing and realizable architectural project. Yet the use of metallic paints—in this case copper, and in a companion drawing gold—adds decorative emphasis in a manner comparable to Marion's use of such pigments.

Brincourt recognized the transformative effect of nature in Garnier's work: "Des cyprès ingénieusement disposés et opposant leurs taches sombres aux clartés d'architectures d'une sèche et massive nudité, font d'un motif indifférent quelque chose de coloré et d'amusant" (Cypress trees, ingeniously arranged, contrast their dark marks to the clarity of the dry, naked architecture and make of an indifferent motif something colorful and amusing).[43] This effect is at work in *Villa au bord de l'eau* (Villa by the water, figure 56); here, cypress trees rise above the waterside villa creating a dark crown under which the pale architecture glows. According to Brincourt, Garnier's inclusion of nature had the capacity to contribute color where there might have been none.

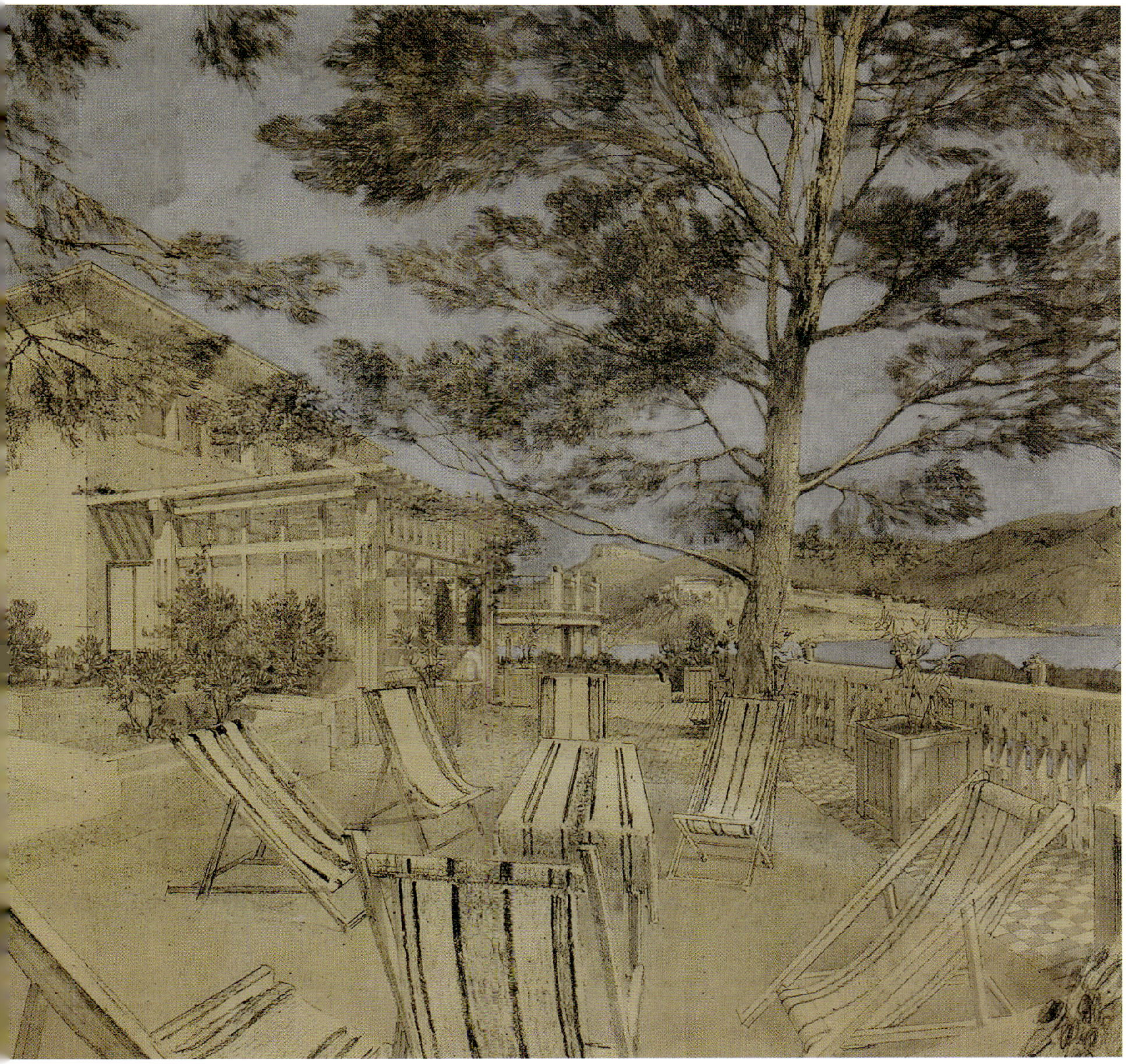

Figure 54
Tony Garnier, *Projet pour une terrasse au bord de la mer* (Project for a Terrace by the Sea), 19[illegible]0; watercolor on paper; [illegible]7 ½ × [illegible]6 in.; Musée des Beaux-Arts de Lyon, 1952-43. Copyright © Lyon MBA / Photograph Alain Basset.

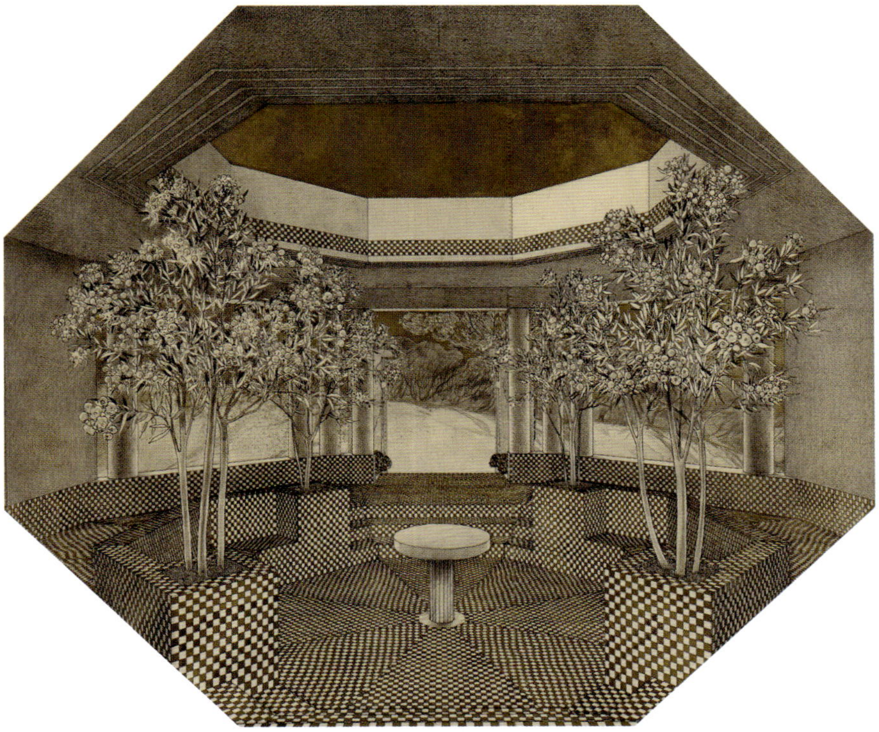

Figure 55
Tony Garnier; *Thalassa*, 1926; ink and gouache on paper; 27 × 36 in.; Musée des Beaux-Arts de Lyon, 1952–90. Copyright © Lyon MBA / Photograph Alain Basset.

Most of the drawings on view were executed in black pencil and charcoal, "expriment un réel sentiment décoratif par la simple opposition nuancée de blanc et de noir" (expressing a real decorative sentiment by their simple nuanced opposition of white and black).[44] Despite the lack of color, Pierre Bourdeix observed in Garnier "all the qualities of a watercolorist," and was struck by the surprising effects of *clair-obscur* (chiaroscuro, or the interplay of light and shadow) in his work.[45]

Standing in front of these works, Brincourt observed Garnier's imagination putting pressure on logic and reason, but lauded the resulting effect as one of powerful unity. "Cet artiste a le sens de l'ensemble, . . . Il sacrifie volontiers le détail, supprime les saillies . . . réduit les corniches à leur plus simple expression, use de fûts de colonnes sans bases ni chapiteaux . . . "(This artist has a sense of the whole . . . He voluntarily sacrifices detail, suppressing relief . . . reducing cornices to their most simple expression, uses column shafts without bases or capitals.)"[46] Bonnier noted comparable paring down of ornament in the Griffins' work, and Brincourt's description is reminiscent of the architecture with which Marion Mahony Griffin populated the Canberra plan.[47] The inventive silhouettes visible in the cross sections certainly trouble reason and logic with their summary effect. One of the most striking elements of the Canberra cross-section drawings is Marion's incorporation of the reflection of the architecture in the lake into her design (figure 57). The effect could not be described as anything but decorative. She was selective in which buildings she chose to reflect and varied the degree of finish in the mirror images, giving them a rhythmic function, adding emphasis and drawing the eye to certain places. Garnier's *Villa au bord de l'eau* employs a similar effect. In this case, some of the lines in the reflected image, especially the staircase at left, are more crisply drawn than in the villa itself, evincing the freedom with which he sketched, unhampered by architectural or even naturalistic accuracy.

Deshairs admired Garnier's ability to construct on paper without constraint, to launch his ideas

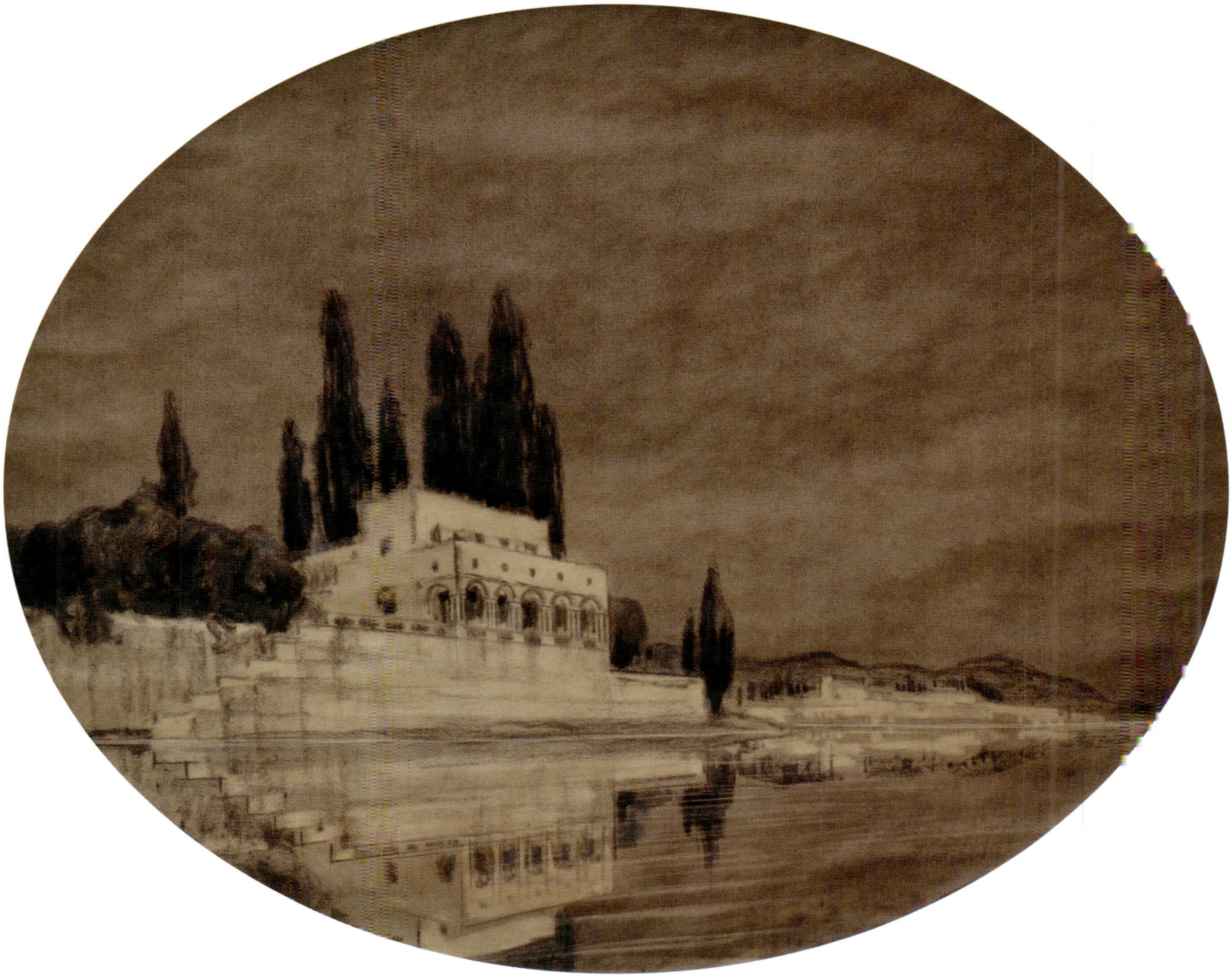

Figure 56
Tony Garnier; *Villa au bord de l'eau* (Villa on the Water), 1921; graphite and charcoal on tracing paper; 27 × 32 ½ in.; Fondation Renaud, Lyon

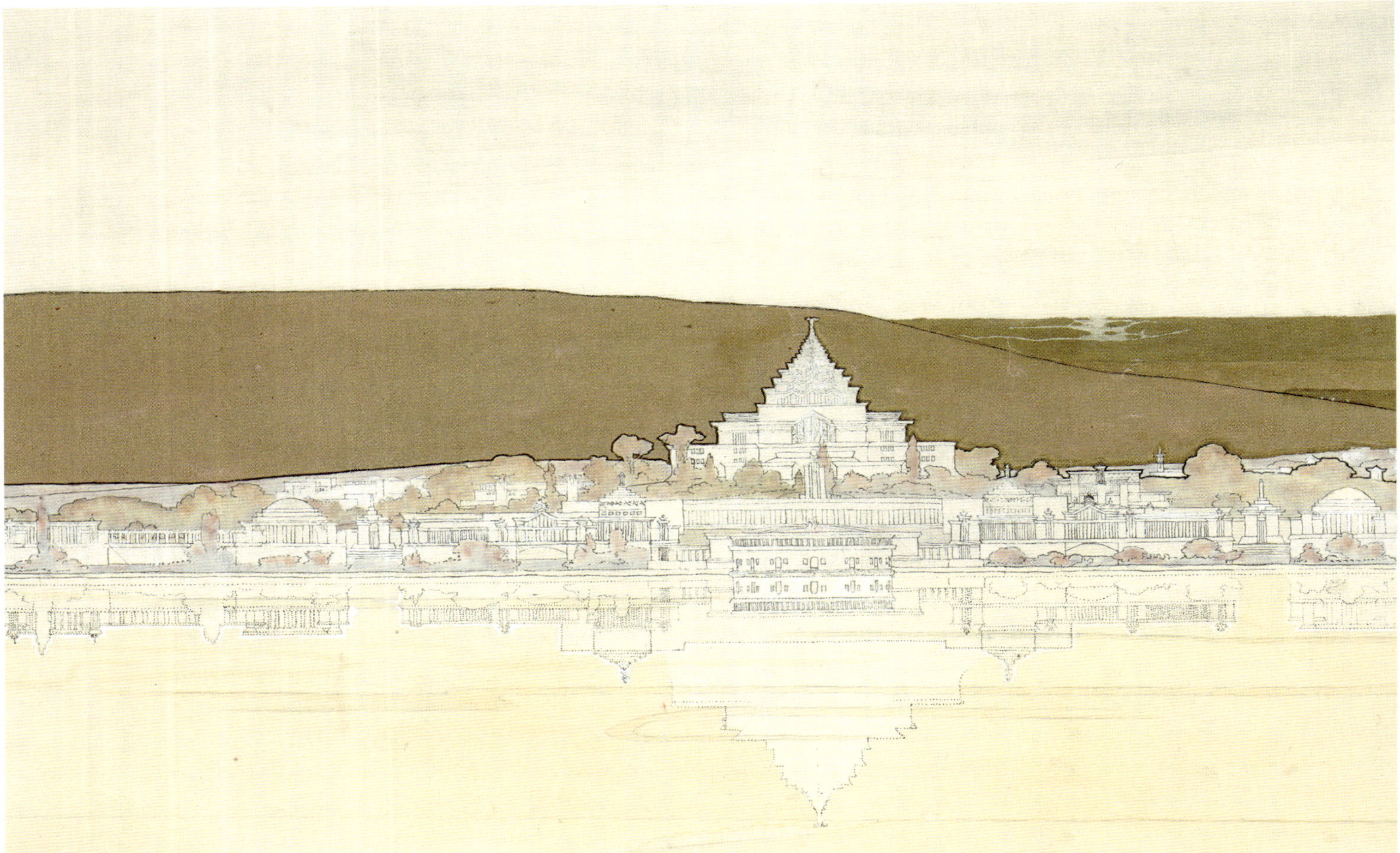

Figure 57
Marion Mahony Griffin and Walter Burley Griffin; detail from *Section B–A Southerly Side of Water Axis: Government Group*, 1911; ink, watercolor, gouache, and metallic paint on linen; National Archives of Australia, A710, 43

on the page, valuing the opportunity to witness the form of the architect's imagination through his sketches.[48] The extent to which the architecture of the Canberra plan was born of Marion's imagination or Walter's is impossible to pinpoint, but the freedom and fantasy evident in her rendering suggest she too might have launched her own ideas upon the page.

Despite the fact that the Musée des Arts Décoratifs chose not to concentrate on the Griffins' and Garnier's city-planning activities, the decorative sensibilities of these architects highlighted by the museum's exhibitions might be credited with enhancing their success in the field of urbanism. Henri Prost, a French urbanist-architect who studied at the Villa Medici in Rome with Garnier, described urbanism as "a visual art which directs itself to our senses; a beautiful city which we love is one where the edifices have a noble beauty, the promenades are agreeable, and where our everyday life is surrounded by an agreeable décor producing a sentiment of profound harmony."[49] Here the city and its architecture become décor, and as we have seen through the exhibitions at the Musée des Arts Décoratifs, its presentation was essential to conveying the desired overall harmony. It has been noted that, at this moment, it was not easy to make distinctions between architecture, its presentation, and its graphic representation.[50] The Musée des Arts Décoratifs's presentation of the Griffins and Garnier embodies this amalgamation and posits their practices as particularly decorative approaches to modern architecture. Connecting the importance of drawing, the search for unity, and stylistic innovation, the Musée des Arts Décoratifs offered the work of the Chicago architects, and subsequently Tony Garnier, as examples of the potential in all of these areas.

Notes

1. This mission is still maintained today. http://www.lesartsdecoratifs.fr/francais/l-institution/presentation/introduction.

2. Marion Mahony Griffin's particular *japoniste* style was developed while working for Frank Lloyd Wright. European audiences may have first been exposed to it as early as 1911 with the publication of *Ausgeführte Bauten und Entwürfe von Frank Lloyd Wright* [Studies and Executed Buildings of Frank Lloyd Wright], for which draftsmen in Wright's studio prepared drawings in her style. As David Van Zanten has recently discovered, an exhibition of Wright's work in Berlin in 1910 may have provided another occasion for Europeans to view Marion's style. *Deutsche Bauzeitung* 44 (October 1, 1910): 641. Christopher Vernon has identified the first international mention and illustration of Walter Burley Griffin's work in Alexander Koch, ed., *Academy Architecture and Architecture Review,* vol. 37 (London: Academy Architecture, 1910). For more of the development of Marion's style, see Paul Kruty, "Graphic Depictions: The Evolution of Marion Mahony's Architectural Renderings," in *Marion Mahony Reconsidered,* ed. David Van Zanten (Chicago: University of Chicago Press, 2011), 51–93.

3. There is very little work on the exhibition of architecture in Paris; however, Barry Bergdoll addressed this topic in his Slade Lectures "Out of Site, in Plain View: The Modernity of the Architecture Exhibition Since 1750" at Cambridge University, winter 2011.

4. *Guide sommaire à travers le Musée des arts décoratifs: Palais du Louvre, Pavillon de Marsan* [Summary Guide Through the Museum of Decorative Arts: Palace of the Louvre, Pavillon de Marsan] (Paris: Lahure, 1905), 15.

5. A more complete quotation is "L'architecture même y est représentée parfois de façon tout à fait intéressante, avec cette série par exemple des dessins de Lebrun pour les façades des pavillons de Marly" [Even architecture is represented here at times in a manner that is quite interesting, for example, with this series of Lebrun drawings for the facades of the pavilions of Marly]. Paul Vitry, "Le Nouveau Musée des Arts Décoratifs" [The New Museum of Decorative Arts], *Art et Décoration* (June 1905): 94.

6. ". . .les dessins originaux exposés mettent sous les yeux des visiteurs des ensembles parfait qui montrent l'ingéniosité et le goût de nos architectes-decorateurs, émules de Boffrand et de Lassurance" [. . . the original drawings exhibited are in the eyes of the visitors perfect ensembles that show the ingenuity and the taste of our architects-decorators, followers of (Germain) Boffrand and of Lassurance (a nickname for Pierre Cailleteau)]. Ibid., 96.

7. *Guide illustré du Musée des arts décoratifs* (Paris: Palais du Louvre, 1923), 173.

8. Sullivan corresponded with museum administrators in 1894. Lauren S. Weingarden, "Louis H. Sullivan: Investigation of a Second French Connection," *Journal of the Society of Architectural Historians* 39, no. 4 (December 1980): 297–303.

9. Vitry, "Le Nouveau Musée des Arts Décoratifs," 104.

10. Bonnier's pamphlet states that they were primarily domestic projects, "isolated private homes and suburban villas." Christopher Vernon posits that the Griffins likely showed the same group of works in Paris as those Walter took to Melbourne in the fall of 1913. The journal *Building* reproduced one of Marion's colored silks, "Plan and Sketches of Hurd Comstock's Two Dwellings, Evanston, Illinois," in its October 11, 1913, issue. "'The Silence of the Mountains and the Music of the Sea': The Landscape Artistry of Marion Mahony Griffin," in Debora Wood, ed., *Marion Mahony Griffin: Drawing the Form of Nature* (Evanston, Ill.: Northwestern University Press and Block Museum of Art, 2005).

11. Walter Burley Griffin's "Report on departmental matters during leave of absence," for the minister of home affairs in Melbourne, dated June 9, 1914. Australian Parliamentary Papers. I owe thanks to David Van Zanten for providing a photocopy.

12. Rapport sur une exposition internationale des arts décoratifs modernes à Paris 1915 [Report on an International Exhibition of Modern Decorative Arts in Paris 1915] (Paris: n.p., June 1, 1911), cited by Nancy J. Troy, *Modernism and the Decorative Arts in France: Art Nouveau to Le Corbusier* (New Haven, Conn.: Yale University Press, 1991), 260 n.20. The other major artists associations to join UCAD and the Société d'Encouragement à l'Art et à l'Industrie in this endeavor were the Société des Artistes Décorateurs, of which Bonnier was also a member; the Société des Artistes Français; the Société Nationale des Beaux-Arts; the Société du Salon d'Automne; and the Union Provincial des Arts Décoratifs.

13. Weisberg had the opportunity to study Bonnier's collection, since dispersed, while it was in the possession of the architect's grandson Bernard K. Bonnier. It included prints by Hiroshige and Hokusai as well as sword guards and *netsuke*. Gabriel P. Weisberg, *Art Nouveau Bing: Paris Style 1900* (New York: Abrams, 1986), 273 n.16.

14. A more complete quotation is ". . . des panneaux de papier ou de soie qui évoquent inévitablement le souvenir de l'art japonais . . . " [. . . paper or silk panels that inevitably evoked the recollection of Japanese art . . .]. Louis Bonnier, *Esquisses d'architecture de l'architecte américain Walter-Burley Griffin* (Paris: Musée des Arts Décoratifs, 1914), unpaginated exhibition pamphlet.

15. For more on Marion's technique, see Debora Wood, "Introduction: Drawing the Form of Nature," in Wood, ed., *Marion Mahony Griffin*, viii–xii.

16. Paul Lafollye, "Exposition d'esquisse d'architecture de l'architecte américain Walter-Burley Griffin," *L'Architecture* 27, no. 29 (July 18, 1914): 247.

17. Louis Bonnier, *Esquisses d'architecture de l'architecte américain Walter-Burley Griffin,* unpaginated.

18. Ibid.

19. Ibid.

20. Lafollye, "Exposition d'esquisse d'architecture de l'architecte américain Walter-Burley Griffin," 247.

21. Ibid.

22. A more complete quotation is "L'Union Centrale n'a pas à intervenir dans les questions d'ordre administratif. Il lui a semblé cependant qu'elle aurait un rôle utile à jouer en initiant le grand public à ces questions d'urbanisme qu'il ignore généralement et que le meilleur moyen de les lui faire connaître serait d'organiser une exposition qui lui en révélerait l'importance." [The Central Union does not have to intervene in administrative matters. It seemed, however, that it could have a useful role to play in introducing the broader public to these planning issues that it generally ignores and that the best way to inform (the public) would be to organize an exhibition that would reveal the importance to them.] Exhibition prospectus in the archives of the Union Centrale des Arts Décoratifs, Bibliothèque des Arts Décoratifs, Paris.

23. Correspondence conserved in the archives of the Union Centrale des Arts Décoratifs, Bibliothèque des Arts Décoratifs, Paris.

24. Debora Silverman, *Art Nouveau in Fin-de-Siècle France: Politics, Psychology, and Style* (Los Angeles: University of California Press, 1989), 186.

25. Paul Vitry, "Le Nouveau Musée des Arts Décoratifs," 66.

26. Exhibition prospectus in the archives of the Union Centrale des Arts Décoratifs, Bibliothèque des Arts Décoratifs, Paris.

27. Regionalism was a form of anticlassicism, an alliance between rustic arts and modernism, which its proponents proposed as an alternative to art nouveau, seen by the 1910s as a passing style, not a solution to the search for authentic French modern form. Jean-Claude Vigato, *L'architecture régionaliste: France 1890–1950* [Regionalist Architecture: France 1890–1950] (Paris: Norma Editions, 1994), 109.

28. *Union centrale des arts décoratifs: Annuaire* (1919): 47.

29. Brincourt, "Tony Garnier," 137.

30. For more on his drawing practice, see Gérard Monnier, "Tony Garnier, dessinateur et peintre" [Tony Garnier, Draftsman and Painter] in *Tony Garnier: L'Œuvre complète* [Tony Garnier: The Complete Works], eds. Alain Guiheux and Olivier Cinqualbre (Paris: Centre Georges Pompidou, 1989), 225–32.

31. An earlier tradition of architectural fantasy drawing can be traced in France.

32. Letter dated December 9, 1924, in the archives of the Union Centrale des Arts Décoratifs. Garnier took a very active role in the planning of his exhibition—he went so far as to send sketches for how he thought his works would best be laid out on the wall.

33. *Union centrale des arts décoratifs: Annuaire* (1926): 163.

34. Ibid., 160.

35. *Meubles par Eugene Gaillard: Quelques Meubles Datés de 1901–1924* [Furniture by Eugene Gaillard: A Few Pieces from 1901–1924].

36. Maurice Brincourt, "A propos d'une exposition de dessins de Tony Garnier" [About an Exhibition of Drawings by Tony Garnier], *L'Architecture* 38, no. 9 (May 10, 1925): 139.

37. Frantz Jourdain, *Exposition Rétrospective de l'œuvre du Maître Orfèvre Charles Rivaud (1859–1923)* [Retrospective Exhibition of the Work of the Master Goldsmith Charles Rivaud (1859–1923)] (Paris: Musée des Arts Décoratifs, 1925), unpaginated.

38. Thilda Harlor, *Les Fers Forgés d'Emile Robert: Exposition retrospective* [The Forged Iron of Emile Robert: Retrospective Exhibition] (Paris: Musée des Arts Décoratifs, 1925), unpaginated.

39. Léon Deshairs, *Exposition d'œuvres de Tony Garnier* (Paris: Musée de Arts Décoratifs, 1925), unpaginated.

40. Ibid.

41. Léon Deshairs, "Les Dessins de Tony Garnier" [The Drawings of Tony Garnier], *Art et Décoration* 49 (1926): 64.

42. Brincourt, "Tony Garnier," 137.

43. Ibid.

44. A more complete quotation is "Ces dessins, traités très largement au crayon noir et au fusain, présentent un aspect très séduisant et expriment un réel sentiment décoratif par la simple opposition nuancée de blanc et de noir" [These drawings, treated very freely with black pencil and charcoal, present a very attractive appearance and express a real decorative sentiment by their simple nuanced opposition of white and black]. Ibid.

45. Pierre Bourdeix, "A propos de l'exposition de Tony Garnier au Musée des Arts décoratifs à Paris," *La Construction Moderne* 40, no. 27 (April 5, 1925): 315.

46. "Devant certaines œuvres de M. Tony Garnier, on se demande si . . . son imagination ne bouscule pas un peu la logique et raison?" [In front of certain works of Mr. Tony Garnier, one wonders if . . . his imagination does not slightly disrupt logic and reason?] Brincourt, "Tony Garnier," 139.

47. "La sincérité de l'appropriation, l'absence de toute ornementation superflue, la franchise du parti donnent à ces esquisses un intérêt tout particulier" [The sincerity of the appropriation, the absence of any unnecessary ornamentation, the frankness of the *parti* (structuring theme) give these sketches a particular interest]. Bonnier pamphlet.

48. Léon Deshairs, "Les Dessins de Tony Garnier," *Art et décoration* 49 (1926): 64.

49. Cited in Paul Rabinow, *French Modern: Norms and Forms of the Social Environment* (Cambridge, Mass.: MIT Press, 1989), 235.

50. "We cannot so easily separate the graphic, the presentational and the architectural in these years. They intertwine—creatively." David Van Zanten, "Modernism/Chicago/Paris: What They Might Have Shared and How They Might Have Shared It," *Cahiers parisiens/Paris Notebooks* 5 (2009): 173.

Rudolph M. Schindler; *Bird's-Eye View Looking Toward Public Library*, 1914; Art, Design and Architecture Museum, University of California, Santa Barbara. See also page 100.

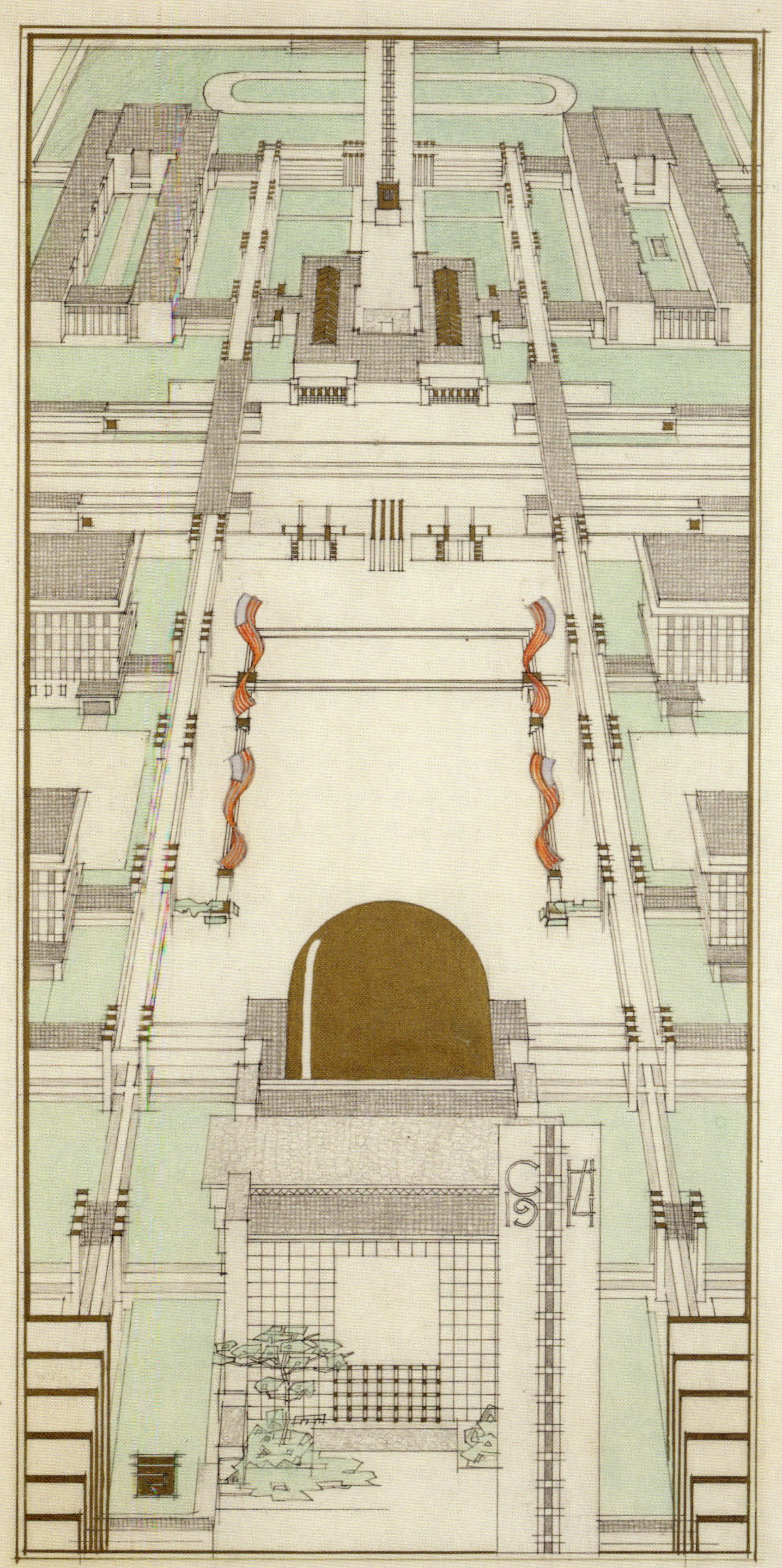

Considering the People

Urban Planning

In 1908, the City Club of Chicago founded a "City Planning Committee" for "the improvement of the street plan and general framework of, and the distribution of functions in, the City of Chicago and its vicinity."[1] From the start, the committee's work was simultaneous with and set against other plans proposed for the city, in particular the 1909 Plan of Chicago by Daniel Hudson Burnham and Edward H. Bennett, which was sponsored by the Commercial Club of Chicago. To the City Club and its progressively minded members, the Commercial Club's plan, popularly known as the "Burnham Plan," was deficient in many ways, most importantly because it had ignored the city's residential areas and "the people on the back streets."[2] To address this problem, the City Club sponsored and then exhibited two city planning competitions between 1912 and 1915. The first contest—*A Competition with Cash Prizes for the Procuring of a Scheme of Development for a Quarter-Section of Land Within the Limits of the City of Chicago, Illinois*—sought suggestions for improved layouts for the subdivision housing developments going up in the expanding outer neighborhoods of Chicago. The second—*A Competition to Be Held by the City Club of Chicago for Plans for a Neighborhood Center*—challenged entrants to propose more rational and convenient arrangements of social and governmental buildings within city neighborhoods throughout the country, in an effort to improve the quality of life for working-class residents and to help unify and stabilize neighborhoods. Unlike some urban plans designed at the time, the proposals produced for these competitions were not fantastical, and their scale was not vast. The

Leslie Coburn

On the Back Streets: At the City Club of Chicago

renderings for many were not even especially pretty. Rather, these projects were realistic, small-scale, and intended to be very practical. The winning entry for the second competition, for example, addressed a particular section of a Bronx neighborhood.

This essay, organized into three sections, focuses on the activities of the City Club's City Planning Committee between its founding and the outbreak of World War I and on the club's two planning competitions. The first section will discuss the City Club's position on the Burnham Plan. The second section will briefly consider the club's Quarter-Section Competition, held in 1912–13. Although this competition has already received considerable attention, a few areas that have remained unclear or unrecognized will be discussed. The remaining section—and the bulk of the essay—addresses the City Club's less-studied Neighborhood Center Competition of 1914 and 1915 and presents details about the entrants and their projects that have been pieced together from City Club records and contemporaneous journal and newspaper reports.

About the City Club of Chicago

The City Club of Chicago was founded in 1903 by leading members of the Municipal Voters' League, who were interested in forming a group that would be both a reform organization and a social club. Its objective was "the investigation and improvement of municipal affairs in the city of Chicago," its methods "nonpartisan and practical."[3] Although the City Club's membership overlapped somewhat with that of other clubs in Chicago, its members were, as a rule, somewhat less affluent.[4] They were also much more left-leaning. Many members had ties to Jane Addams and her Hull-House Settlement, the settlement house Addams founded in a poor immigrant neighborhood on the West Side of Chicago, and to other settlement houses in the city. Many City Club members had connections to the University of Chicago. Architects later associated with the "Prairie Style" and former employees of Frank Lloyd Wright—many with offices in Steinway Hall, where Wright had a studio—were also well represented.

The orientation of the City Club was therefore closely aligned philosophically with some of Chicago's most progressive thinkers, and in many ways the club could be viewed as diametrically opposed to a group like the Commercial Club of Chicago, which had more conservative and capitalist concerns. This alignment makes the activities of the City Club, and especially of its City Planning Committee, particularly interesting between the years of 1909 and 1915, when the Commercial Club's Plan of Chicago was first published and promoted. Many of the Planning Committee's activities involved study and critique of the Commercial Club's plan. By illuminating the plan's deficiencies, compiling their own data, and educating and persuading the public through lectures, exhibitions, and publications, the City Club attempted both to complement the Burnham Plan by expanding its scope and to provide a counterview. The City Club's activities were thus a very real (albeit polite) voice of dissent, and its work can be seen as an attempt to create a different version of an improved Chicago, an alternative to the Burnham Plan.

The City Club was extremely active during this period. In 1912, after residing in a series of rental spaces, the club moved into its own new permanent headquarters building in downtown Chicago, at 315 Plymouth Court. Designed by club members Irving K. Pond and Allen B. Pond, the six-story structure provided members with several large dining areas, a lounge and library, numerous meeting rooms, and ample space in which to mount the club's exhibitions (figure 58).[5]

The City Planning Committee and the Burnham Plan

The City Club's work was done largely through its civic committees, the first twenty-one being set up in 1906. The City Planning Committee was started two years later, in the spring of 1908. In his annual report to the club's Board of Directors, written in April 1909, the committee's first chairman, Allen B. Pond, explained how the committee had positioned itself vis-à-vis the anticipated Commercial Club plan:

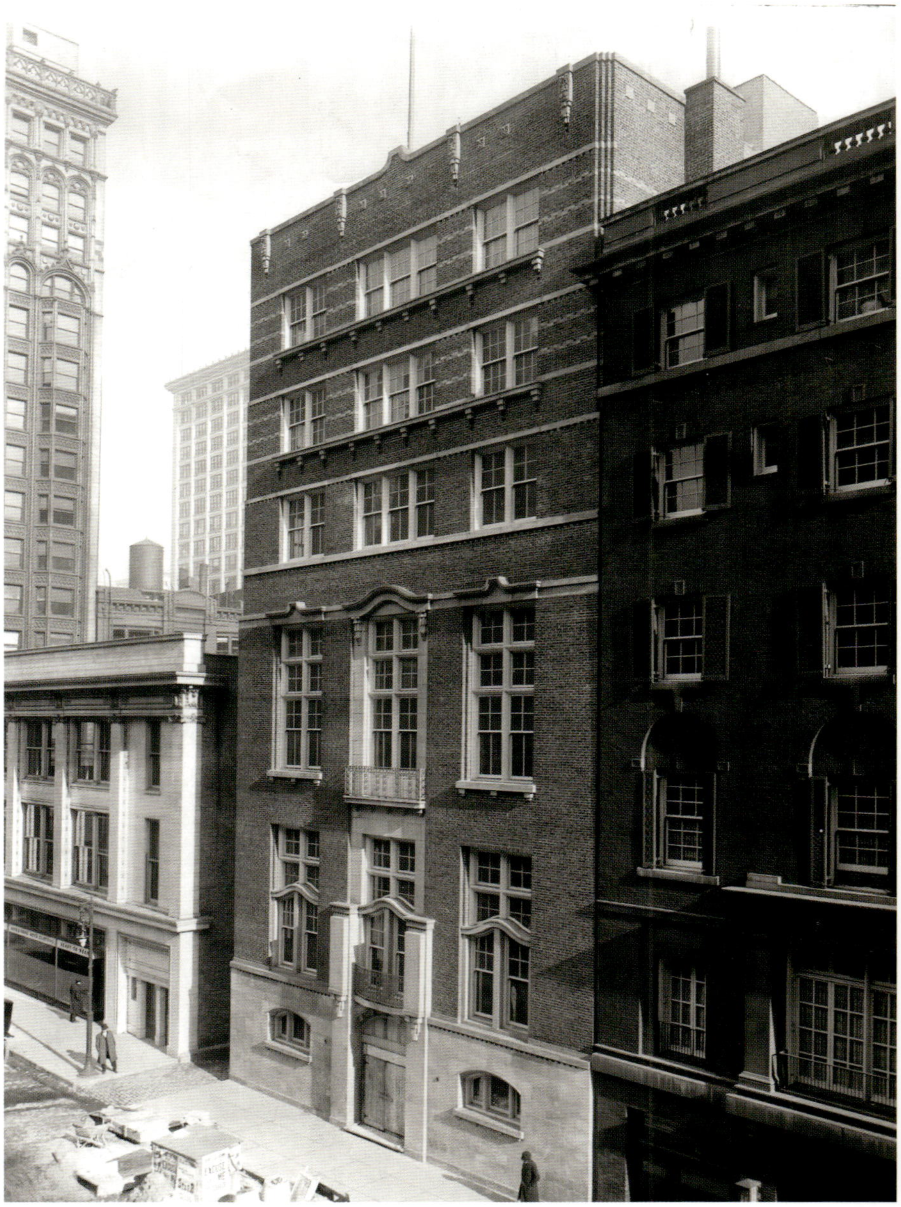

Figure 58
Pond and Pond, Architects (Irving K. Pond and Allen B. Pond); City Club of Chicago Clubhouse, 315 Plymouth Court, 1912. Photograph by Henry Fuermann and Sons, 1912; approximately 7 ¼ x 9 ½ in. Private collection.

> In view of the nearness of the date for the issuance of the program of the Commercial Club I judged that it would not be wise for the City Club to undertake an independent investigation and report, and that for the present at least its wiser function would be to study the report of the Commercial Club committee and experts and criticize their program rather than parallel it . . . Unfortunately the expectations of the Commercial Club Committee have not been fulfilled and their full program has not yet been published . . . In view of this delay it appears questionable whether it would not have been wiser if this Committee had pushed its own investigations without awaiting the move of the Commercial Club Committee.[6]

Incidentally, one of the first reviews and criticisms of the Commercial Club's plan came from George Ellsworth Hooker. Hooker was a founding and honorary City Club member and perhaps its most important driving force during the club's early years. Hooker served for many years as its salaried civic secretary, a position that made him an ex officio member of all the club's committees, and as a liaison between the committees and the club's Board of Directors. Hooker was trained in New York as a lawyer. After coming to Chicago, he became a close friend of social activist and reformer Jane Addams and lived as a resident of Hull-House from 1899 until his death in 1939. In 1902, Hooker had been commissioned by the Chicago City Council to investigate and gather literature about municipal administration in Europe, and "such methods and principles employed in such administration, particularly in dealing with housing, local transportation, open spaces and rapid city expansion."[7] Hooker presented a report of his findings to the City Council in 1904. In the years that followed, he continued to keep abreast of developments in housing, transportation, and city planning; attended and spoke at national planning conferences; and corresponded with important American advocates of urban planning, such as Benjamin C. Marsh, John Nolen, and Charles Mulford Robinson.

In his review of the Commercial Club's plan, which was largely a summary of the plan's contents, Hooker ended by touching on the areas he found weak. In particular, he expressed concern about the plan's lack of supporting data, its overuse of Paris as a model, and its insufficient attention to transportation issues, crosstown railway lines, and housing conditions of the "common people."[8]

The City Club's City Planning Committee was initially composed of ten members. After 1910, its numbers swelled considerably, perhaps in response to the publication of the Burnham Plan and a heightened interest in the topic. The committee was reorganized in 1909, and landscape architect Jens Jensen took over as chair, a position he held until 1913 when Walter Burley Griffin assumed the chairmanship. Although Griffin's tenure was brief, and records of it are few, there is an interesting account of one meeting he presided over in April 1913 when "Mr. Pond suggested the advisability of having a committee to formulate an ideal plan for the city. After some discussion it was voted to have the chairman appoint such a sub-committee to be called the 'Organic Plan' sub-committee."[9] At a meeting a few weeks later, it is mentioned that the "sub-committee on Organic Plan" was working on a solution to the city's railroad terminal problem.[10] It is not clear whether the subcommittee did further work or ever formulated its own ideal plan for Chicago.[11]

After winning the competition to design the Australian capital of Canberra in 1912, discussed elsewhere in this volume, Griffin's attendance at the City Planning Committee meetings was often interrupted by travel, and he resigned from the chairmanship in April 1914. He and his wife, Marion Mahony Griffin, left Chicago and moved to Australia.

R. F. Schuchardt assumed the chairmanship from Griffin and, shortly afterward, the committee decided it would focus its attention during the spring and summer of 1914 on understanding the work of the Chicago Plan Commission. This decision resulted in a most interesting series of meetings. The minutes for these meetings are unusually detailed and provide us with a record of the attitudes and concerns of the committee's members regarding the Chicago Plan Commission and the Burnham Plan itself.

The Chicago Plan Commission had been established soon after the publication of the Commercial

Club's Plan of Chicago, mostly to assist with its promotion. Walter Moody, managing director of the Chicago Plan Commission, was invited to speak to the City Planning Committee on two occasions. In response to his visits, the committee drafted a letter that posed lingering questions. Four letters exchanged between the committee and Charles Wacker, chairman of the Chicago Plan Commission, are also included in the City Club's papers. What follows are highlights of these meetings and written correspondence, beginning with the minutes from the meeting of May 26, 1914 (Moody's second visit):

> Mr. Moody answered a number of questions. One of them was what relation does the plan of Chicago bear to housing? Answer: the Commission considered that the question of housing was a field in itself of sufficient size and importance to be handled separately. He said that the Chicago Plan was essentially a street plan. He said that it was not a hard and fast plan and that any suggestion as to housing would be gladly received by the committee and if it were worthy would receive the commission's backing. He believed that the housing proposition could be better handled by men familiar with legal matters . . .
>
> Question: Is there a precedent for a city plan in which housing has been a feature? Answer: Yes, the Wrenn [*sic*] plan of London in 1666. The Council of London never adopted this plan and it has since been considered a great mistake upon the part of the Council.[12]

Meeting of June 9, 1914:

> The chairman asked for a discussion on the relations of the City Club Committee with the Chicago Plan Commission. He desired to know what action the City Club Committee should take toward the Chicago Plan Commission. . . . Mr. Pond and Mr. Drummond suggested that the organization of the Chicago Plan Commission was not wholly satisfactory and that frequently general principles of action were lost sight of by them in the exigencies of special cases. Mr. [Herman] Von Holst thought it was allright [*sic*] to support the Plan Commission in things obviously right but to carry the work further ourselves along the lines of the broader developments in zone planning, etc.[13]

The committee next received a six-page letter from Charles Wacker, written in response to a letter from them (not included in the records), in which he attempted to explain the workings of the Chicago Plan Commission and its immediate plans for the future. Although appreciative of Wacker's lengthy letter, the committee was not altogether satisfied with his reply. At the committee's next meeting, each member was asked to comment on Wacker's letter. Here are excerpts from minutes of the July 14, 1914 meeting:

> Mr. Von Holst read clipping from the last night's News, being an editorial based on interview with Captain George A. Taylor, Secretary of the Town Planning Association of Australia. This editorial referred especially to Captain Taylor's remarks that the people on the back streets were evidently not being considered in the Chicago Plan.[14] Mr. Von Holst maintained that the widening of boulevards and such improvements do not materially affect the condition of the residential section of the city. He said he believed the fundamentals of light, air and cleanliness have not been considered. Nothing is said regarding the prevention of smoke. . .
>
> Mr. [Edward] Bangs said he was struck especially by the absence of figures or statistics in the reports of the Plan Commission . . .
>
> Mr. [John] Van Bergen brought out the point that there are few experts on the Plan Commission.
>
> Mr. [Irving] Pond spoke of the same point, namely, the lack of experts on the Commission. He said the housing and back-yards of the city have been given no attention. He thinks it is vital that the location of residences, factories, railways, etc., should be determined by a city plan. He believes the planning of the city should be gone about in the same way as the planning of a house . . . He maintained that the Plan Commission can and ought to consider the housing conditions and the zone principle . . .
>
> Mr. [William] Drummond spoke of the personnel of the Plan Commission as an unhopeful sign of real progress. He believed the Commission had not the right organic relation with the city. He believed that our committee can not co-operate. He believed we ourselves should formulate some definite principle.[15]

The committee drafted a follow-up letter to Wacker, and in his reply of September 22 Wacker again explains that "housing in its restricted sense of provision for the congested population was regarded in the Plan of Chicago as a matter requiring special study. There has been organized by the mutual effort of Chicago housing advocates the Chicago Housing Board for the special study of these questions, to which all such matters might be properly referred."[16]

In the City Planning Committee's annual report to the club's Board of Directors, Chairman Schuchardt summarized this set of meetings, the exchange of correspondence, and the committee's subsequent discussion. He stated that the committee had decided that:

> While the organization and the methods of the Commission may be properly subject to criticism, the Commission is an official body and such of its acts as are found by us after investigation to be for the good of Chicago and in accordance with our best judgment should receive our very hearty support. In the same way, such acts as we cannot agree with should receive such active opposition from us as the facts may warrant. In other words, we should meet all the problems with which the Commission is wrestling fairly and squarely, co-operate where we agree and oppose where we disagree. This has been the governing spirit of our Committee during the past year with reference to the Commission.[17]

The Quarter-Section Competition

In 1912 and 1913, the City Club sponsored the Quarter-Section Competition, a design competition held in conjunction with its Housing Exhibition. The arrangements for the Housing Exhibition were, not surprisingly, handled by the Housing Conditions Committee, and the City Planning Committee appears to have had no involvement with it—or the Quarter-Section Competition—at all. Most of the arrangements for the competition seem to have been taken care of by George Hooker personally, who in turn received assistance in the writing of the competition program from the Illinois chapter of

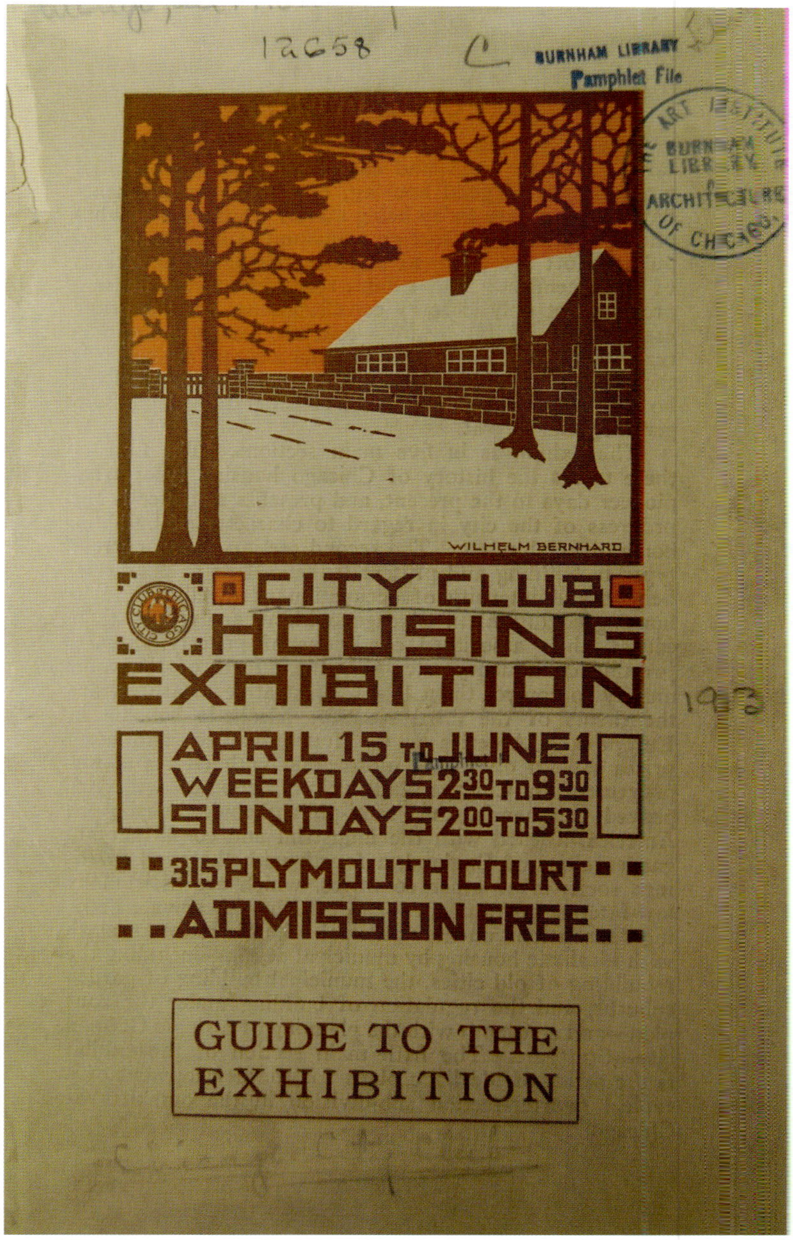

Figure 59
Wilhelm Bernhard, Cover of *City Club Housing Exhibition: Guide to the Exhibition* (Chicago: City Club of Chicago, 1913); approximately 8 x 5 in.; The Art Institute of Chicago, Ryerson and Burnham Libraries

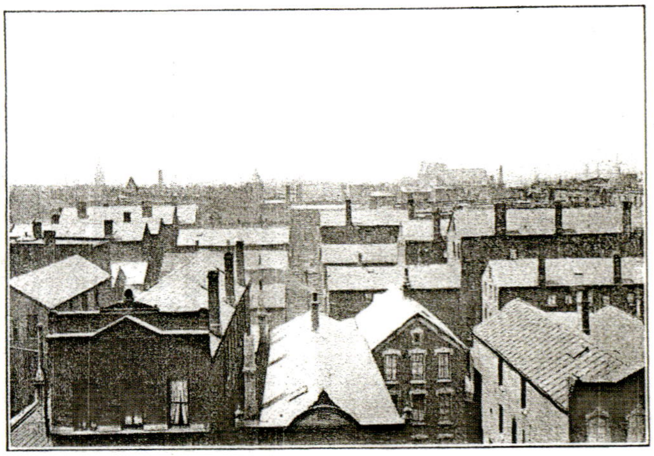

219.—House-top View in Tenth Ward
A Typical view in a Crowded Area.

Figure 60
House-Top View in Tenth Ward; displayed in the exhibition section "'Darker Chicago'—Bad Housing in the City"; reproduced in *City Club Housing Exhibition: Guide to the Exhibition* (Chicago: City Club of Chicago, 1913); The Art Institute of Chicago, Ryerson and Burnham Libraries

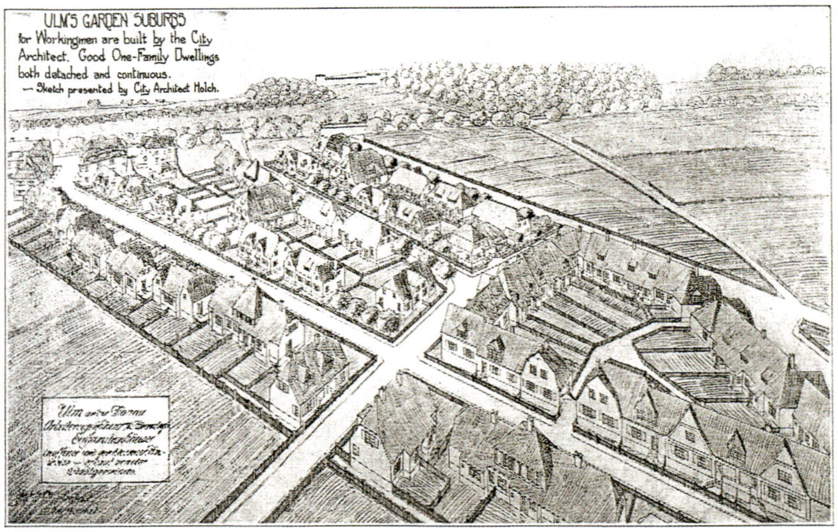

1197.—Workingmen's Dwellings Planned by City Architect, Römerstrasse, Ulm.

Figure 61
Workingmen's Dwellings Planned by City Architect, Römerstrasse, Ulm; reproduced in *City Club Housing Exhibition: Guide to the Exhibition* (Chicago: City Club of Chicago, 1913); The Art Institute of Chicago, Ryerson and Burnham Libraries

the American Institute of Architects. The Housing Exhibition was held in the new clubhouse and occupied nearly the entire building (figures 58 and 59). In addition to the competition drawings, hundreds of other drawings and photographs were displayed that contrasted existing poor housing conditions in Chicago with the latest Garden City and municipal housing projects of Europe and America (figures 60 and 61).

The Housing Exhibition was held concurrently with the Fifth National Conference on City Planning, which met in Chicago from May 5 to 7, 1913. This timing was almost certainly by design. George Hooker had attended and participated in the earlier national conferences, and was on the organization's executive committee. As early as 1910, Hooker had suggested to the City Club's City Planning Committee the possibility of holding a national exposition on city planning, and the committee had then voted that Hooker propose this to the "conference on city planning to be held in Rochester next week."[18] It seems likely that the City Club was at least aware of, and possibly involved with, the decision to hold the National Conference on City Planning in Chicago, and would thus have taken this into account as it planned its own programming. Interestingly, the National Conference also sponsored a planning competition, which also considered how to arrange streets, parks, and buildings on a tract of land on the outskirts of a large city, and we know that both competitions were viewed by at least some of the conference attendees.[19]

Because the Quarter-Section entry drawings and supporting text were published in book form by the City Club of Chicago, the competition has been well known and, especially in recent years, the subject of considerable scholarship.[20] Its most discussed aspect has been the noncompetitive entry by Frank Lloyd Wright, a subdivision design that incorporated his earlier Quadruple Block Plan for the arrangement of its single family houses (figures 62 and 63). The asymmetrical arrangement of Wright's park areas and streets, and the overall quality of the renderings, make Wright's entry stand out among the other designs. The architectural historian Gwendolyn Wright (no relation to Frank Lloyd Wright) has observed that it took "pride of place" in the publication.[21]

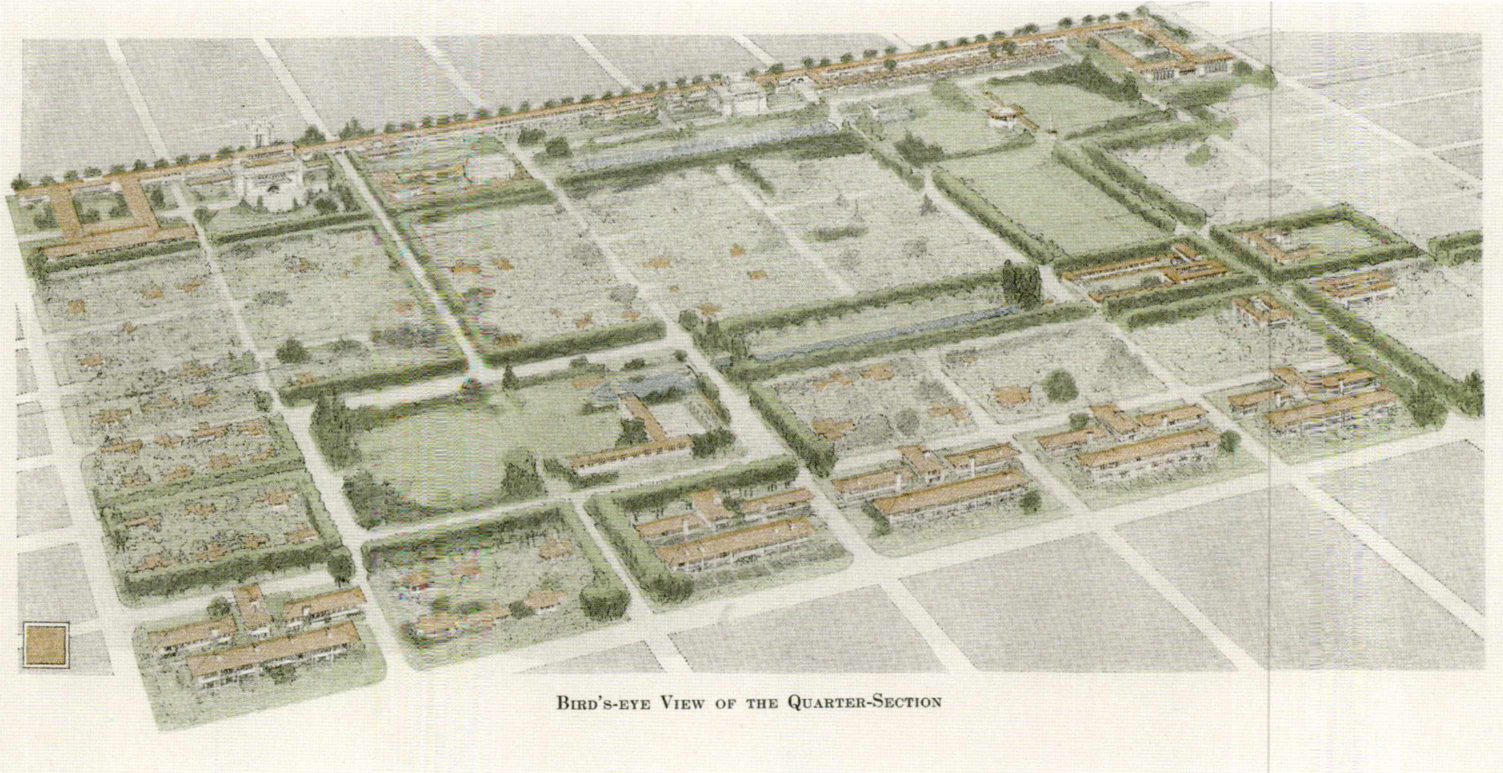

Figure 62
Frank Lloyd Wright; *Bird's-Eye View of the Quarter-Section;* from Alfred B. Yeomans, *City Residential Land Development,* 4 ¼ x 8 ½ in. (Chicago: University of Chicago Press, 1916); Charles Deering McCormick Library of Special Collections, Northwestern University Library. Copyright © 2012 Frank Lloyd Wright Foundation/Artists Rights Society (ARS), New York.

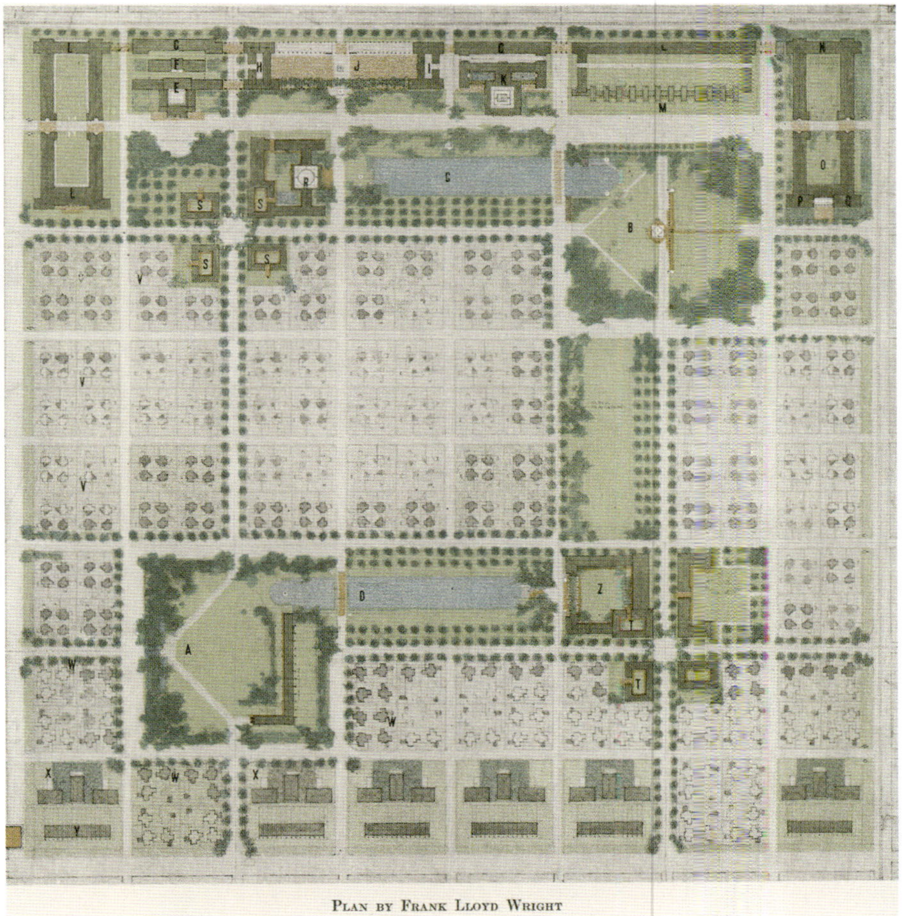

Figure 63
Frank Lloyd Wright; *Plan of the Quarter Section;* from Alfred B. Yeomans, *City Residential Land Development;* approximately 6 ½ x 6 ½ in. (Chicago: University of Chicago Press, 1916); Charles Deering McCormick Library of Special Collections, Northwestern University Library. Copyright © 2012 Frank Lloyd Wright Foundation/Artists Rights Society (ARS), New York.

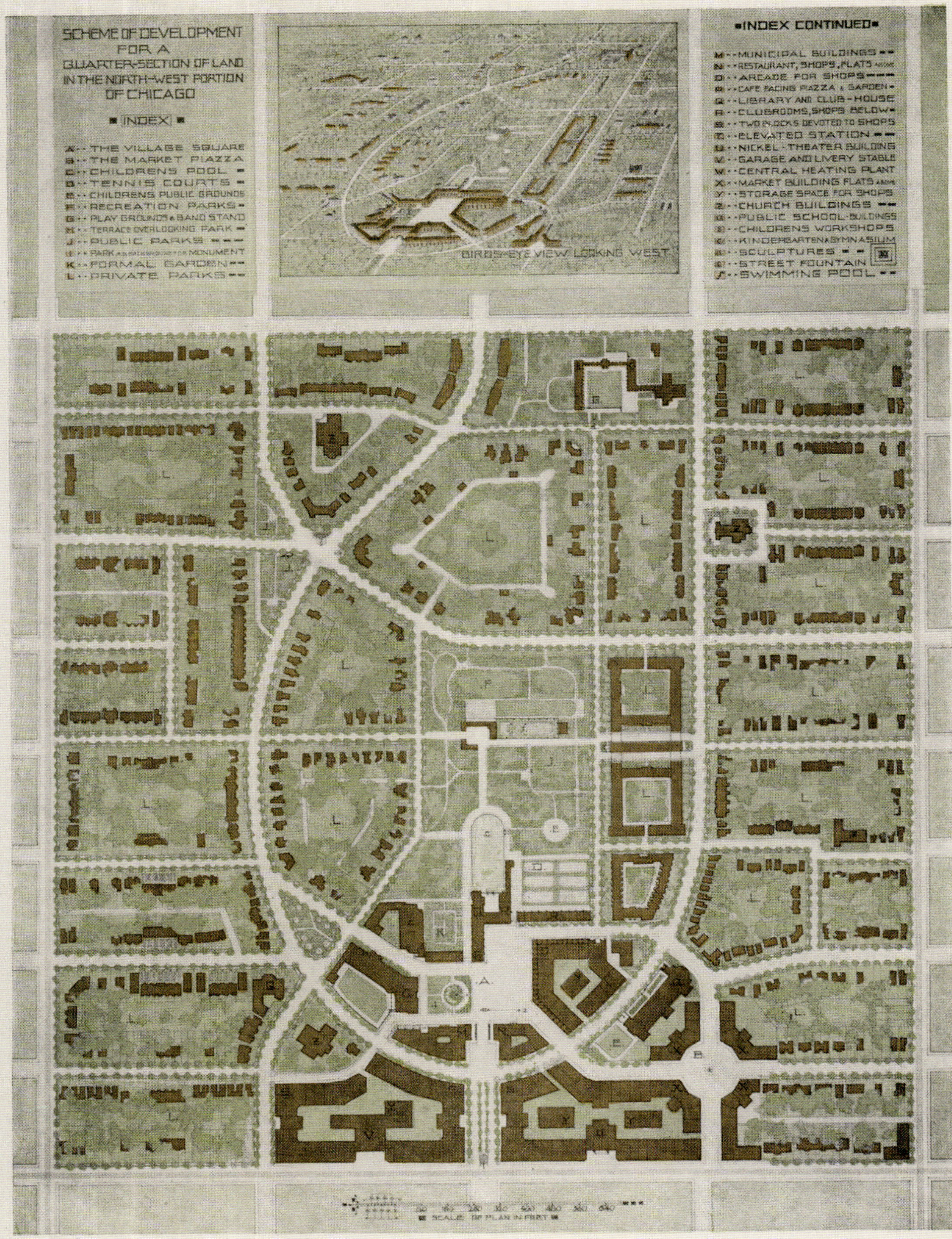

First Prize Plan by Wilhelm Bernhard

For statistical data relating to this plan see tables pp. 134–137, Plan No. 1.

Despite the attention paid to this competition, many of the details of the Quarter-Section Competition generally, and Wright's involvement in particular, have not yet been thoroughly understood. For example, it has been suggested that Wright's entry was not treated as a competitive entry because he was "an active member of the City Club and a charter member of its City Planning Committee," and therefore "could not officially enter the competition."[22] The club's papers, and a comparison with other entries for both competitions, reveal that this cannot be the explanation. Although Wright was indeed a "charter member" of the City Planning Committee—his name appeared on the list of the committee's original ten members—the committee's minutes indicate that he was hardly active. There is no record that he attended a single meeting, and his name, in fact, was dropped from the membership list when the committee was reorganized in February 1910. But membership in the City Club or its committees did not seem to preclude individuals from participating in these competitions. A number of City Club members entered either the Quarter-Section or the Neighborhood Center competition, and one member participated competitively in both.[23] It remains unclear, then, whether it was by Wright's choice, or the City Club's, or for some other reason, that his entry was not judged competitively against the others submitted.

In total, thirty-nine entries were evaluated by the jury. The entrants largely came from Chicago or the Midwest, although a number of East Coast entries were also received. First prize was won by Wilhelm Bernhard, an architect practicing in Chicago, who had trained in Dresden and previously worked with Frank Lloyd Wright (figure 64).[24] Third place was

Figure 65
Edgar H. Lawrence; *Quarter-Section Plan;* from Alfred B. Yeomans, *City Residential Land Development;* approximately 6 ½ x 6 ½ in. (Chicago: University of Chicago Press, 1916); Charles Deering McCormick Library of Special Collections, Northwestern University Library

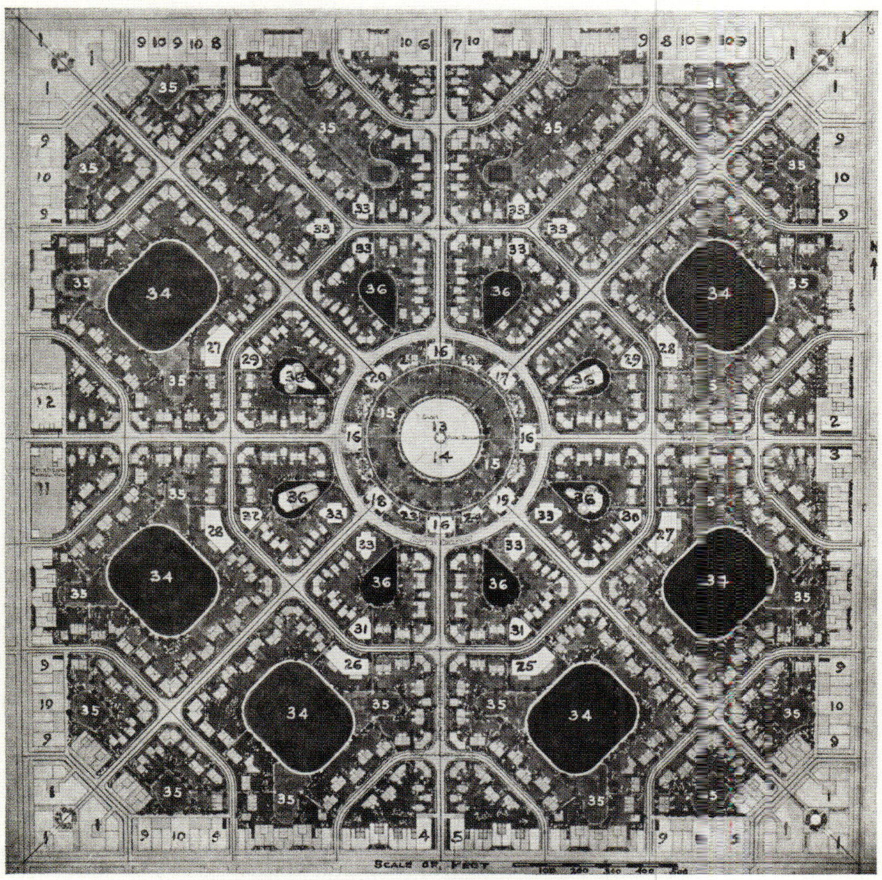

Plan by Edgar H. Lawrence. Walter B. Griffin, Advisory

Figure 64 *(facing page)*
Wilhelm Bernhard; *Scheme of Development for a Quarter-Section of Land;* from Alfred B. Yeomans, *City Residential Land Development,* approximately 9 ½ x 6 ½ in. (Chicago: University of Chicago Press, 1916); Charles Deering McCormick Library of Special Collections, Northwestern University Library

won by a husband-and-wife team from Gothenburg, Sweden.[25] Walter Burley Griffin served in an advisory capacity for an entry submitted by Edgar H. Lawrence, an employee of Griffin's at the time. Lawrence's plan, like many of the others, had a pleasing radial symmetry which, if repeated in adjacent quarter-sections, created an elegant interlocking network of residential streets, shopping arcades, and water basins (figure 65).[26]

In 1916, the City Club's Quarter-Section Competition results were published by the University of Chicago Press. Titled *City Residential Land Development: Studies in Planning: Competitive Plans for Subdividing a Typical Quarter-Section of Land in the Outskirts of Chicago,* the book contained numerous color illustrations, was printed in a fairly large format, and had a hard-cover binding. Because the City Club of Chicago was not as well financed as organizations like the Commercial Club, it is somewhat surprising that the Quarter-Section Competition actually made it into print, and even more so that the publication was as lavish as it was.[27] Little attention has been paid to this feat, and several observations can be made regarding it. First, it is clear that the City Club realized the importance of getting its work published and before the public. The Commercial Club's Plan of Chicago may have provided the City Club with an extra incentive to publish its Quarter-Section Competition, to provide a public alternative to the Burnham Plan. Second, it seems that the City Club wanted to produce a book of as fine a quality as it could afford, possibly so its work would not be discounted out of hand as less important than the Commercial Club's. Finally, it is interesting to note that the City Club's Quarter-Section book not only resembles the Commercial Club's but also was designed to have exactly the same dimensions. Was it hoped that the two books would stand, literally side-by-side, on the city's bookshelves?

Given the club's tight finances, how then was the book published? The answer is found in minutes of the City Club's Board of Directors meetings, which show that on two occasions the board extended a "vote of thanks" to Helen Culver for making possible publication of the Quarter-Section Competition results.[28] Culver was one of Jane Addams's most important benefactors. She had inherited the Hull-House property from her uncle and subsequently provided it to Addams for her settlement work. Culver's sponsorship of the Quarter-Section publication, and of other City Club work, provides another example of how closely intertwined were the connections between the City Club and Hull-House.

The Neighborhood Center Competition

The City Club followed up its successful Housing Exhibition and competition with another exhibition focusing on "the great public estate." Titled the Public Properties of Chicago Exhibition, the exhibit displayed various civic buildings and other properties and assets of Chicago. In conjunction with this exhibit, the City Planning Committee organized the Neighborhood Center Competition. The object of the program was to "bring before the public, in graphic form, the practical possibilities of enhancing neighborhood life in our cities by better, and especially better grouped, buildings and grounds for neighborhood activities."[29] After a preliminary round, a smaller group of entries would be selected to advance to the final competition. Entrants could design a neighborhood center for Chicago or any other large city, or for a center of a smaller town, and for actual or assumed conditions.

Basic information about the winning participants and their designs has been found in issues of *The City Club Bulletin* and in the journal *The Survey.* From these sources, we know that the competition jury was composed of University of Chicago sociology professor and City Club member George H. Mead; Mary McDowell, of the University of Chicago Settlement House; Chicago architects and City Club members Robert C. Spencer, Irving K. Pond, and Howard Van Doren Shaw; and Charles Mulford Robinson, a City Beautiful advocate and planner who became, with his appointment at the University of Illinois in 1913, the first professor of civic design at an American university. There were twenty entrants to the preliminary competition, and from this group ten were selected to participate in the final competition. The jury was said to have been, in general, disappointed in most of the plans, which it viewed "as having vital solutions of a very important problem, some indicating the greatest technical ability showing the tendency to interpret the center in too monumental and elaborate terms."[30]

At a meeting of the City Club held on March 5, 1915, when the finalists presented each of their plans and the winners were announced, George Mead summarized the main conclusions he drew from the competition:

> Two points seem to me pretty definitely settled. One is that the neighborhood center should gather about the child and the adolescent life. The school should be the focal point for the interests of all the family . . . In the second place, we should have means of recreation, and in this adults as well as children should be able to participate.
>
> There should also be some representation of the central government at such a central point. Provision should be made in the center so that those who have inquiries or complaints to report could come into direct touch with the City Hall or its representatives . . . bringing the political life right home to the people.[31]

The winners of the cash prize, which was to be distributed equally to the authors of the best eight plans, were:

> First honors: Anna Pendleton Schenck and Marcia Mead, architects, New York. Second honors: Louis Guensel [sic] and William Drummond, architects, Chicago. Third honors (divided): Prof. Joseph Hudnut, Alabama Polytechnic Institute, Auburn, Ala.; Carl Berg, civil engineer, Chicago. Others participating in the cash award were: George A. Damon, dean of engineering, Throop College of Technology, Pasadena, Cal. Bremer W. Pond and Elbert Peets, Harvard University, Cambridge, Mass. E. Post Tooker and Reginald E. Marsh, architects and landscape engineers, New York. George W. Jacoby, architect, New York.[32]

Because the two finalists who did not receive a cash award were not mentioned in this article, their identities are still uncertain. In addition to the above-mentioned contestants, noncompetitive entries were also received from Jens Jensen, Dwight H. Perkins, and Wilhelm Bernhard. Three of the entrants—Marcia Mead, Wilhelm Bernhard, and William Drummond—had also competed in the earlier Quarter-Section Competition.

Small reproductions of some of the Neighborhood Center entries were published in issues of *The City Club Bulletin*, and descriptions and images of other entries can be found in contemporary newspapers, architectural and planning journal articles, and other archival records. From these various sources, the competition entries have been partially reassembled.

Elbert Peets and Bremer W. Pond were students in the landscape architecture program at Harvard School of Design when they submitted their entry in the Neighborhood Center Competition. Although their entry drawings appear to have been lost, a draft of their twenty-two page general thesis, as well as a verbal description of the entry itself, which accompanied their submission, still exists.[33] The thesis includes a detailed analysis of the competition program, followed by a discussion of "general principles"—specifically, the value of neighborhoods, a sociological discussion of neighborhood units and boundaries, a statement regarding the ideal population size and density for a neighborhood, and an argument for the value of planning as a means of strengthening neighborhood stability. Their actual Neighborhood Center design was "an application of these principles to a particular neighborhood in a large Eastern City," and with "perspective sketches . . . intended merely to indicate the type of architectural expression which seems to us to be suited to that plan and to that neighborhood."[34] Although the city is not identified, it seems likely to have been Boston. Their study first identified an existing natural center for the working-class neighborhood they were looking at. They then worked to improve the adjacent street plan while preserving business buildings around the existing public square, and grouped new social buildings around a courtyard nearby. The authors believed the advantages of their plan were that "it recognizes existing conditions and tendencies, and that it expresses the spirit of citizenship, the broadest basis for cooperative effort in a modern American city."[35]

Reconstructing the entry from William Drummond and Louis Guenzel, which was awarded second place, is difficult. William Drummond had also participated in the Quarter-Section Competition, and his work is included in the Quarter-Section publication. Unlike the other entries in the book, Drummond's section is expanded and does not include a single Quarter-Section plan and bird's-eye view, but rather several larger scale plans of interconnecting quarter-sections, as well as detailed sketches of "social centers" and a discussion of "neighborhood units." It also includes a plan showing transportation and manufacturing belts. It seems possible, because this book was published after the Neighborhood Center Competition, that some of Drummond's Neighborhood Center drawings were included in it. Also supporting this possibility is the observation that at least one of the sketches in the book indicates that the drawings are by "Drummond & Guenzel." Both names are mentioned in relation to the Neighborhood Center Competition, but the Quarter-Section entry is listed as being by William Drummond alone. On the other hand, because there were plans to eventually publish the Neighborhood Center Competition in a separate volume, one would think that Drummond's Neighborhood Center drawings would have been held in reserve, to be used for that. Several small reproductions of Drummond and Guenzel drawings do exist elsewhere, however, which seem more certainly to have been part of their Neighborhood Center Competition entry. These were published in an article that appeared in the February 1915 issue of *Western Architect* and depict a detail of a building grouping that is very similar to ones in the Quarter-Section sketches; however in this case it is labeled "Neighborhood Center." The article's caption explains: "On this page is illustrated a scheme which is designed to bring about a reconstruction of our social and political urban life. The scheme aims at a pronounced 'individualization' of neighborhood districts in cities. A whole city like Chicago would be composed of 'units,' each having a neighborhood center or 'little capitol.' " The text goes on to say, "The 'little capitol' would have a large public meeting house, school rooms, a library and halls for exhibition and recreation, as well as gymnasia and contiguous park and play space."[36]

An image and description of the entry from George A. Damon appeared shortly after the competition in the *Los Angeles Times*.[37] His proposals were also later reprinted by the Pasadena Woman's Civic League, to whom he spoke on several occasions (figure 66).[38] Damon was dean of engineering at the Throop College of Technology—later the California Institute of Technology—and his design focused on creating a civic center for downtown Pasadena, which would function as a social and an educational center. His proposal also included a plan to relocate railroad lines and create a union station. The *Los Angeles Times* reported that Damon's design, "intended only as a suggestion . . . has been taken up by the Woman's Civic League of Pasadena as the basis for a vigorous city beautiful movement." Although Damon did work to incorporate existing public buildings to best advantage within the area, overall his design went a bit afield of the stated program, as it was somewhat grander than other proposals and addressed a civic center rather than a neighborhood center. As the *Times* reported, it did indeed spur a movement in Pasadena. The Woman's Civic League took up the cause, and its lobbying eventually led to passage of a bond issue to finance construction of a civic center for Pasadena. In 1927, a resplendent city hall, along with a new police station, YMCA, YWCA, post office, and library, were all constructed in the area initially sketched out by Damon in his Neighborhood Center design.[39]

Regarding the three entries that were submitted outside the competition—from Bernhard, Jensen, and Perkins—two images published of Wilhelm Bernhard's entry show that his Neighborhood Center design was a detailed working out of the commercial and social center indicated in his prize-winning Quarter-Section proposal (figure 67). Jens Jensen's entry appears to have been for the newly created Harrison Park—in Chicago's present-day Pilsen neighborhood—and depicted an arrangement of school buildings, young men's and women's buildings, lodging halls, a police station, fire department, and other specific public buildings, and adjacent business blocks. Not surprisingly, all were

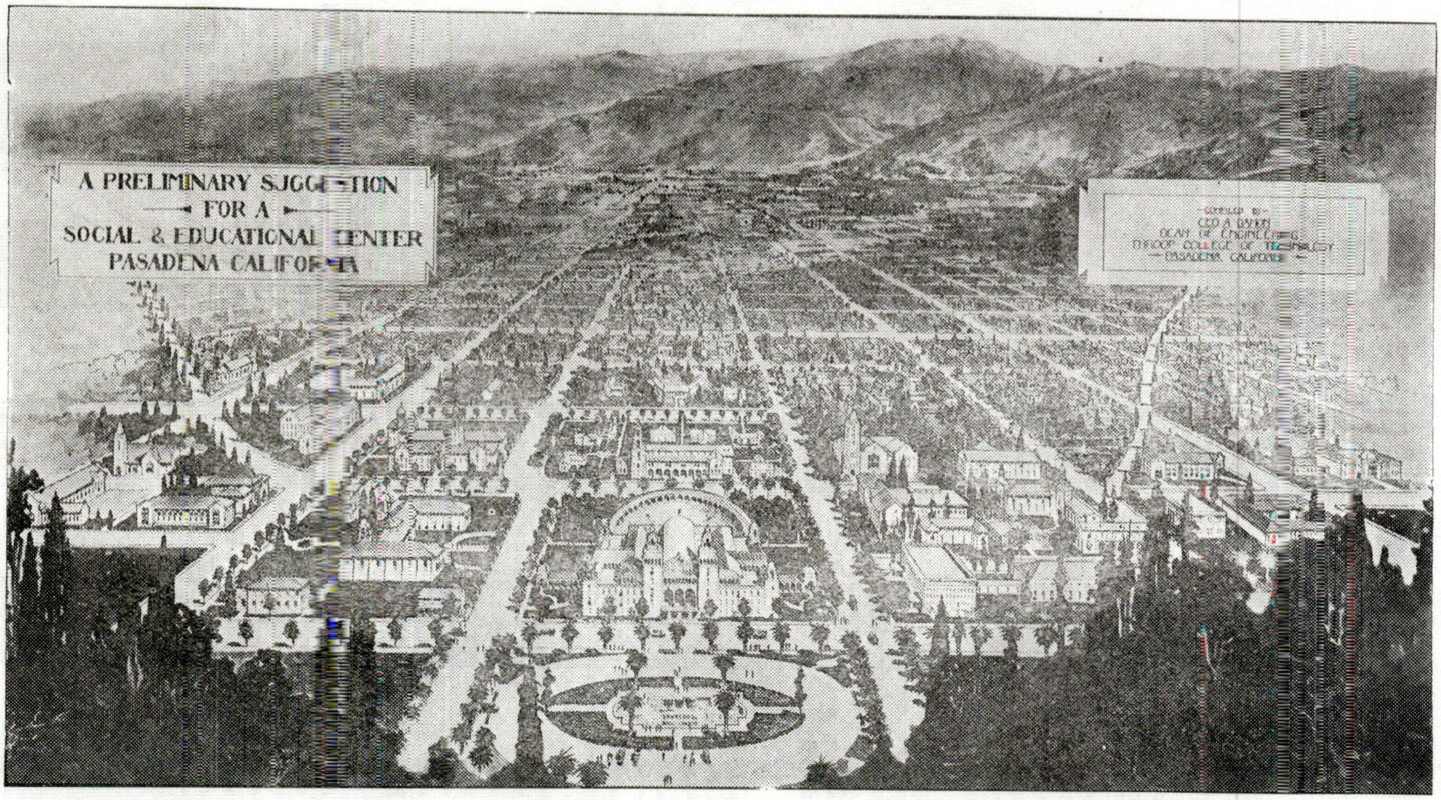

What might be done with the "blighted district" when the Santa Fe tracks are removed from north of Colorado street is shown by this birdseye view. The central point of interest is the auditorium located where the lumber yard now is. Directly to the east is shown a special group occupying the site of the present Wilson school and on the west a new library building has been located in Library Park. Broadway has been opened directly through to Summit; Lincoln avenue has been cut through to Library Park, and a new diagonal street suggested to the northeast. Other interesting suggestions make the plan worthy of thought and study. See plan below for details.

Figure 66
George A. Damon; *A Preliminary Suggestion for a Social and Educational Center, Bird's-Eye View for the Neighborhood Center Competition*; from *Some Preliminary Suggestions for a "Pasadena Plan"* (Pasadena, Calif.: Woman's Civic League, 1915)

somewhat secondary to the center's landscaped areas, which included a "council hill" for outdoor assemblies (figure 68). Nothing specifically identified as Dwight Perkins's Neighborhood Center entry has been located. Because Perkins was active in school design and had been advocating the use of schools as community centers, it is likely that his entry dealt with a school plan. Later that year, for example, Perkins wrote that a properly planned school could serve as "a neighborhood or social center for daytime use by children" and, outside of school hours, in a similar function for adults—the only difference, he said, "relates to the size of the furniture."[40] In an article entitled "The Social Center," published in the *Architectural Record* in 1919, Perkins's New Trier Township High School plans were included, along with Bernhard's and Jensen's Neighborhood Center Competition drawings, and a design by Joseph Hudnut for a Harrison Park Center.[41] Might this be because Perkins had submitted the New Trier Township High School project, which was designed and built by 1912, as his Neighborhood Center entry?[42]

Joseph Hudnut, who would later be appointed first dean of Harvard's Graduate School of Design and would be responsible for bringing Walter Gropius and Berlin city planner Martin Wagner to the United States, was a professor at Auburn Polytechnic Institute at the time of the Neighborhood Center Competition. This competition seems to have been Hudnut's first foray into city planning.[43]

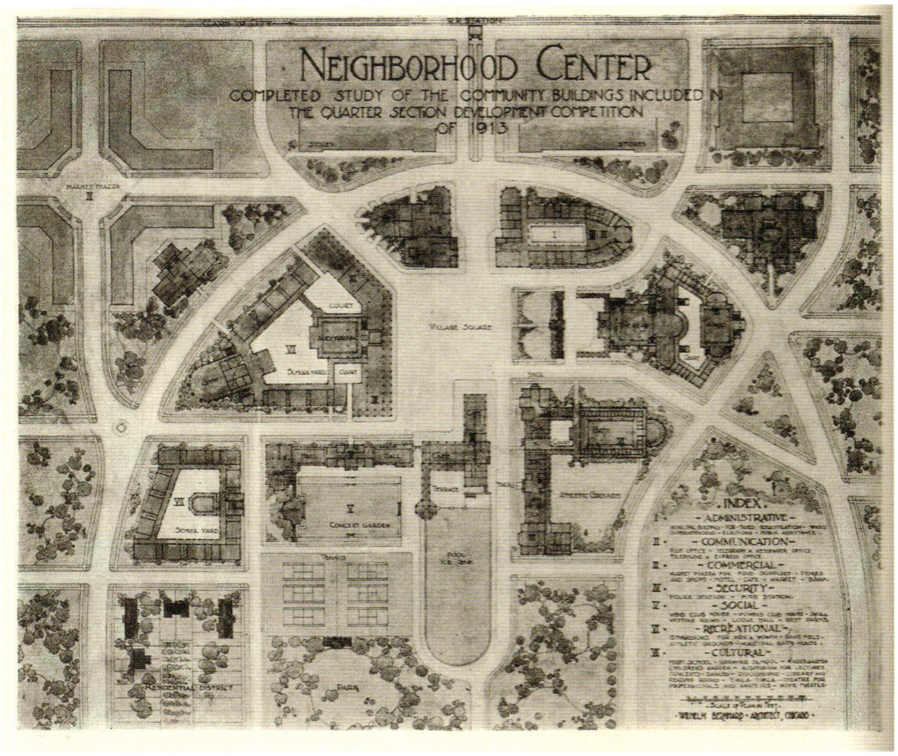

Figure 67
Wilhelm Bernhard; *Neighborhood Center;* from *Architectural Record* 46 (July 1919)

Although his original entry drawings have been lost, we know that the club found them interesting, as it decided to retain Hudnut over the summer of 1915 for the purpose of developing working proposals for two specific neighborhood center projects in Chicago. Hudnut was also to make preparations for a publication that would include the Neighborhood Center Competition drawings and the two Chicago projects.[44] Regarding the Chicago projects, one was to address an already built-up area and the other an undeveloped tract of land. Hudnut worked with Jens Jensen on plans for the built-up area, which was a sixteen-acre site in the West Side Chicago neighborhood that included Harrison Park. The neighborhood center there was to include a school, branch library, theater, assembly hall, and gymnasium (figure 69). An interesting aspect of the plan was its picturesque incorporation of an old quarry. The second project was for a tract of land owned by a W. A. Peterson on the northwest side of Chicago. Called "The Peterson Center," the scheme took advantage of the sanitary canal for landscape and recreational purposes; recommended sites for an assembly hall, school buildings, an outdoor court, and theater; provided a layout of streets, elevated train tracks, and streetcar lines; and indicated a convenient location for the neighborhood's business center.

No drawings or records have yet been located regarding the entries submitted by Tooker and Marsh (E. Post Tooker and Reginald Marsh), Carl Berg, and William Jacoby.[45]

Before discussing the first-place entry, one final set of Neighborhood Center drawings, which remains a bit of a mystery, should be mentioned. These five drawings were created by Rudolph Schindler.[46] Three are inked drawings (two bird's-eye perspectives, looking down at an angle, and one plan view from directly above) and several are labeled "Competition Held by the City Club of Chicago for a Neighborhood Center" (figure 70). Because Schindler's name does not appear on the list of winning entries, the question remains whether Schindler actually entered these drawings in the competition or not. If he did, his entry was either one of the original twenty submissions that

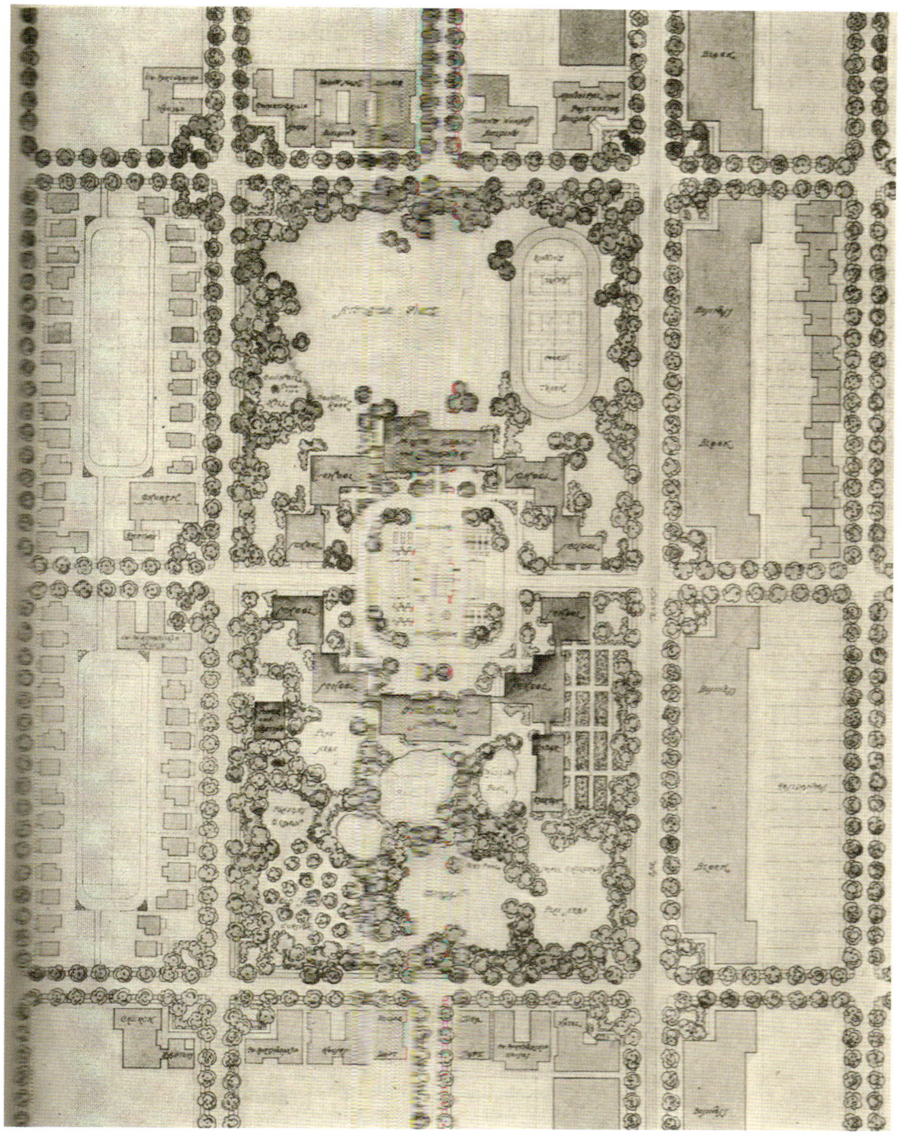

Figure 68
Jens Jensen; *Plan for a Neighborhood Center* from *Architectural Record* 46 (July 1919)

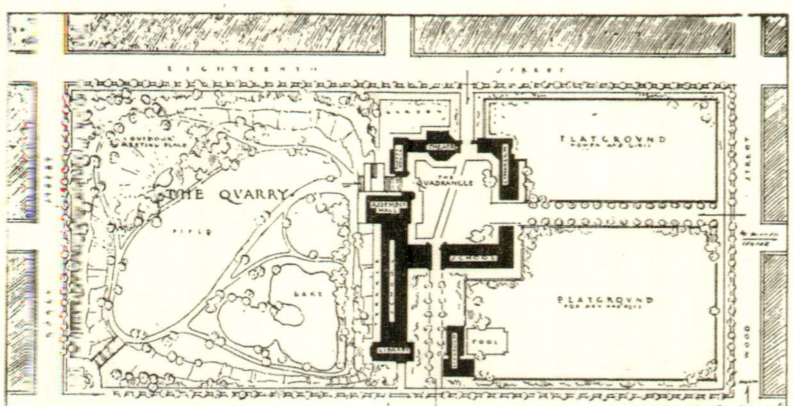

HARRISON PARK CENTER, CHICAGO.
Joseph Hudnut, Architect.

Figure 69
Joseph Hudnut; *Harrison Park Center, Chicago*; from *Journal of the American Institute of Architects* 4 (February 1916)

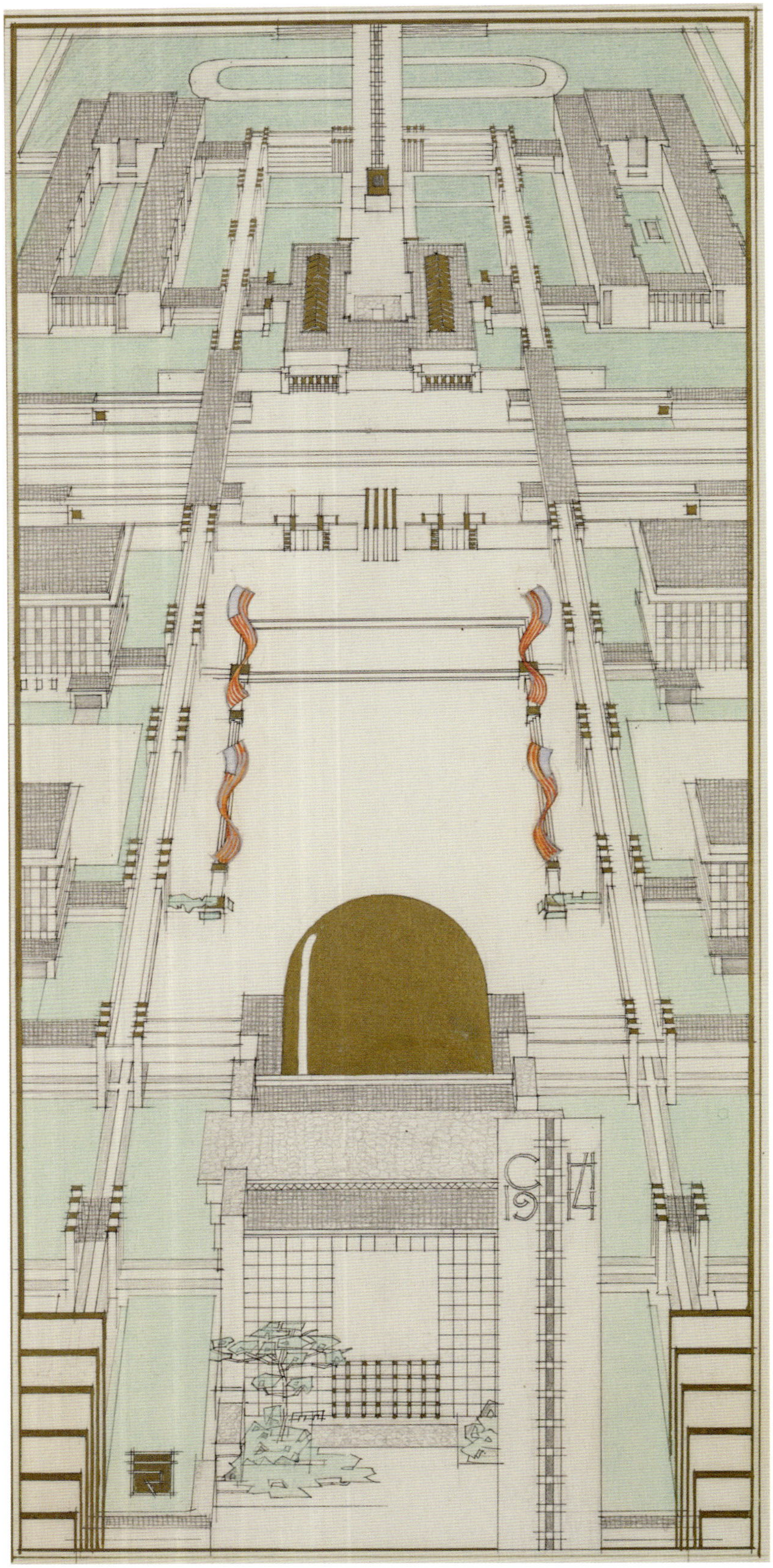

Figure 70
Rudolph M. Schindler; *Bird's-Eye View Looking Toward Public Library*, 1914; ink, watercolor, and crayon on paper; 24 ¾ × 15 in.; Art, Design and Architecture Museum, University of California, Santa Barbara

did not advance to the final competition, or was one of the two finalists that were not awarded prizes.

Until shortly before the competition, Schindler had been studying in Vienna with Otto Wagner, but he had completed his studies and graduated in 1913 and arrived in the United States in March 1914.[47] Schindler arrived first in New York City but is said to have left soon afterward for Chicago, where he began work at the firm of Ottenheimer, Stern and Reichert. Because the Neighborhood Center Competition was not announced until June 1914, Schindler would almost certainly have been settled in Chicago by this time and aware of the competition. Interestingly, and also somewhat confusingly, Wagner had asked Walter Burley Griffin for a copy of the Neighborhood Center Competition program, which he translated into German.[48] Although it seems clear that Schindler produced these drawings while he was working in Chicago, it is possible that other project drawings were made in Vienna, by other students of Wagner.

Another point of confusion regarding these drawings is that, in some accounts, they have been identified as for a competition held by the Chicago Architectural Club.[49] This seems to be an error, as there is no indication that the Chicago Architectural Club was involved with the City Club's competition, and the legend on the drawings themselves identifies them as for the "City Club of Chicago." However, because Schindler was active in the Chicago Architectural Club at this time, it is possible that he drew them as an exercise for the Architectural Club—and noted or remembered them as such—and never entered them in the City Club's competition.

Schindler's drawings basically adhered to the Neighborhood Center Competition requirements; he created plan and bird's-eye views, and community buildings were numbered and identified in a legend. At least one of the drawings included Schindler's initials, however. If this drawing was submitted in the preliminary competition, these initials might have disqualified the entry, as guidelines required that they be identified by a "nom de plume." If Schindler's drawings had advanced to the final competition, why did they not win a prize? Possibly jurors were put off by Schindler's Viennese aesthetic, or considered his design "too monumental," or simply found his proposal less well-developed than other entries.

The judges awarded first place to the designs entered by two, now almost entirely forgotten, women architects named Anna Pendleton Schenck and Marcia Mead. Together, Schenck and Mead had started an architectural firm in 1914 that was believed, at the time, to be the first in New York City composed solely of women architects.[50] The opening of their firm made news (figure 71). Although the newspaper stories patronizingly made much of Schenck and Mead's supposed attention to closets and other "women's" concerns, their interest in housing and, in particular, housing for the poor, was also detailed.

Although little information can now be found on the two women, we do know that Mead was the first woman to graduate from the School of Architecture at Columbia University, where she received her degree in 1913.[51] She also participated in the City Club's Quarter-Section Competition that same year and placed among the first ten.[52] Schenck was the youngest daughter of a prominent Brooklyn clergyman. News accounts described her as the "senior" member of the firm, suggesting she was older than Mead. Information about Schenck's professional training is unclear. She was said to have worked previously as a draftswoman for the architect Grosvenor Atterbury. Some accounts say that she was trained in Paris, while others report that she, like Mead, studied at Columbia University.[53] Regarding her Paris training, several sources state that she studied or worked in the atelier of "Aubretin," or "M. Aubretin." This comment suggests an intriguing possibility. Although no Parisian architects with the name of Aubretin have been found, the name is very similar to and may simply have been a repeated misspelling of "Auburtin," an architect and planner who *was* working in Paris during this period. Jean-Marcel Auburtin taught at the École des Beaux-Arts and was a friend of Alfred Agache, with whom he cofounded the Société Française des Architectes Urbanistes in 1913.[54] Records indicate that at least one other American woman studied with Auburtin around this same time.[55] That Schenck had studied

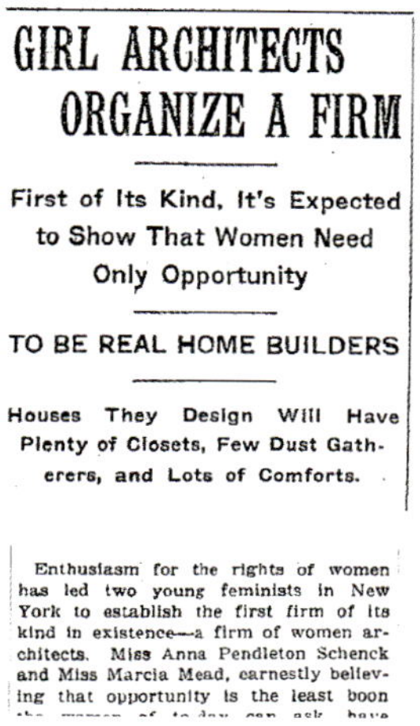
GIRL ARCHITECTS ORGANIZE A FIRM

First of Its Kind, It's Expected to Show That Women Need Only Opportunity

TO BE REAL HOME BUILDERS

Houses They Design Will Have Plenty of Closets, Few Dust Gatherers, and Lots of Comforts.

Enthusiasm for the rights of women has led two young feminists in New York to establish the first firm of its kind in existence—a firm of women architects. Miss Anna Pendleton Schenck and Miss Marcia Mead, earnestly believing that opportunity is the least boon

Figure 71
Article published in the *New York Times*, March 8, 1914

with Auburtin would therefore make a good deal of sense, given Mead and Schenck's interest in urban housing, their familiarity with European housing models, and their later success with several worker housing projects.

Unlike many of the entries, Mead and Schenck's addressed the needs of an actual community. Their area of study was a one-square-mile section of the Bronx, between the Washington Bridge and Macombs Dam Park. In an article published in the *New York Times*, Mead explained that they wanted to provide Bronx residents with everything necessary to make families living in that district feel at home, and not perceive the need to go elsewhere in search of pleasure. "We wanted to show what could be done for real people . . . not what might be done for ideal beings in Utopia. I think that was why we won the prize, because our plans were entirely possible and workable."[56] Their plan recommended retaining all of the existing permanent buildings and streets (except for 167th Street, which they suggested be widened). They sited a new community center—consisting of a high school, kindergarten, playground, gymnasium, clubhouse, library, and other facilities—on a bluff facing the Harlem River (figure 72). Beneath the center, the bluff would be landscaped and parked, and the railroad tracks along the river would be spanned by a pedestrian bridge that led to a pleasure pier (figure 73).

A series of talks and other programs were scheduled to complement the exhibition and competition, and Schenck discussed her firm's entry at

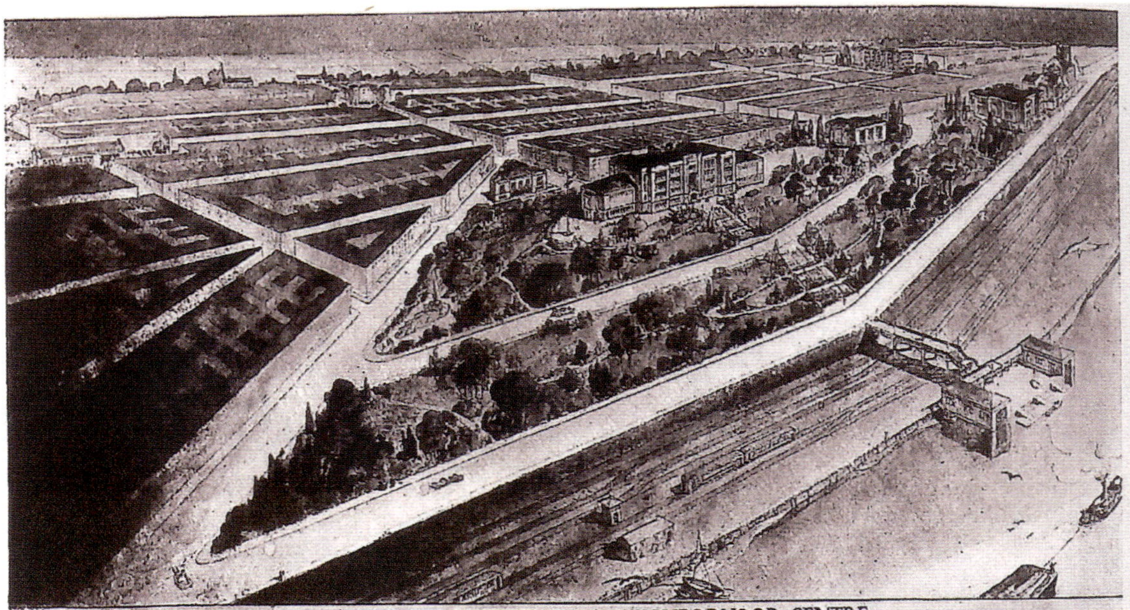

BIRD'S-EYE PERSPECTIVE OF A NEIGHBORHOOD CENTRE
View of Bronx Development Looking from the North, Showing Relation of the Main Axis to the Different Buildings in the Group
Awarded first honor in the Chicago City Club's Neighborhood Center Competition
By Anna Pendleton Schenck and Marcia Mead, Architects, New York

Figure 72
Anna Pendleton Schenck and Marcia Mead; *Bird's-Eye Perspective of a Neighborhood Centre*; from George B. Ford, "Neighborhood Centers," *Journal of the American Institute of Architects* 3:5 (May 1915)

an evening program held by the club on March 5, 1915. A few days later, she met with the Committee on Housing Conditions and presented the firm's designs for the Ellen Wilson Memorial Homes, a block of model homes to be built in Washington, D.C.[57] This presentation may have planted a seed with the Housing Conditions committee, as the following year "discussion was had of possible sites [in Chicago] for a two story flat housing scheme with separate yards for each family, similar to certain types in Washington."[58]

Tragically, less than two months after winning the City Club competition, Schenck died of pneumonia. Mead continued the firm's work on her own for several years, retaining the name "Schenck and Mead," and in 1917 she completed an impressive project in Bridgeport, Connecticut, for the Bridgeport Housing Company, a limited-dividend company formed by local manufacturers and utilities to address the city's growing housing problem. The project was built for factory workers on a triangular piece of land in an industrial district, and the main block of row houses was arranged to enclose a shared court and garden space. The arrangement, scale, and style of the buildings were reminiscent of European worker housing, such as the project built in Ulm, Germany, that had been featured in the City Club's Housing Exhibition (figure 74; see also figure 61). The development also shared some similarities to Grosvenor Atterbury's Forest Hills Gardens community, built in 1910 for the Russell Sage Foundation. In addition to this development—and YWCA buildings in Bridgeport, Connecticut; Jersey City, New Jersey; and Buffalo, New York—Mead's later work involved teaching, composing professional and popular articles on housing, and writing a book titled *Homes of Character*.[59]

During the years of World War I, the membership and income of the City Club of Chicago dwindled, and its activities focused largely on war-specific needs. A balance remained on the club's books, however, toward a publication of the Neighborhood Center Competition. In August 1918, the board finally ruled to move any "unused

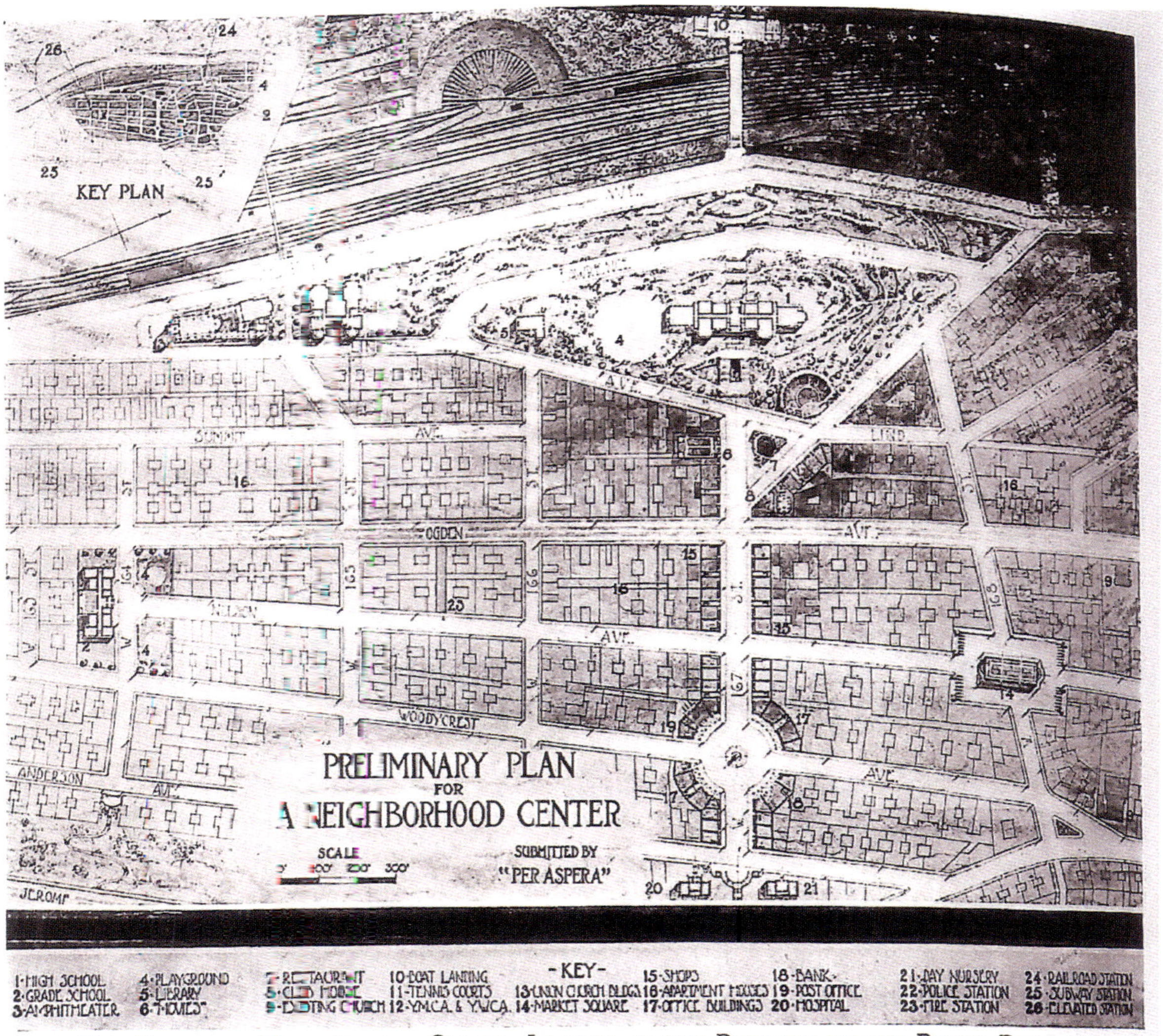

THE PLAN OF A NEIGHBORHOOD CENTER, LOCATED IN THE BOROUGH OF THE BRONX BETWEEN WASHINGTON BRIDGE AND McCOMBS DAM PARK, NEW YORK

Awarded First Honor in the Chicago City Club's Neighborhood Center Competition. By Anna Pendleton Schenck and Marcia Mead, Architects, New York

Figure 73

Anna Pendleton Schenck and Marcia Mead; *Preliminary Plan for a Neighborhood Center*; from George B. Ford, "Neighborhood Centers"; *Journal of the American Institute of Architects* 3:5 (May 1915)

special funds" into a newly created "Publication and Contingent Fund," and, after this date, the "Neighborhood Center Publication" line item disappeared from the treasurer's reports.[60] The club appeared to be abandoning hope of ever publishing the Neighborhood Center proposals. This outcome was finally assured in early 1920, when the Board of Directors authorized Hooker to return the Neighborhood Center plans to their respective owners.[61]

Although interrupted by the war, many of the ideas that the City Club of Chicago and its City

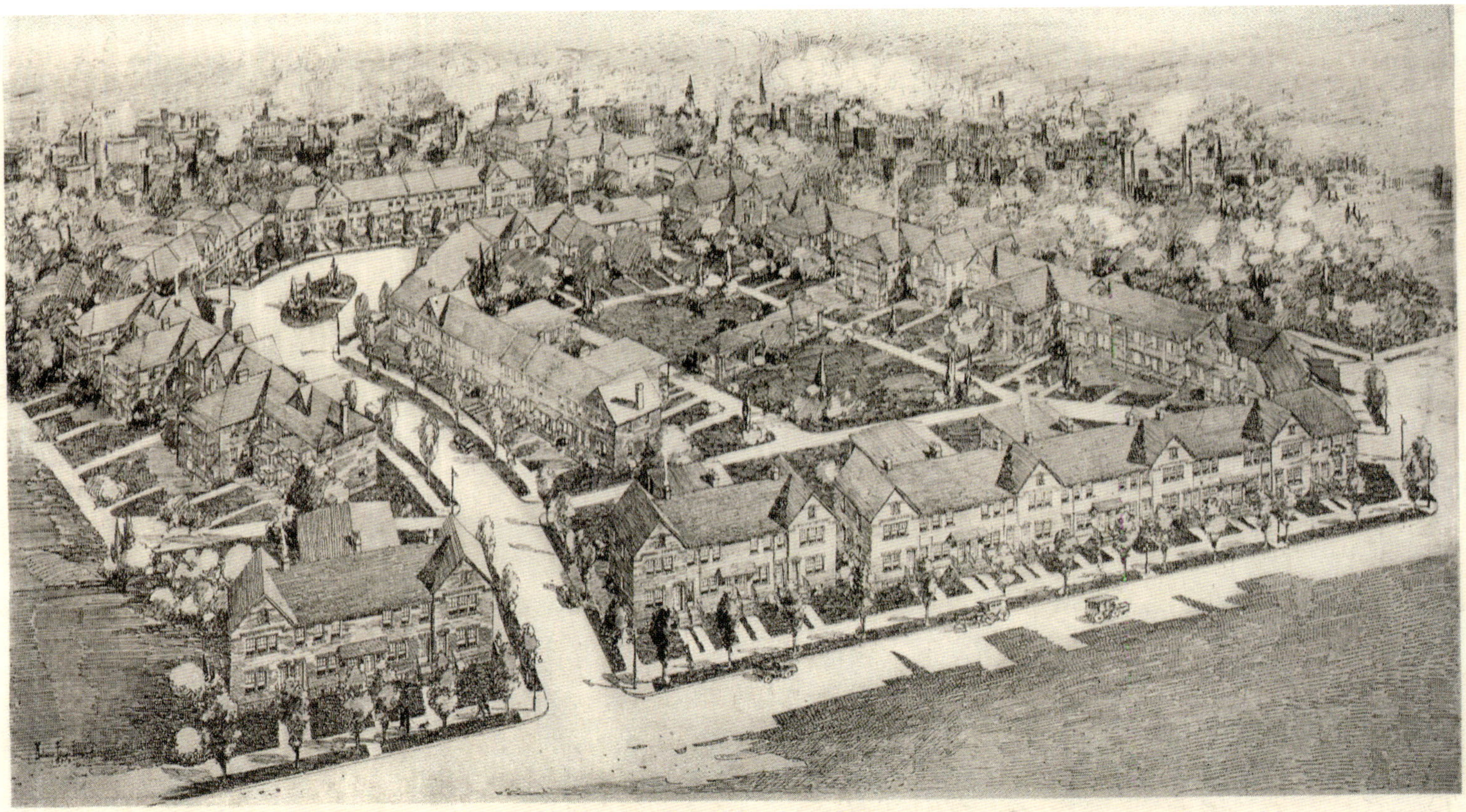

FIG. 33. BIRD'S-EYE VIEW OF CONNECTICUT DEVELOPMENT—BRIDGEPORT HOUSING CO. SCHENCK & MEAD, ARCHITECTS.

Figure 74
Schenck and Mead, Architects; *Bird's-Eye View of Connecticut Development, Bridgeport Housing Co.*; from "The Bridgeport Housing Development"; *American Architect* 113 (February 6, 1918)

Planning Committee were exploring during the 1910s—such as zoning, neighborhood units, and neighborhood centers—would become established planning concepts in the decades that followed. And much of the later work of the competitions' participants—of Damon, Griffin, Hudnut, Jensen, Peets, and Perkins—can also be seen as further advancements of the club's interests from this period. In the end, however, it appears that the only realized project to directly come out of either of the City Club's competitions was George Damon's "Pasadena Suggestion"—ironically the grandest and most "Burnhamesque" of the lot—which also seemingly confirmed Burnham's famous admonition: "Make no little plans; they have no magic to stir men's blood."

Notes

1. Civic Committees and Their Duties, May 14, 1908. City Club of Chicago Records, 1903–78, Chicago History Museum.

2. Minutes of the City Planning Committee, July 14, 1914. City Club of Chicago Records, 1903–78 (Box 16, folder 16–1), Chicago History Museum.

3. James L. Merriner, *The City Club of Chicago: A Centennial History* (Chicago: City Club of Chicago, 2003), 5.

4. Because of this, the club made a point of keeping its dues lower than other clubs. Ibid., 10.

5. The building still stands and is occupied by the John Marshall Law School, which has owned the structure since the 1930s.

6. Annual Report of the City Planning Committee, April 14, 1909. City Club of Chicago Records, 1903–78, Chicago History Museum.

7. This information comes from the biographical notes in the finding aid for the George Ellsworth Hooker City Planning, Transportation and Housing Collection, 1882–1932, University of Chicago Library.

8. *The Survey* 22: 778–90.

9. Its members were to be Irving K. Pond, William Drummond, and Herman von Holst. Minutes of the City Planning Committee, April 25, 1913. City Club of Chicago Records, 1903–78, Chicago History Museum.

10. Minutes of the City Planning Committee, May 13, 1913. City Club of Chicago Records, 1903–78, Chicago History Museum.

11. It is possible that the Organic Plan subcommittee lost its steam after Griffin's departure for Australia.

12. Minutes of the City Planning Committee, May 26, 1914. City Club of Chicago Records, 1903–78 (Box 16, folder 16–1), Chicago History Museum.

13. Minutes of the City Planning Committee, June 9, 1914. City Club of Chicago Records, 1903–78 (Box 16, folder 16–1), Chicago History Museum.

14. George Taylor was Walter Burley Griffin's closest Australian friend and may have been Griffin's mouthpiece on the matter. (My thanks to Christopher Vernon for this observation.)

15. Minutes of the City Planning Committee, July 14, 1914. City Club of Chicago Records, 1903–78 (Box 16, folder 16–1), Chicago History Museum.

16. Letter from Charles Wacker to the City Planning Committee, September 22, 1914. City Club of Chicago Records, 1903–78 (Box 16, folder 16–1), Chicago History Museum.

17. Annual report of the City Planning Committee, 4–5. City Club of Chicago Records, 1903–78 (Box 16, folder 16–1), Chicago History Museum.

18. Minutes of the City Planning Committee, April 27, 1910. City Club of Chicago Records, 1903–78, Chicago History Museum.

19. *Proceedings of the Fifth National Conference on City Planning Chicago, Illinois* (Boston: University Press, 1913), 189.

20. See Alfred B. Yeomans, *City Residential Land Development: Studies in Planning: Competitive Plans for Subdividing a Typical Quarter Section of Land in the Outskirts of Chicago* (Chicago: University of Chicago Press, 1916). Also Gwendolyn Wright, *Moralism and the Model Home: Domestic Architecture and Cultural Conflict in Chicago, 1873–1913* (Chicago: University of Chicago Press, 1980); Donald Leslie Johnson, "Origin of the Neighbourhood Unit," *Planning Perspectives* 17, no. 3 (July 2002): 227–45; Neil Levine, "The Quadruple Block Plan and Frank Lloyd Wright's Obsession with the Grid," *AV (Enseignement architecture ville)* 11 (2005/2006): 62–84; Neil Levine, "Making Community out of the Grid," in Richard Cleary et al., *Frank Lloyd Wright: From Within Outward* (New York: Rizzoli, 2009), 58–73; R. Samuel Roche and Aric Lasher, *Plans of Chicago* (Chicago: Architects Research Foundation, 2009, distributed by the University of Chicago Press); and Gwendolyn Wright, *Frank Lloyd Wright's Progressive Suburbia* (Lincoln: Hixson-Lied College of Fine and Performing Arts, University of Nebraska-Lincoln, 2010).

21. Wright, *Frank Lloyd Wright's Progressive Suburbia*, 16.

22. Ibid.

23. The club member who participated in both competitions was William Drummond.

24. Wilbert R. Hasbrouck, *The Chicago Architectural Club: Prelude to the Modern* (New York: Monacelli Press, 2005), 404.

25. Architect and planner Albert Lilienberg and his wife, Ingrid Lilienberg.

26. The bird's-eye perspective for Lawrence's entry, unlike any of the others submitted, was unusually wide and narrow. This scroll-like format is reminiscent of some of Marion Mahony Griffin's Canberra competition renderings. Christopher Vernon has pointed out that Walter Burley Griffin later, on more than one occasion, republished this plan in Australia, suggesting that his role in its design may have extended beyond "advisory."

27. The City Club had previously published several small pamphlets and books, most notably *The Railway Terminal Problem of Chicago* in 1913, which included plans and addresses by Guenzel and Drummond, Pond and Pond, D. H. Burnham and Co., and Jarvis Hunt. Although well written and well illustrated, overall this was a much more modest publication, having a smaller format, fewer pages, black-and-white illustrations, and a soft-cover binding.

28. Minutes of the Board of Directors Meeting, July 17, 1913, and March 30, 1916. City Club of Chicago Records, 1903–78, Chicago History Museum.

29. City Club of Chicago. *Program of a Competition to*

Be Held by the City Club of Chicago for Plans for a Neighborhood Center (Chicago: City Club, 1914), 1.

30. *The Survey* 34: 66.

31. *Journal of the American Institute of Architects* (May 1915): 223.

32. *The City Club Bulletin* (March 23, 1915): 77–78.

33. Their thesis is held by the Special Collections Department at the Frances Loeb Library of the Harvard Graduate School of Design.

34. Bremer Pond and Elbert Peets, "Neighborhood Center Competition, City Club of Chicago" (typescript manuscript, 1914), 2.

35. Bremer Pond and Elbert Peets, "A Neighborhood Center for a New England City" (Cambridge, Mass., undated), 7. Pond continued to work in the field of landscape architecture and later taught at Harvard, while Peets went on to an important career in town planning, working on the designs for Greendale, Wisconsin, and Park Forest, Illinois, and writing with Werner Hegemann, in 1922, *The American Vitruvius: An Architects' Handbook of Civic Art.* (New York: Architectural Book Publishing Co., 1922).

36. *Western Architect* 21: 15.

37. "Preliminary Study for Social and Educational Center in Crown City," *Los Angeles Times,* April 4, 1915.

38. Woman's Civic League, *Some Preliminary Suggestions for a "Pasadena Plan"* (Pasadena, Calif.: Woman's Civic League, 1915).

39. A number of wealthy Chicagoans moved to Pasadena, or had established winter residences there, during the early part of the twentieth century. It is interesting to consider whether their presence played a role in the enthusiasm with which Damon's "Pasadena Plan" was met and the manner in which it was eventually executed.

40. *The Brickbuilder* 24 (1915): 293.

41. *The Architectural Record* 46, no. 1 (1919): 29–46.

42. Also of interest and possibly relevant is the fact that in 1912 and 1913,Walter Burley Griffin laid out the "New Trier Centre" residential subdivision on property that abutted New Trier Township High School.

43. Jill E. Pearlman, *Inventing American Modernism: Joseph Hudnut, Walter Gropius, and the Bauhaus Legacy at Harvard* (Charlottesville: University of Virginia Press, 2007), 24.

44. Minutes of Board of Director's meeting, June 17, 1915. City Club of Chicago Records, 1903–78, Chicago History Museum.

45. We do know, however, that Tooker and Marsh was a newly created firm when it competed in the Neighborhood Center Competition, having been formed in 1914. The pair of architects went on to have a long and successful practice, perhaps best known for their design of the Bear Mountain Inn, built in 1915 in Rockland County, New York. George W. Jacoby was a 1902 graduate of the Columbia School of Architecture, studied for two years in Paris and Rome as a McKim fellow, and was associated with the firm of Trowbridge and Livingston from 1905 until his death in 1937 ("George W. Jacoby: Architect Helped Plan Many Important Buildings," *New York Times* [February 24, 1937]).

46. The originals are in the Rudolph M. Schindler Collection at the University Art Museum, University of California, Santa Barbara. They have been reproduced in David Gebhard's *The Architectural Drawings of R. M. Schindler: The Architectural Drawing Collection, University Art Museum, University of California, Santa Barbara* (New York: Garland, 1993).

47. Judith Sheine, *R. M. Schindler: Works and Projects* (Barcelona, Spain: Editorial Gustavo Gili, 1998), 230.

48. David Van Zanten, "The Walter Burley Griffin-Otto Wagner Correspondence, 1914–1915," in *The Chicago Architectural Journal: Vol. 6–1987* (New York: Rizzoli, 1987), 22–25.

49. See August Sarnitz, ed., *R. M. Schindler, Architect: 1887–1953: A Pupil of Otto Wagner, Between International Style and Space Architecture* (New York: Rizzoli, 1988), 16, 173; and Judith Sheine, *R. M. Schindler* (London: Phaidon, 2001), 24.

50. There is some uncertainty about whether this claim is actually correct. See "Miss Anna P. Schenck, Architect, Dies," *New York Times* (April 30, 1915); "Death of Two Notable Architects," *Western Architect* (May 1915): 38; and Sarah Allaback, *The First American Women Architects* (Urbana: University of Illinois Press, 2008), 219.

51. "Women at Columbia: A Century of Change." *Progressive Architecture* 63 (June 1982): 22–23.

52. Allaback, 135, and *New York Times* (March 8, 1914).

53. See note 50.

54. Agache was also a former student of Victor Laloux, an entrant in the Canberra competition, and an admirer of Tony Garnier. See www.library.cornell.edu/Reps/DOCS/agache.htm.

55. Mary Rockwell Hook, who went to Paris in 1905. International Archive of Women in Architecture Newsletter, Fall 1991, no. 3 (accessed June 13, 2012), spec.lib.vt.edu/IAWA/news/news3.html.

56. *New York Times* (March 6, 1915).

57. Their designs were accepted by the United States Housing Corporation, and were eventually built in Washington, D.C., sometime after World War I. Allaback, 136, 219.

58. Minutes of the Committee on Housing Conditions meeting, February 5, 1916. City Club of Chicago Records (manuscript), 1903–78, Chicago History Museum.

59. Allaback, 136.

60. Minutes of Board of Directors' meeting, August 12, 1918. City Club of Chicago Records, 1903–78, Chicago History Museum.

61. Minutes of Board of Directors' meeting, March 22, 1920. City Club of Chicago Records, 1903–78, Chicago History Museum.

Contributors

David Van Zanten is the Mary Jane Crowe Professor in Art and Art History at Northwestern University. He specializes in American and European architecture and urbanism after 1800. He wrote *Sullivan's City: The Meaning of Ornament for Louis Sullivan* (2000) and edited *Marion Mahony Griffin Reconsidered* (2011). His *Designing Paris: The Architecture of Duban, Labrouste, Duc, and Vaudoyer* won the 1988 Alice Davis Hitchcock Book Award from the Society of Architectural Historians. He extended this work in *Building Paris: Architectural Institutions and the Transformation of the French Capital, 1830–1870* (1994). In 2012, he was elected a Fellow of the American Academy of Arts and Sciences.

Ashley Elizabeth Dunn is a graduate student in art history at Northwestern University, focusing on nineteenth-century French visual culture. She previously studied at the University of Oxford, where her master's dissertation, " 'The Philosophy of Vice': The Yvette Guilbert Album Reconsidered," examined Henri de Toulouse-Lautrec's 1894 folio of lithographs. She has also written on etching in relation to communication discourse in late nineteenth-century America.

Leslie Coburn is a graduate student at the University of Illinois at Chicago. Her research focuses on the nineteenth- and twentieth-century built environment in the United States, especially Chicago. Her publications include articles for *Chicago History* magazine and *Dwell* magazine. She also contributed an essay, "Hyde Park A & B Urban Renewal Project," to *The Architecture of Harry Weese* (2010) by Robert Bruegmann and Kathleen Skolnik.

INDEX